SUPREME COURT JUDGMENTS ON IBC

MUKESH KUMAR SUMAN

Second Edition @ 2026

First Edition @ 2025

Contents

Preface

I am pleased to present second edition of this book. This book covers summaries of ninety five judgments passed by the Supreme Court of India on Insolvency and Bankruptcy Code, 2016 upto March, 2026. These judgments have been arranged topic wise, so that a reader could comprehend development of jurisprudence on each aspect of the Code.

Insolvency and Bankruptcy Code, 2016 is a landmark legislation enacted by Parliament, which has brought a paradigm shift in insolvency framework in India. The Supreme Court of India has delivered several judgments on different aspects of the Code, which have enriched jurisprudence in this branch of law.

This book is a must resource for lawyers, chartered accountants and company secretaries who are working in this domain particularly in litigation. This book is also useful for all those who have interest in this emerging area.

I am thankful to my family and friends for supporting me in this endeavour.

CONSTITUTIONAL CHALLENGE

SWISS RIBBONS PVT. LTD. Vs. UNION OF INDIA

The Supreme Court in Swiss Ribbons Pvt. Ltd. Vs. Union of India (2019) 4 SCC 17 upheld the constitutional validity of several provisions of IBC including classification of financial creditor and operational creditors, exclusion of operational creditors from IBC, Section 29A, and liquidation waterfall under Section 53.

Case Title : Swiss Ribbons Pvt. Ltd. & Anr Vs. Union of India & Ors
Date of Decision : 25.01.2019
Bench: R. F. Nariman, J; Navin Sinha, J

FACTS OF THE CASE

After the enactment of the Insolvency and Bankruptcy Code, 2016, several affected stakeholders filed writ petitions before the Supreme Court challenging the constitutional validity of various provisions of the Code. The lead petition was filed by Swiss Ribbons Pvt. Ltd., and the Supreme Court heard it along with a batch of writ petitions. Since the challenge was directed against the legislative framework itself, the Court did not examine the individual facts of each petitioner's dispute. Several provisions of the IBC, including classification of financial creditor and operational creditors, exclusion of operational creditors from IBC, Section 29A, and liquidation waterfall under Section 53, were challenged.

FINDINGS OF THE SUPREME COURT

The Supreme Court deliberated upon the following aspects of IBC.

Whether procedure of appointment of members of NCLT is in accordance with judgment of the Supreme Court in Madras Bar Association v. Union of India, (2015) 8 SCC 583 ?

The Supreme Court found that there is no infirmity in procedure of appointment of members of NCLT. A selection committee has been constituted as per direction of Supreme Court in Madras Bar Association to appoint the members of NCLT in 2015 itself.

The Supreme Court also directed to establish circuit bench of NCLAT within six months.

Whether classification of Financial Creditor and Operational Creditor is arbitrary?

The Supreme Court held that classification of Financial Creditor and Operational Creditor is based on intelligible differentia as Financial Creditors and Operational Creditors have different characteristics. Financial Creditors from the very beginning are involved in assessing the viability of the Corporate Debtor while operational creditors are not. Relevant para is as under:

28. Most importantly, financial creditors are, from the very beginning, involved with assessing the viability of the corporate debtor. They can, and therefore do, engage in restructuring of the loan as well as reorganization of the corporate debtor's business when there is financial stress, which are things operational creditors do not and cannot do. Thus, preserving the corporate debtor as a going concern, while ensuring maximum recovery for all creditors being the objective of the Code, financial creditors are clearly different from operational creditors and therefore, there is obviously an intelligible differentia between the two which has a direct relation to the objects sought to be achieved by the Code.

Whether Section 12 A of the Code is arbitrary?

It was contended before the Supreme Court that Section 12A is arbitrary as it derails the settlement process by requiring the approval of at least ninety per cent of the voting share of the Committee of Creditors. Unbridled and uncanalised power is given to the Committee of Creditors to reject legitimate settlements entered into between creditors and the Corporate Debtor. The Supreme Court rejected such arguments. The Supreme Court observed that once the Code gets triggered, the proceedings become collective proceedings and CoC must be consulted before any settlement is arrived. At the stage when Committee of Creditors is not constituted, NCLT can permit withdrawal after hearing all the concerned parties. The Supreme Court also justified the ninety percent voting requirement as all financial creditors have to put their heads together. Relevant para is as under:

53. The main thrust against the provision of Section 12A is the fact that ninety per cent of the committee of creditors has to allow withdrawal. This high threshold has been explained in the ILC Report as all financial creditors have to put their heads together to allow such withdrawal as, ordinarily, an omnibus settlement involving all creditors ought, ideally, to be entered into. This explains why ninety per cent, which is substantially all the financial creditors, have to grant their approval to an individual withdrawal or settlement. In any case, the figure of ninety per cent, in the absence of anything further to show that it is arbitrary, must pertain to the domain of legislative policy, which has been explained by the Report (supra). Also, it is clear, that under Section 60 of the Code, the committee of creditors do not have the last word on the subject. If the committee of creditors arbitrarily rejects a just settlement and/or withdrawal claim, the NCLT, and thereafter, the NCLAT can always set aside such decision under Section 60 of the Code. For all these reasons, we are of the view that Section 12A also passes constitutional muster.

Whether Resolution Professional has administrative powers or quasi-judicial powers?

The Supreme Court held that while the Liquidator has quasi-judicial power under the Code, the Resolution Professional has only administrative powers. The Resolution Professional has no adjudicatory powers.

61. Unlike the liquidator, the resolution professional cannot act in a number of matters without the approval of the committee of creditors under Section 28 of the Code, which can, by a two-thirds majority, replace one resolution professional with another, in case they are unhappy with his performance. Thus, the resolution professional is really a facilitator of the resolution process, whose administrative functions are overseen by the committee of creditors and by the Adjudicating Authority.

Whether Section 29A is constitutionally valid?

Several aspects of Section 29A were challenged before the Supreme Court. Writ Petitioners had questioned that retrospective application of Section 29A on the ground it takes away vested rights of Resolution Applicant. The Supreme Court relied on ArcelorMittal India Pvt. Ltd Vs Satish Kumar Gupta (2019) 4SCC17 held the Resolution Applicants have no vested rights for being considered as Resolution Applicant.

The Supreme Court also did not find period given under 29A (c) as unreasonable as a person who cannot service a debt for the aforesaid period is obviously a person who is ailing itself. The legislative policy, therefore, is that a person who is unable to service its own debt beyond the grace period referred to above, is unfit to be eligible to become a Resolution Applicant.

The court also dispelled the argument that 29 A (j) is invalid. The relevant para is as under:

75. We are of the view that persons who act jointly or in concert with others are connected with the business activity of the resolution applicant. Similarly, all the categories of persons mentioned in Section 5(24A) show that such persons must be connected with the resolution applicant within the meaning of Section 29A(j). This being the case, the said categories of persons who are collectively mentioned under the caption relative obviously need to have a connection with the business activity of the resolution applicant. In the absence of showing that such person is connected with the business of the activity of the resolution applicant, such person cannot possibly be disqualified under Section 29A(j). All the categories in Section 29A(j) deal with persons, natural as well as artificial, who are connected with the business activity of the resolution applicant. The expression —related party, therefore, and —relative contained in the definition Sections must be read noscitur a sociis with the categories of persons mentioned in Explanation I, and so read, would include only persons who are connected with the business activity of the resolution applicant.

Whether Section 53 violates Article 14 of the Constitution ?

Section 53 has been also challenged on the ground that Operational Creditor will not get anything under the hierarchy given under Section 53 in case of liquidation. The Supreme Court held that intelligible differentia exists between operational debt and financial debt as financial debt infuses capital into the economy. Relevant para is as under:

84. It will be seen that the reason for differentiating between financial debts, which are secured, and operational debts, which are unsecured, is in the relative importance of the two types of debts when it comes to the object sought to be achieved by the Insolvency Code. We have already seen that repayment of financial debts infuses capital into the economy inasmuch as banks and financial institutions are able, with the money that has been paid back, to further lend such money to other entrepreneurs for their businesses. This rationale creates an intelligible differentia between financial debts and operational debts.

OVERRIDING EFFECT OF IBC

INNOVENTIVE INDUSTRIES Vs. ICICI BANK & ANR

The Supreme Court in Innoventive Industries Ltd Vs ICICI Bank (2018) 1 SCC 407 held that certain provisions of Maharashtra Relief Undertakings (Special Provisions) Act, 1958 are repugnant to IBC under Article 254 of the Constitution and are , therefore, void to that extent. The Supreme Court also held that non-obstante clause contained in Section 238 IBC will overrides limited non-obstante clause in Maharashtra Act.

Case Title : M/S Innoventive Industries Vs. ICICI Bank & Anr Date of Decision : 31.08.2017 Bench : R.F.Nariman, J; Sanjay Kishan Kaul, J

FACTS OF THE CASE

The Appellant was a multi-product company. The Appellant began to suffer losses due to labour problems. As the Appellant was not able to service financial assistance given to it, the Appellant proposed corporate debt restructuring. Joint Lender Forum approved the restructuring plan. Section 7 Application was filed by ICICI Bank seeking initiation of CIRP against the Appellant. In the reply the Appellant contended that there is no debt legally due as liabilities and enforcement thereof has been temporarily suspended for a period of one year vide notification dated 22nd July, 2015 and another year vide notification dated 18th July, 2016 under Maharashtra Relief Undertakings (Special Provisions) Act, 1958.

By order dated 17th January, 2017, NCLT held that the IBC would prevail against Maharashtra Act in view of non-obstante clause in Section 238 of the Code. Parliamentary Statute will prevail over State statute. Application was admitted by the NCLT. The appeal filed by the Appellant before the NCLAT was also dismissed.

FINDINGS OF THE SUPREME COURT

The Supreme Court noted that one of the objective of the IBC is to bring the insolvency law in India within a single umbrella with the object of speeding up the insolvency process. The Supreme Court made a detailed survey of several provisions of the Code.

The Supreme Court observed that repugnancy under Article 254 arises only if both Parliamentary and the State law are referrable to List III in 7th Schedule of the Constitution of India. Doctrine of Pith and Substance has to be applied in order to test that both statutes fall under Concurrent List. The language of Article 254 speaks of repugnancy of not only merely a statute but also "any provision" thereof. The onus of showing that a statute is repugnant has to be on the party attacking its validity. Inconsistency must be clear and direct and be of such nature as to bring two acts or parts into direct collision between each other. Repugnant state statute is void to the extent of repugnancy. Only that portion of the State's statute which is found to be repugnant is to be declared void.

The Supreme Court held that Maharashtra Act is repugnant to IBC, which has been enacted by Parliament as under the Maharashtra Act the State Government may take over management of the undertaking after which a temporary moratorium takes place under Section 4 of Maharashtra Act. Moratorium under Section 4 of Maharashtra Act directly clashes with moratorium under Section 14 IBC. Thus Central enactment being repugnant to the earlier state enactment by virtue of Article 254 (1) would operate to render Maharashtra Act void vis-à-vis action taken under later Central enactment.

The Supreme Court also relied on Section 238 of IBC and observed that later non-obstante clause of Parliamentary enactment will prevail over the limited non-obstante clause contained in Section 4 of Maharashtra Act.

The Supreme Court observed that Maharashtra Act cannot stand in the way of the Corporate Insolvency Resolution Process under the Code.

The Supreme Court was of the view that NCLT and NCLAT rightly admitted the application for initiation of CIRP and dismissed the appeal filed by the Appellant.

DUNCANS INDUSTRIES LTD. Vs. A. J. AGROCHEM

The Supreme Court in Duncans Industries Ltd. Vs. A J Agrochem 2019 (9) SCC 725, held that the provisions of Insolvency and Bankruptcy Code, 2016 will have overriding effect over the Tea Act, 1953.

Case Title : Duncans Industries Ltd. Vs. A. J. Agrochem Date of Decision : 04.10.2019 Bench : Arun Mishra, J; M. R. Shah, J; B. R. Gavai, J

FACTS OF THE CASE

Duncans Industries Ltd. (Corporate Debtor) owned and managed fourteen tea gardens out of which control of seven tea gardens were taken over by the Central Government under Section 16 E of the Tea Act, 1953 . A J Agrochem (Operational Creditor) used to supply pesticides, insecticides and herbicides to the Corporate Debtor. Insolvency Proceedings were initiated against Corporate Debtor under Section 9 IBC as Corporate Debtor had defaulted in payment of Rs. 41, 55, 500/-. Insolvency proceedings were opposed by the Corporate Debtor solely on the ground that under 16 (1) (c) of the Tea Act, 1953, once management of tea unit has been taken over by the Central Government, the proceedings of winding up or appointment of receiver cannot be initiated without the consent of the Central Government.

The NCLT held that as prior consent has not been taken from the Central Government, the Application under Section 9 was not maintainable.

The NCLAT reversed the finding of the NCLT and held that Section 9 Petition will be maintainable even without consent of the government.

FINDINGS OF THE COURT

The short issue before the Supreme Court was whether Section 9 Petition was maintainable without consent of the Central Government as provided under Section 16 E of Tea Act, 1953.

The Supreme Court noted that the Central Government vide notification dated 28.01.2016 under Section 16 E of the Tea Act, authorized Tea Board to take over control of seven tea gardens as tea gardens were managed by the Appellant in a manner detrimental to tea industry and public interest. The said notification was challenged by the Appellant before the High Court of Calcutta. Division Bench of Calcutta passed interim order whereby the management continues with the Corporate Debtor. The Supreme Court observed that provisions of the Tea Act will only be applicable if the management of tea undertaking has been taken over. Taking over actual management and control is sine qua non for applicability of the Section 16 G of the Tea Act.

The Supreme Court observed that IBC is a complete Code in itself. Section 16 (E) 1 (c) of the Tea Act refers to only winding up or appointment of receiver in respect thereof. Section 9 proceedings is not limited to winding up or appointment of receiver only. The winding up will be of last resort under IBC in case Corporate Insolvency Resolution Process for revival of the Corporate Debtor fails. The Supreme Court noted that in Swiss Ribbons Pvt. Ltd. Vs. Union of India AIR (2019) 4 SCC it has been observed that the primary purpose of the IBC is to ensure revival and continuation of the Corporate Debtor by protecting the Corporate Debtor from its own management. Corporate Insolvency Resolution Process cannot be equated with winding up proceedings.

The Supreme Court held that Section 238 of Insolvency and Bankruptcy Code, 2016 which was passed subsequent to the Tea Act, 1953 would be applicable and provisions of IBC will have overriding effect over the Tea Act. If consent of Central Government is required then the main objective of time bound resolution of CIRP will be frustrated. The Supreme Court concluded that Section 7 or Section 9 Application under Insolvency and Bankruptcy Code, 2016 will be maintainable even without prior consent of the Central Government.

The judgment of NCLAT was affirmed by the Supreme Court.

APPLICABILITY OF LIMITATION ACT

B. K. EDUCATIONAL SERVICES PVT. LTD. Vs. PARAG GUPTA & ASSOCIATES

The Supreme Court in B. K. Educational Services Pvt. Ltd. Vs. Parag Gupta and Associates (2019) 11 SCC 633 held that Section 238A of the Code , the Insolvency and Bankruptcy Code (Second Amendment) Act 2018 is clarificatory in nature and shall be applicable with retrospective effect.

Case Title : B. K. Educational Services Pvt. Ltd. Vs. Parag Gupta & Associates Date of Decision : 11.10.2018 Bench : R. F. Nariman, J; Navin Sinha, J

FACTS OF THE CASE

Parliament amended Insolvency and Bankruptcy Code, 2016 vide Insolvency and Bankruptcy Code (Second Amendment) Act, 2018 and inserted inter alia Section 238A , whereby the provisions of Limitation Act, 1963 were made applicable to Insolvency and Bankruptcy Code, 2016. Section 238A reads as under:

238 A. Limitation - The Provisions of the Limitation Act, 1963 (36 of 1963) shall, as far as may be, apply to the proceedings or appeals before the Adjudicating Authority, the National Company Law Appellate Tribunal, the Debt Recovery Tribunal or the Debt Recovery Appellate Tribunal, as the case may be.

The main issue before the Supreme Court in this case was whether Provisions of Limitation Act would apply from retrospective effect.

The NCLAT has held that the Limitation Act is not applicable for initiation of the Corporate Insolvency Resolution Process but doctrine of Limitation and Prescription is necessary to be looked into for determining the question whether the application under Section 7 or Section 9 can be entertained after long delay, amounting to laches.

FINDINGS OF THE SUPREME COURT

The Supreme Court noted that National Company Law Tribunal has been constituted under Section 408 of the Companies Act, 2013. It discharges such powers and functions that are conferred on it not merely under the Companies Act but also under any other law for the time being in force.

The Supreme Court also noted that Section 433 provides that provisions of Limitation Act, 1963 will apply to proceedings and appeals before the Tribunal or Appellate Tribunal.

The Supreme Court also noted that winding up applications, compromise, arrangements and reconstruction have to be transferred from the High Courts to NCLT. Limitation Act was applicable to these proceedings. After such transfer it cannot be the case that Limitation Act will not apply to these proceedings.

The Supreme Court held that Section 433 of the Companies Act, 2013 would apply to the Tribunal even when it decides applications under Section 7 and Section 9 of the Code.

The Supreme Court relied on judgments in M. P. Steel Corporation Vs. CCE (2015) 7 SCC 58 and held that limitation , being procedural in nature, would ordinarily be applied retrospectively, save and except that the new law of limitation cannot revive a dead remedy. In the present case an application which is filed in 2016 or 2017 after the Code has come into force, cannot suddenly revive a debt , which is no longer due as it is time-barred.

The Court held that amendment to Section 238A would not serve its object unless it is construed as being retrospective, as otherwise, applications seeking to resurrect time -barred claims would have to be allowed, not being governed by law of limitation.

The Supreme Court observed that the Code cannot be triggered in the year 2017 for a debt which was time barred in 1990, as that would lead to absurd consequences. The expression "debt due" in the definition sections of the Code would obviously refer to debts that are "due and payable" in law i.e. the debts that are not time barred.

The Supreme Court also held that the expression "default" bears the same meaning in Section 7 and 8 of the Code making it clear that the CIRP against the Corporate Debtor can only be initiated by a Financial or Operational Creditor in relation to debts which have not become time-barred.

The Supreme Court concluded that the Limitation Act is applicable to Section 7 or Section 9 application from inception of the Code. If default has occurred over three years prior to the date of filing of the application, the application would be barred under Article 137 of the Limitation Act, save and except in those cases where, in facts of the case, Section 5 of the Limitation Act may be applied to condone the delay in filing such application.

JIGNESH SHAH Vs. UNION OF INDIA

The Supreme Court in Jignesh Shah Vs. Union of India (2019) 10 SCC 750 has held that a suit for recovery and a winding-up petition are separate and distinct remedy. A suit of recovery instituted prior to winding-up petition will not impact the limitation within which the winding-up proceedings are to be filed by keeping the debt somehow alive for the purpose of winding-up proceedings.

Case Title : Jignesh Shah Vs. Union of India
Date of Decision : 25.09.2019
Bench : R. F. Nariman, J; R. Subhash Reddy, J; Surya Kant, J

FACTS OF THE CASE

Share purchase agreement was executed between MCX Stock Exchange Ltd. and IL & FS whereby IL & FS agreed to purchase 442 lakh equity shares of MCX -SX from MCX. Pursuant to this agreement La-Fin, a group company of MCX, issued a letter of undertaking to IL & FS wherein it was stated that La-Fin would offer to purchase from IL & FS the shares of MCX-SX after a period of one year but before a period of three years from a date of investment. Period of three years expired in August, 2012.

IL & FS by letter dated 3rd August, 2012 exercised its option to sell its entire holding of shares MCX -SX and called upon La -Fin to purchase shares. La-Fin replied that it was under no obligation to buy the aforesaid shares. IL & FS filed suit for specific performance against La -Fin or in the alternative, damages.

Statutory notice was also issued under Section 433 and 434 of the Companies Act, 1956 on 3rd November, 2015 by IL & FS. Winding-up petition was filed by IL & FS on 21st October, 2016 in Bombay High Court under Section 433 (e) of the Companies Act, 1956.

After coming in force of the IBC, winding-up petition was transferred to NCLT. Winding-up Petition was admitted as Section 7 Application by NCLT on 28th August, 2018. Appeal filed before NCLAT was also dismissed.

FINDINGS OF THE SUPREME COURT

The Supreme Court observed that with the introduction of Section 238A in IBC , the provisions of the Limitation Act apply to applications made under IBC. After coming into force of the Code, winding-up petitions have been converted into Petitions under the Code.

In the instant case, it has to be decided whether on the date when winding-up petition was filed was barred by limitation. If such petition is time-barred, Section 238A will not give a new lease of life to time barred petition. Winding-up petition has been filed beyond three years as such it was time barred

The Supreme Court analysed several judgments and held that a suit of recovery based upon a cause of action that is within limitation cannot in any manner impact the separate and independent remedy of winding-up proceedings. A suit for recovery, which is a separate and independent proceedings distinct from the remedy of winding-up would , in no manner, impact the limitation within which the winding-up proceedings is to be filed, by keeping the debt somehow alive for the purpose of winding-up proceedings.

The Supreme Court also rejected the argument that in case of winding-up petitions, cause of action for purposes of limitation would include the commercial insolvency or loss of substratum of the company. The Supreme Court observed that in case of winding-up petitions the trigger of limitation is the inability of a company to pay debts. The trigger occurs when a default takes place. It is this date alone which is relevant for filing winding-up Petition. The stage at which the Court examines whether the company is commercially insolvent is once it begins to hear winding-up petition for admission on merits.

The Supreme Court held that winding-up petition filed on 21st October, 2016 being beyond the period of three years mentioned under Article 137 of the Limitation Act is time barred and cannot be proceeded with any further. Accordingly, the Supreme Court set aside orders of NCLT and NCLAT.

BABULAL VARDHARJI GURJAR Vs. VEER GURJAR ALUMINIUM INDUSTRIES PVT. LTD.

The Supreme Court in Babulal Vardharji Gurjar Vs. Veer Gurjar Aluminium Industries Pvt. Ltd. (2020) SCC Online SC 647 held that Limitation will start running in case of Section 7 application from the date of default and not from the commencement of IBC. The Supreme Court also held that Section 7 IBC application is not for enforcement of mortgage and limitation prescribed under Article 62 of Limitation Act will not apply on Section 7 Applications.

Case Title : Babulal Vardharji Gurjar Vs Veer Gurjar Aluminium Industries Pvt. Ltd. Date of Decision : 14.08.2020 Bench : A. M. Khanwilkar,J ; Dinesh Maheshwari, J

FACTS OF THE CASE

The lender banks i.e. Corporation Bank, India Overseas Bank, and Bank of India sanctioned and advanced credit facilities to the Corporate Debtor. The Corporate Debtor defaulted in payment of loan. The Banks initiated recovery proceedings under SARFAESI Act.

Respondent No. 2 also filed an Application under Section 7 IBC for initiation of CIRP. The Adjudicating Authority admitted the Application vide order dated 09.08.2018.

An appeal was filed against order of the NCLT dated 09.08.2018 before NCLAT which dismissed the same. Subsequently, an appeal was filed before the Supreme Court. The Supreme Court noted that aspect of limitation has not been considered and remanded the matter back to the NCLAT. The NCLAT again dismissed the application by observing that the Application is not barred by limitation mainly on two grounds – (i) Right to apply under Section 7 only accrued on 01.12.2016 and (ii) period of recovery of mortgaged property is twelve years.

THE FINDINGS OF THE SUPREME COURT

The Supreme Court observed that CIRP is not intended to be adversarial to the Corporate Debtor but is essentially to protect its interests.

The Supreme Court noted that Section 238A provides that provisions of Limitation Act, as far as may be, shall apply to the proceedings under IBC or appeals.

The supreme Court surveyed the provisions of the Code and several judgments and observed that the period of limitation for an application seeking initiation of CIRP under Section 7 of the Code is governed by Article 137 of the Limitation Act and is therefore three years from the date when right to apply accrues. Limitation period starts to run from the date of default on the Corporate Debtor and not from date of commencement of IBC. There is nothing in IBC to suggest even remotely that the period of limitation for the purposes of Section 7 Application will commence from commencement of the Code itself. Further such observation is in the teeth of law declared by the Supreme Court in B. K. Educational Services Pvt. Ltd. Vs. Parag Gupta & Associates AIR 2019SC5601.

The Supreme Court observed that in Sagar Sharma Vs Phoenix Arc (2019) 10 SCC 353 it has been held that date of coming into force of the IBC does not and cannot form a trigger point of limitation for applications under the Code.

On the aspect of mortgage, the Supreme Court held that Application under Section 7 of IBC is not for enforcement of mortgage liability and Article 62 of the Limitation Act does not apply to such applications.

The Supreme Court observed that the date of default has been mentioned as 08.07.2011 in application under Section 7. No other date of default has been mentioned in the application or any suggestion for acknowledgement has been made. The question of limitation is mixed question of law and fact and when a party seeks to invoke any particular provision for extension or enlargement of the period of limitation, the relevant facts are required to be pleaded and requisite evidence is required to be adduced. In the instant case the Respondent never came out with any pleading other that the date of default as such no case of extension of the period of limitation is available to be examined.

The Supreme Court set aside the order of NCLAT and rejected application filed under Section 7 IBC for initiation of CIRP

RADHA EXPORTS (INDIA) PVT. LTD Vs. K P JAYARAM & ORS

The Supreme Court in Radha Exports (India) Pvt. Ltd. Vs. K. P. Jayaram & Ors (2020) 10 SCC 538 held that the Application filed by the Respondents for initiation of CIRP was barred by limitation. The Application was also not maintainable as there was no financial debt in existence.

Case Title : Radha Exports (India) Pvt. Ltd. Vs K. P. Jayaram & Ors Date of Decision : 28.08.2020 Bench : Arun Mishra, J; Indira Banerjee, J

FACTS OF THE CASE

The Respondents had advanced a loan to Radha Exports, a Proprietorship firm. The loan was unsecured and free of interest. The Appellant company was incorporated to take over the business of proprietorship firm on or about 19th July, 2004. At the time of incorporation, total liability towards the Respondents was Rs. 1,11, 85, 350/-.

After incorporation of the Appellant company the Respondents requested the Appellant to convert Rs. 90,00,000/- of the loan amount into share application money for allotment of shares in the name of Respondent No. 2. Accordingly, Rs. 90,00,000/- was converted in share application money and the remaining loan amount was Rs. 21, 85, 350/-. According to the appellant company loan amount was fully repaid by March, 2006.

The Respondent No. 2 resigned from the Board of Directors and at the time of resignation, the Respondent No. 2 requested the Appellant company to treat the share application money of Rs. 90,00,000/- as share application money of Mr. M. Krishnan. Rs. 90,00,000/- was to be treated as loan amount From Respondent No. 2 to Mr. M. Krishnan. The Appellant Company claimed to have issued shares of Rs. 90,00,000/- in the name of Mr. M. Krishnan in 2008. The Appellant claimed that there had been no financial transaction between the Appellant company and the Respondents.

The Respondents issued legal notice dated 19th November, 2012 for payment of sum of Rs. 1, 49,60,000/-. The said amount was not paid as such the Respondents filed Petition before High Court of Madras for winding-up of the Appellant Company. The said petition was transferred to the NCLT, Chennai Bench. On 4th August, 2017 winding up petition was dismissed by the NCLT.

The Respondents again filed fresh Petition under Section 9 IBC before NCLT which was withdrawn. The Respondents again filed fresh Petition under Section 7 IBC before the NCLT. NCLT held that Respondents were not Financial Creditors. The NCLT also held that Petition is barred by limitation and dismissed the Petition.

Respondents preferred appeal before the NCLAT wherein the NCLAT set aside the order of the NCLT.

FINDINGS OF THE SUPREME COURT

The Supreme Court observed that it was for the Applicant, who invokes corporate insolvency resolution process, to prima facie show the existence in his favour a legally recoverable debt. Such Applicant has to show that the debt is not barred by limitation.

The period of limitation for suit for recovery of money lent is three years from the date money was lent under the Limitation Act. The last loan amount was advanced in 2004-05. In the instant case debt was time barred even in 2012 when winding-up proceedings were initiated.

The Supreme Court observed that the NCLT has rightly rejected the Application on the ground that it was barred by limitation.

The Supreme Court also held that the Petition was not maintainable under Section 7 of the IBC as there was no financial debt in existence. The definition of "financial debt" in Section 5 (8) makes it clear that "financial debt" means a debt along with interest, if any, disbursed against time value of money. The transaction in this matter did not fall within definition of financial debt.

SESH NATH SINGH Vs. BAIDYABATI SHEORAPHULI CO-OPERATIVE BANK LTD.

The Supreme Court held in Sesh Nath Singh Vs. Baidyabati Sheoraphuli Co-operative Bank Ltd AIR 2021 SC 2637 that delay in filing an Application under Section 7 or Section 9 can be condoned even in the absence of an application for condonation of delay. The Supreme Court also held that Section 14 of Limitation Act, 1963 is applicable on application under Section 7 or Section 9.

Case Title : Sesh Nath Singh & Anr Vs. Baidyabati Sheoraphuli Co-operative Bank Ltd Date of Decision : 22.03.2021 Bench : Indira Banerjee, J; Hemant Gupta, J

FACTS OF THE CASE

The Financial Creditor had extended finance facilities to the Corporate Debtor, which was declared NPA on 31st March, 2013. On 18th January, 2014 the Financial Creditor issued notice to the Corporate Debtor under Section 13 (2) of the SARFAESI Act. The Corporate Debtor made a representation dated 3.3.2014 to the Financial Creditor under Section 13 (3A) of the SARFAESI Act, which was rejected by the Financial Creditor. The Financial Creditor vide notice dated 13th December, 2014 called upon the Corporate Debtor to hand over peaceful possession of the secured immovable assets.

The Corporate Debtor challenged the said notices in Writ Application before Calcutta High Court under Article 226 of the Constitution.

During the pendency of the Writ Petition the Financial Creditor took into possession the secured assets on 24th December, 2014 under Section 13 (4) of the SARFAESI Act. On 11th May, 2017, the District Magistrate issued an order under the SARFAESI Act for possession of assets of the Corporate Debtor.

The High Court vide order dated 24th July, 2017 passed an interim order restraining the Financial Creditor from taking steps against the Corporate Debtor under the SARFAESI Act until further orders. The High Court was of prima facie opinion that Financial Creditor, being a Cooperative Bank, could not invoke the provisions of the SARFAESI Act.

The Financial Creditor filed an application under Section 7 of the Code on 10th July, 2018 for initiation of CIRP before NCLT, Kolkata Bench. The NCLT admitted the application and appointed IRP.

An appeal was filed before NCLAT where it was contended for the first time that account of the Corporate Debtor was declared NPA on 31st March, 2013 and Application before NCLT has been filed on 27th August , 2018 after almost five years and therefore was barred by Limitation.

The NCLAT dismissed the Appeal on the ground that plea of the limitation has been raised for the first time in appeal and further that Financial Creditor was entitled to exclusion under Section 14(2) of the Limitation Act.

FINDINGS OF THE SUPREME COURT

The following two issues arose for consideration in this matter (i) Whether delay beyond three years can be condoned in Section 7 Application in absence of an application for condonation of delay ? (ii) Whether Section 14 of the Limitation Act will apply to applications under Section 7 of the IBC ?

The Supreme Court noted that Section 238A provides that the provisions of Limitation Act are applicable to proceedings before Adjudicating Authority. The Supreme Court also noted that in several judgments including B. K Educational Services Private Ltd Vs Parag Gupta (2019) 11 SCC 633 , it has been held that NCLT or NCLAT has the discretion to entertain application or appeal after prescribed period of limitation if sufficient cause is shown.

The Supreme Court held that it is not mandatory to file an application in writing before any relief can be granted under Section 5 of the Limitation Act. However, the Court can always insist that an application or an affidavit showing cause for the delay be filed. No applicant or appellant can claim condonation of delay under Section 5 of the Limitation Act as of right, without making an application.

Section 14 (2) of the Limitation Act provides for exclusion of time in computing the period of limitation in certain circumstances. Similarly Section 18 of the Limitation Act, an acknowledgment of present subsisting liability, made in writing in respect of any right claimed by the opposite party and signed by the party against whom the right is claimed, has the effect of commencing of a fresh period of limitation, from the date on which the acknowledgment is signed. However such acknowledgment must be made before the period of limitation expires.

The Supreme Court observed that Section 238A IBC makes the provisions of the Limitation Act applicable to proceedings before NCLT or NCLAT. The IBC does not exclude the application of Section 6, or 14 or 18 or any other provision of the Limitation Act.

The conditions for exclusion under Section 14 are that the earlier proceedings should have been prosecuted diligently and in good faith and the proceedings should have been prosecuted in a forum which due to a defect of jurisdiction or other cause of a like nature was unable to entertain it.

The Supreme Court in Consolidated Engineering Enterprises Vs Principal Secretary, Litigation Department and Ors (2008) 7 SCC 169 held that in absence of any provision in the Arbitration and Conciliation Act, 1996 which excluded the applicability of Section 14 of the Limitation Act, there was no reason why Section 14 of the Limitation Act should not apply to an application for setting aside an arbitral award.

The Supreme Court in Commissioner, M. P. housing Board Vs Mohanlal (2016) 14 SCC 199 held that Limitation Act has to be interpreted to advance the cause of justice.

The Supreme Court held that Section 14 (1) (2) and (3) do not say that Section 14 can only be invoked on termination of the earlier proceedings prosecuted in good faith.

The Supreme Court held that Explanation (a) cannot be construed in a narrow pedantic manner to mean that Section 14 can never be invoked until and unless the earlier proceedings have actually been terminated for want of jurisdiction or other cause of a like nature. Explanation (a) only restricts the period of exclusion to the period between the date of initiation and the date of termination. An applicant cannot claim any further exclusion. Section 14 excludes the time spent in proceeding in a wrong forum, which is unable to entertain the proceedings for want of jurisdiction or other such cause. Where such proceedings have ended, the outer limit to claim exclusion under Section 14 would be the date on which proceedings ended.

The Supreme Court held that since proceedings in the High Court were still pending on the date of filing of the Application under Section 7 of the IBC in NCLT, the entire period after the initiation of proceedings under the SARFAESI Act could be excluded.

The Supreme Court observed that an Adjudicating Authority under the IBC is not a substitute forum for a collection of debts in the sense it cannot reopen debts which are barred by law or debts, recovery whereof have become time-barred. The Adjudicating Authority does not resolve disputes in the manner of suits, arbitrations and similar proceedings. However, the ultimate object of an application under Section 7 or 9 of IBC is the realization of debt by invocation of Insolvency Resolution Process. Further cause of invocation of Insolvency proceedings is default as is the case with SARFAESI proceedings. As such there is no reason why Section 14 or 18 should not apply to the insolvency proceedings.

The Supreme Court observed that Section 238A of the IBC makes the provisions of the Limitation Act applicable to proceedings before the NCLT/NCLAT "as far as may be", that is, to the extent they are capable of being applied. The words “as far as may be " are not otiose. These words are to be understood in a manner which harmonise with the subject matter of the legislation and the object which the Legislature has in view. In the context of IBC, Section 14 could not be interpreted in a rigid and pedantic manner to hold that only civil proceedings in Court would enjoy exclusion.

The Supreme Court concluded that keeping in mind the scope and ambit of proceedings under IBC before NCLT/NCLAT, the expression "Court" in Section 14 (2) would be deemed to be any forum for civil proceedings including any Tribunal or any forum under the SARFAESI Act. The Supreme Court also held that Section 5 and Section 14 are not mutually exclusive. Even where Section 14 does not strictly apply, the principles of Section 14 can be invoked to grant relief to an applicant under Section 5 of the Limitation Act by purposively construing “sufficient cause”.

The Supreme Court held that NCLAT has rightly refused to stay the proceedings before the NCLT.

ASSET RECONSTRUCTION COMPANY (INDIA) LTD. Vs. BISHAL JAISWAL

The Supreme Court in Asset Reconstruction Company (India) Ltd. Vs. Bishal Jaiswal & Anr (2021) SCC Online SC 321 held that an entry made in balance sheet may constitute as acknowledgment under Section 18 of Limitation Act and will depend on facts of each case.

Case Title : Asset Reconstruction Company (India) Ltd. Vs Bishal Jaiswal & Anr
Date of Decision : 15.04.2021
Bench : R. F. Nariman, J ; B. R. Gavai, J; Hrishikesh Roy, J

FACTS OF THE CASE

The Corporate Power Ltd (Corporate Debtor) set up thermal power project in Jharkhand and for which availed loan facilities from various lenders including the State Bank of India in 2009. The account of the Corporate Debtor was declared NPA on 31.07.2013. SBI issued loan recall notice on 27.03.2015. On 31.03.2015, some of the lenders assigned debt to the appellant. The appellant issued notice under Section 13 (2) of the SARFAESI Act.

The Appellant also filed an application under Section 7 of IBC for a default amounting to Rs. 5997, 80,02,973/- against the Corporate Debtor. As the application did not indicate date of default, a supplementary affidavit was filed showing date of default and annexing copies of balance sheets of the Corporate Debtor which periodically acknowledged the debt that was due. NCLT admitted the application considering the entries in a balance sheet as acknowledgment under Section 18 of the Limitation Act, 1963.

An appeal was filed before NCLAT, which allowed the same on the ground that Full Bench of NCLAT in V. Padmakumar Vs. Stressed Assets Stabilisation Fund (Company Appeal (AT) Insolvency No 57 of 2020) has held that an entry made in a balance sheet would not amount to acknowledgement of debt for the purpose of extending limitation under Section 18 of Limitation Act.

Aggrieved by the same, the Appellant approached the Supreme Court. The Supreme Court set aside the findings of NCLAT.

FINDINGS OF THE SUPREME COURT

Section 238A of the IBC makes the provisions of the Limitation Act, 1963 applicable to proceedings under the Insolvency and Bankruptcy Code, 2016. The Supreme Court relied on Shesh Nath Singh Vs Baidyabati Sheoraphuli Co-operative Bank Ltd (2021) 7 SCC 321 and Laxmi Pat Surana Vs Union of India (2021) 8 SCC 481 and observed that Section 14 and Section 18 of the Limitation Act are applicable to IBC proceedings..

The Supreme Court relied on Mahabir Cold Storage Vs CIT , 1991 Supp 1 SCC 402 , A. V. Murthy Vs. B. S. Nagabasavanna (2002) 2 SCC 642, S. Natarajan Vs. Sama Dharman Crl. A. No. 1524/2014 and observed that an entry made in books of accounts, including the balance sheet, can amount to an acknowledgement of liability within the meaning of Section 18 of the Limitation Act.

The Supreme Court observed several relevant sections of the Companies Act, 2013 and observed that filing of balance sheet is mandatory under Companies Act. The notes forming part of such financial statements are expressly recognized by Section 134 (7). The Supreme Court noted that law contained in Bengal Silk Mills Co. Vs. Ismail Golam Hosaain Ariff 1961 SCC Online Cal 128 to the effect that there is a compulsion of law to prepare a balance sheet but no compulsion to make any particular admission is correct in law. It will depend on facts of each case as to whether an entry made in balance sheet qua a particular creditor is unequivocal or has been entered into with caveats, which has to be examined on a case to case basis to establish whether an acknowledgement of liability has , in fact, been made.

The Supreme Court held that majority decision of the Full Bench in V Padmakumar is contrary to the several judgments. The minority judgment has reached correct conclusion. The supreme Court set aside the majority judgment.

The Supreme Court also set aside judgment of NCLAT dated 22.12.2020 and remanded the matter to NCLAT for fresh consideration in accordance with law.

RAJENDRA NAROTTAMDAS SHETH VS. CHANDRA PRAKASH JAIN

The Supreme Court in Rajendra Narottamdas Seth Vs. Chandra Prakash Jain (2021) SCC Online 843 approved the view taken by the NCLAT in Palogix Infrastructure Pvt. Ltd. Vs. ICICI Bank Ltd. (2017) SCC Online NCLAT 266 regarding institution of Section 7 IBC Application through power of attorney holder. The Supreme Court reiterated that Section 18 of the Limitation Act is applicable on proceedings under IBC.

> Case Title : Rajendra Narottamdas Sheth & Anr Vs. Chandra Prakash Jain & Anr.
> Date of Decision : 30.09.2021
> Bench : L. Nageswara Rao, J; B. R. Gavai, J; B. V. Nagarathna; J

FACTS OF THE CASE

The Corporate Debtor was in business of setting up underground fiber network in some cities of Gujarat. Union Bank of India extended credit facility to the Corporate Debtor. Corporate Debtor defaulted in the repayment of loan amount , consequently on 30.09.2014 the account of Corporate Debtor was declared NPA. Subsequent thereto the Financial Creditor filed application under Section 19 of the Recovery of Debt due to Banks and Financial Institutions Act , 1993 for recovery of dues.

The Financial Creditor also filed an Application under Section 7 of Insolvency and Bankruptcy Code, 2016 which was admitted on 01.06.2020. An appeal was filed before the NCLAT which was also dismissed.

FINDINGS OF THE SUPREME COURT

There were two issues involved – (i) whether an application under Section 7 IBC filed through attorney holder is maintainable? (ii) whether application was barred by limitation?

The NCLAT in Palogix Infrastructure has held that "power of attorney holder" is not competent to file an application under Section 7 on behalf of the Financial Creditor. At the same time, The NCLAT was of the opinion that general authorization given to an officer of the Financial Creditor by means of a power of attorney, would not disentitle such officer to act as an authorized representative of the Financial Creditor while filing application under Section 7 of the Code, merely because authorization was granted through power of attorney. The NCLAT has further held in Palogix that if officer was authorized to sanction loans, Application filed by him under Section 7 cannot be rejected on the ground that there is no separate authorization. Corporate Debtor cannot take plea that while the officer has power to sanction loan, he has no power to recover loan or initiate CIRP. The Supreme Court approved the view taken in Palogix by the NCLAT.

The Supreme Court observed that in the present case Sh. Praveen Kumar Gupta has been given general authorization with respect to all business and affairs of the bank including commencement of legal proceedings before any Court or Tribunal. Such authorization given through a power of attorney does not impair Mr. Gupta's ability to file an application under Section 7 of the Code.

It was contended before the Supreme Court that the date of default is shown as 30.09.2014 in the Section 7 Application. The Application was filed on 25.04.2019 as such Application was time barred.

The Supreme Court relied on Asset Reconstruction Company (India) Ltd Vs. Bishal Jaiswal & Anr (2021) 6 SCC 366 and Dena Bank Vs. C. ShivKumar Reddy & Anr (2021) SCC Online SC 543 and observed that non-furnishing of information by the Financial Creditor at the time of filing of application under Section 7 of the Code need not necessarily entail dismissal of the application. An opportunity can be provided to the Financial Creditor to provide additional information required for satisfaction of the Adjudicating Authority.

The Financial Creditor has contended that Section 18 of the Limitation Act is applicable in view of Corporate Debtor having acknowledged its debt by way of letters written in and after 2018 giving details of amount paid, acknowledging the amount outstanding and requesting consideration of one-time settlement proposal.

The Supreme Court observed that it is no more *res integra* that Section 18 of the Limitation Act is applicable to applications filed under Section 7 of the Code. In case debt is acknowledged within initial period of three years, a fresh period of limitation commences and application can be filed within the extended period.

The Supreme Court observed that there are sufficient materials in the present case to justify enlargement of limitation under Section 18 of the Limitation Act, which has rightly been considered by NCLT.

The Supreme Court dismissed the appeal.

STATUS OF HOME BUYERS

PIONEER URBAN LAND & INFRASTRUCTURE LTD. Vs. UNION OF INDIA

The Supreme Court in Pioneer Urban Land & Infrastructure Ltd. & Ors. Vs. Union of India & Ors (2019) 8 SCC 416 held that amendment to the Insolvency and Bankruptcy Code, 2016 is constitutionally valid whereby amounts raised from allottees under real estate projects were clarified to constitute financial debt and homebuyers were included in the category of Financial Creditors. .

Case Title : Pioneer Urban Land & Infrastructure Ltd. & Ors. Vs. Union of India & Ors
Date of Decision : 09.08.2019
Bench : R. F. Nariman, J; Sanjiv Khanna, J; Surya Kant, J

FACTS OF THE CASE

The Insolvency and Bankruptcy Code (Second Amendment) Act, 2018 amended Section 5(8)(f) of the IBC by clarifying that amounts raised from allottees under real estate projects constitute financial debt. Consequently, homebuyers were treated as Financial Creditors and became entitled to initiate corporate insolvency resolution proceedings under Section 7 of the IBC and participate in the committee of creditors through Authorized Representatives.

Several real estate developers, led by Pioneer Urban Land & Infrastructure Ltd., challenged the constitutional validity of these amendments before the Supreme Court.

FINDINGS OF THE SUPREME COURT

(i) Deference to legislative judgment in economic matters

The Supreme Court held that deference should be shown to legislative judgment in economic matters. The relevant para is as under :

15. In Swiss Ribbons (supra), this Court was at pains to point out, referring, inter alia, to various American decisions in paragraphs 17 to 24, that the legislature must be given free play in the joints when it comes to economic legislation. Apart from the presumption of constitutionality which arises in such cases, the legislative judgment in economic choices must be given a certain degree of deference by the courts.

(ii) Harmonious construction of RERA & IBC

The Supreme Court held that RERA and IBC must coexist but in case of conflict RERA must give way to the Code.

28. It is clear, therefore, that even by a process of harmonious construction, RERA and the Code must be held to co-exist, and, in the event of a clash, RERA must give way to the Code. RERA, therefore, cannot be held to be a special statute which, in the case of a conflict, would override the general statute, viz. the Code.

(iii) Whether classification of home buyers as Financial Creditor violates Article 14 ?

The Supreme Court held that money raised from allottees has many elements of financial debt and hence classification cannot be said to be arbitrary.

The Supreme Court observed that in the case of real estate developers, the developer who is the supplier of the flat/apartment is the debtor inasmuch as the home buyer/allottee funds his own apartment by paying amounts in advance to the developer for construction of the building in which his apartment is to be found. Another vital difference between operational debts and allottees of real estate projects is that an operational creditor has no interest in or stake in the corporate debtor, unlike the case of an allottee of a real estate project, who is vitally concerned with the financial health of the corporate debtor, for otherwise, the real estate project may not be brought to fruition. Also, in such event, no compensation, nor refund together with interest, which is the other option, will be recoverable from the corporate debtor. One other important distinction is that in an operational debt, there is no consideration for the time value of money –

the consideration of the debt is the goods or services that are either sold or availed of from the operational creditor. Payments made in advance for goods and services are not made to fund manufacture of such goods or provision of such services. Examples given of advance payments being made for turnkey projects and capital goods, where customisation and uniqueness of such goods are important by reason of which advance payments are made, are wholly inapposite as examples vis-à-vis advance payments made by allottees. In real estate projects, money is raised from the allottee, being raised against consideration for the time value of money.

When a person supplies goods and services, such person is the creditor and the person who has to pay for such goods and services is the debtor.

Even the total consideration agreed at a time when the flat/apartment is non-existent or incomplete, is significantly less than the price the buyer would have to pay for a ready/complete flat/apartment, and therefore, he gains the time value of money.

Likewise, the developer who benefits from the amounts disbursed also gains from the time value of money. The fact that the allottee makes such payments in instalments which are co-terminus with phases of completion of the real estate project does not any the less make such payments as payments involving "exchange", i.e. advances paid only in order to obtain a flat/apartment. What is predominant, insofar as the real estate developer is concerned, is the fact that such instalment payments are used as a means of finance qua the real estate project. One other vital difference with operational debts is the fact that the documentary evidence for amounts being due and payable by the real estate developer is there in the form of the information provided by the real estate developer compulsorily under RERA. This information, like the information from information utilities under the Code, makes it easy for home buyers/allottees to approach the NCLT under Section 7 of the Code to trigger the Code on the real estate developer's own information given on its webpage as to delay in construction, etc. It is these fundamental differences between the real estate developer and the supplier of goods and services that the legislature has focused upon and included real estate developers as financial debtors. This being the case, it is clear that there cannot be said to be any infraction of equal protection of the laws.

MANISH KUMAR VS UNION OF INDIA

The Supreme Court in Manish Kumar Vs Union of India (2021) 5 SCC 1 held that Sections 3, 4 and 10 of Insolvency and bankruptcy Code (Amendment) Act, 2020 are constitutionally valid.

Case Title : Manish Kumar Vs Union of India & Anr Date of Decision : 19.01.2021 Bench : R. F. Nariman, J; Navin Sinha, J; K. M. Joseph, J

FACTS OF THE CASE

Several Writ Petitions were filed before the Supreme Court challenging Sections 3, 4 and 10 of Insolvency and bankruptcy Code (Amendment) Act, 2020.

Section 3 of the Amendment Act incorporates three provisos to Section 7 (1) :

Provided that for the financial creditors, referred to in clauses (a) and (b) of the sub-section (6A) of section 21, an application for initiating corporate insolvency resolution process against the corporate debtor shall be filed jointly by not less than one hundred of such creditors in the same class or not less than ten per cent of the total number of such creditors in the same class, whichever is less,

Provided further that for financial creditors who are allottees under a real estate project, an application for initiating corporate insolvency resolution process against the corporate debtor shall be filed jointly by not less than one hundred of such allottees under the same real estate project or not less than ten percent of total number of such allottees under the same real estate project, whichever is less

Provided also that where an application for initiating the corporate insolvency resolution process against a corporate debtor has been filed by a financial creditor referred to in the first and second provisos and had not been admitted by the Adjudicating Authority before the commencement of the Insolvency and Bankruptcy Code (Amendment) Act, 2020 such application shall be modified to comply with the requirements of the first or second proviso within thirty days of the commencement of the said Act, failing which the application shall be deemed to be withdrawn before its admission.

Section 4 of Amendment Act added Explanation II to Section 11 of IBC, which is as under:

Explanation II For the purposes of this section, it is hereby clarified that nothing in this section shall prevent a corporate debtor referred to in clauses (a) to (d) from initiating corporate insolvency resolution process against another corporate debtor.

Section 10 of the Amendment Act added Section 32 A which exempted Corporate Debtor from Criminal Liability for offences committed prior to initiation of CIRP.

FINDINGS OF THE SUPREME COURT

The Supreme Court observed that grounds on which plenary legislation can be challenged are well established. Firstly, a law can be challenged if Parliament has usurped powers and made law which does not come within its domain and is against separation of powers. Secondly, a law contravening Fundamental Rights can also be declared void. Thirdly, apart from Fundamental Rights, Supremacy of Constitutional Rights are preserved against ordinary legislation.

One of the grounds of challenge to the amendment was that this amendment has been brought under pressure from Real Estate Developers. The Court rejected this argument and held that malice does not furnish a ground to attack a plenary law. Another ground was raised before the Supreme Court that Union of India had argued in Pioneer Urban Land that Home Buyers are Financial Creditors. Parliament is therefore estopped from principle of promissory estoppel. The Supreme Court held that Supreme Legislature cannot be cribbed, cabined or confined by the doctrine of promissory estoppel or estoppel.

It was contended that provision that an application by an allottee can be made only if there are hundred allottees or a number representing one-tenth of the total number of allottees, whichever is less, with a further rider that the allottees must be part of the same Real Estate Project is vague. Following questions are raised – (i) Is total number of the allottees to be calculated qua the units proposed ? (ii) Is it to be based on number of units constructed or is it to be based on number of units allotted or units where agreement of sale is entered into ?

A Real Estate Project is a development of a building or apartment or development of land into plots or apartments. It would also include common area. The expression apartment has been defined widely under RERA and includes blocks, chambers, dwelling units, flats, offices, show-rooms, shops, Godown, premises, suite, tenement, unit or by any other name and which is separate and self-contained part of any immovable property. It can be used for residential or commercial use. Allotment under RERA can be in form of plot, building or an apartment.

Explanation to Section 5 (8) (f) incorporates definition of "allottee" from RERA. Section 2 (d) of RERA defines allottee. An allottee may be allottee of a plot or an apartment or building. An allottee would include a person to whom an apartment is allotted or sold. Allottee will also include a person to whom the promotor has transferred the apartment otherwise by way of sale.

Promotor under RERA has been defined as person who constructs or causes to be constructed an independent building or apartments or convert an existing building or a part thereof into apartments for purpose of selling. Promotor also includes such persons who develops land into project.

Real Estate Project has been defined under Section 2 (zn) of RERA which consists of - (i) Development of building (ii) a building which consists of apartment (iii) Converting an existing building or part thereof into apartment (iv) the development of land into plots or apartments as the case may be.

The Supreme Court observed that the term "allottees" as defined under Section 2 (d) must be understood undoubtedly on its own terms. But at the same time other provision which form part of the Act and therefor scheme must also be borne in mind.

If applicant is able to garner a magical figure of 100 allottees, then he can file Application before NCLT under Section 7. One tenth number is meant to apply in those cases where one tenth number is less than 100 allottees.

All allottees and assignee of allotment would qualify both to be considered for the purpose of calculating the total number of allottees but confined to the particular real estate project and therefore for arriving at a figure of 100 allottees or one -tenth of allottees as the case may be.

It was also contended that 10% is dynamic will change frequently. The Supreme Court observed that contention that 10% is dynamic and is untenable in law.

The issue of default and limitation

It was contended that default in different agreement may be different. This will prejudice the right of the allottee to file Section 7 Application. The Supreme Court observed that explanation to Section 7 makes it clear that a financial debt which is owned to any other financial creditor of the Corporate Debtor would suffice to make an application on the basis that the default has occurred.

Requirement of allottees from the same project

The Supreme Court observed that rationale behind confining the allottees to the same real estate project is to promote the object of the code. Different Real Estate Projects may be at different stages. The requirement of allottees drawn from the same project stands to reason.

Point of time to comply with threshold requirements

The Supreme Court held that required number of allottees has to be seen at the time of filing of an Application under Section 7 IBC and not at time of admission stage.

Joint holding of a Unit

If a unit is jointly owned by two or more persons, they will be treated as one member for purpose of filing of an application under Section 7 of IBC.

Order 1 Rule 8 CPC & the Amendment

It was contended that more liberal approach has been provided under Order 1 Rule 8 CPC wherein if several persons are having the same interest, one person, with the consent of the Court, can sue or defend suit. The decision of the Court will be binding on all similarly situated persons. The Supreme Court held that the objective of IBC is different wherein

Corporate Debtor has to go through CIRP and if the CIRP fails then through liquidation. The Court further observed that this is a legislative domain and Court cannot interfere in the same.

Information Asymmetry

The Supreme Court also rejected that there is case of any information asymmetry. The Court observed that under RERA several information are required to be disclosed. Section 11 (1) (b) of RERA makes it compulsory to disclose information regarding booking. Similarly, under Section 88 (1) of Companies Act, 2013 registers of debenture holders and security holders have to be maintained.

Classification of Allottees and Other Financial Creditors

The Supreme Court observed that Article 14 does not interdict creation of a class within a class absolutely. Should there be rational basis for creation of class within a class, that is not impermissible. Allottees although belonging to Financial Creditors have certain distinct features – (i) Numerosity (ii) Heterogeneity and (iii) individuality in decision making, which the Supreme Court considered to be intelligible differentia. In Real Estate Project there would be large number of allottees. If a single allottee is allowed to file Application under Section 7 IBC, interests of all other allottees may be put in peril.

Classification of allottees and other Operational Creditors

It was contended that classification between allottees and Operational Creditors are arbitrary. The same was rejected by the Supreme Court relying on Swiss Ribbons Pvt. Ltd Vs Union of India (2019) 4 SCC 17 and Pioneer Urban Land & Infrastructure Land Vs Union of India (2019) 8 SCC 216.

Debenture Holders and Security Holders

The Supreme Court held that first proviso is invulnerable. The intention of legislature by inserting sub-section 6A in Section 21 and Section 25A is to treat Financial Creditors differently. They are marked by unique features in terms of numerosity and heterogeneity.

Challenge to Explanation II to Section 11

It was contended that an explanation cannot modify the main provision. Explanation II effectively repeals Section 11 (a) and (d).

The Court observed that Section 11 purports to declare that an application for initiating CIRP cannot be made by categories expressly detailed in Section 11. The Supreme Court held that explanation is clarificatory. Section 11 (a) and (d) remains intact and is not whittled down by Explanation II to Section 11.

Constitutionality of Section 32 A

It was contended that Article 32 A is arbitrary, ultra vires, and violative of Article 300A and Articles 14, 19 and 21. It provides undeserved immunity which would be acquired through proceeds of crime.

The Supreme Court observed that the provision is well thought out. It is not that if the wrongdoers are allowed to get away. They remain liable. Only criminal liability of Corporate Debtor is extinguished.

Constitutionality of third proviso of Section 7

3rd proviso of Section 7 also made the amended provisions applicable on those applications which had been filed but has not been admitted. It was contended that amendment could not have been applied with retrospective effect as it takes away vested rights of such applicants.

The Court observed that right of action is, undoubtedly, a vested right. Role of the Applicant fades out after admission of application is made under Section 7 (5). The right which is given is in rem. The application may result in liquidation of the Corporate Debtor if CIRP is unsuccessful.

The Supreme Court held that imposing the threshold requirement under the 3rd proviso is not a mere matter of procedure. It impairs vested rights. Legislature has purported to equate persons who had not filed applications with persons like the Petitioners who had filed applications under unamended law.

The Supreme Court observed that a vested right can be taken away by retrospective law. The Supreme Court observed the public interest behind amendment cannot be ignored. The sheer numbers in which applications proliferated combined with the results it could produce, cannot be brushed aside as an irrational or capricious aspect to have been guided by in making the law.

ELEGNA CO-OP HOUSING AND COMMERCIAL SOCIETY LTD. Vs. EDELWEISS ASSET RECONSTRUCTION COMPANY LIMITED

The Supreme Court in Elegna Co-op Housing and Commercial Society Ltd. Vs Edelweiss Asset Reconstruction Company Ltd (Civil Appeal 10261/2025) held that the right to initiate or participate in insolvency proceedings is statutory, not equitable. The Supreme Court further held that a society or Resident Welfare Association, not being a creditor in its own right and not recognised as an authorised representative of allottees under the IBC, has no *locus standi* to intervene in proceedings arising out of a Section 7 petition.

Case Title : Elegna Co-op Housing and Commercial Society Ltd. Vs Edelweiss Asset Reconstruction Company Ltd Date of Decision : 15.01.2026 Bench : J. B. Pardiwala, J; R. Mahadevan, J

FACTS OF THE CASE

The Corporate Debtor availed financial assistance of Rs. 70 Crore from ECL Finance Ltd. under two loan agreements for developing project the Takshila Elegna and executed requisite documents. The loan accounts were classified NPA on 30.12.2021. On 09.05.2022 loan was assigned to Edelweiss Asset Reconstruction Company Ltd. Subsequent to that Financial Creditor initiated recovery proceedings for amount of Rs. 57,24,96,064/- before DRT. One -time settlement was entered which also failed. Subsequently, the Financial Creditor also filed a Section 7 Petition for initiation of insolvency proceedings against the Corporate Debtor. During the pendency of proceedings the Financial Creditor issued notice for sale of secured assets. NCLT dismissed the Petition on the ground that IBC was invoked as recovery mechanism rather than a tool of insolvency resolution. The NCLT also observed that the project was viable and admitting the corporate debtor into insolvency will adversely affect the interests of home buyers.

The Financial Creditor preferred an appeal before the NCLAT. Elegna Co-op. Housing and Commercial Society also filed an intervention application. NCLAT allowed the appeal and also rejected the intervention application on the ground of lack of *locus standi*. Appeal was filed before t Supreme Court.

FINDINGS OF THE SUPREME COURT

The Supreme Court determined two issues in the matter –

(i) Whether the NCLAT was correct in admitting the Corporate Debtor into the Corporate Insolvency Resolution Process ?

The Supreme Court reiterated the well settled principle that once the Adjudicating Authority is satisfied that a financial debt exists and a default has occurred, it must admit the application unless it is incomplete. The Supreme Court relied on judgments of the Supreme Court in Innoventive Industries Vs ICICI Bank (2018)1SCC407, E. S. Krishnamurthy Vs. Bharath Hi-Tech Builders Pvt. Ltd. (2022)3SCC161, M. Suresh Kumar Reddy Vs. Canara Bank and Ors (2023 SCC Online SC608) and Indus Biotech Pvt. Ltd. Vs Kotak India Venture (Offshore) Fund (2021)6SCC436. The Supreme Court observed that the Vidarbha Industries is a narrow exception on its peculiar facts and is not applicable.

The Supreme Court observed that reliance on business viability, unsold inventory, project status, or anticipated receivables does not constitute "good reasons" in law to defer or deny admission of CIRP.

The Supreme Court also observed that the Code does not prohibit a financial creditor from invoking CIRP merely because recovery proceedings under the SARFAESI Act or before the DRT are pending or have been initiated. Allegations of mala fide invocation can be examined only within the framework of Section 65 of the Code, which requires specific pleadings and proof of abuse of process by the Corporate Debtor.

The Supreme Court observed that the concept of revival under the IBC does not exclude recovery altogether; it excludes abuse of insolvency as a pressure tactic. The Adjudicating Authority retains a crucial gatekeeping role at later stages, particularly at the time of approval of the resolution plan, to ensure compliance with the Code while respecting the primacy of the commercial wisdom of the Committee of Creditors.

The Supreme Court concluded that the debt and default having been conclusively established, and the narrow exception carved out in Vidarbha Industries being clearly inapplicable, the NCLAT was fully justified in admitting the Corporate Debtor into the CIRP.

(ii) Whether the NCLAT was correct in rejecting the intervention application filed by the Society ?

The Supreme Court observed that in GLAS Trust Co. LLC v. BYJU Raveendran (2025) 3 SCC 625, it held that while there is no rigid requirement restricting the right to appeal only to the applicant creditor and the corporate debtor, such latitude applies when proceedings are *in rem* post-admission of CIRP. At the pre-admission stage, proceedings under Section 7 remain in personam, and neither the Adjudicating Authority nor the Appellate Authority is required to hear other creditors, much less unrelated third parties. When proceedings are in personam, no right of audience inheres in persons who are strangers to the debt and default forming the basis of the application.

The Supreme Court observed that a financial creditor under Section 5(7) must be a person to whom a financial debt is owed. While the Explanation to Section 5(8)(f) deems individual allottees to be financial creditors, it does not extend such status to societies or associations unless the entity is itself a creditor in its own right, or is statutorily recognised as an authorised representative under the Code. A society is a distinct juristic entity separate from its members. Unless it has itself advanced funds, executed allotment agreements, or received allotments, it cannot claim financial creditor status. The right to initiate or participate in CIRP flows from the debt transaction and the statute, not from associative or representational interest.

The Supreme Court concluded that in the present case, the appellant Society is neither a financial nor an operational creditor. It is a maintenance society not constituted for insolvency representation. No documentary proof of registration, collective authorisation, or general body resolution has been produced. Membership is automatic and mandatory, negating consensual representation. Reliance on compulsory membership to claim representational authority on behalf of allottees is nothing but a *brutum fulmen*. Notably, the intervention application was filed only at the appellate stage and not before the NCLT. The Society is not a party to the financial transaction forming the substratum of the Section 7 application. Hence, no statutory right of appeal inheres in the appellant.

Although the Supreme Court affirmed the findings of the Hon'ble NCLAT, it issued following directions for safeguarding the interests of home-buyers- (i) The Information Memorandum shall mandatorily disclose comprehensive and complete details of all allottees; (ii) Where the Committee of Creditors, upon due consideration, finds it not viable to approve handover of possession in terms of Regulation 4E of the CIRP Regulations, it shall mandatorily record cogent and specific reasons in writing for such decision. (iii)Any recommendation for liquidation by the Committee of Creditors shall be accompanied by a reasoned justification recorded in writing,

CLASSIFICATION OF CREDITORS

NEW OKHLA INDUSTRIAL DEVELOPMENT AUTHORITY Vs. ANAND SONBHADRA

The Supreme Court in New Okhla Industrial Development Authority Vs Anand Sonbhadra (2023) 1 SCC 724 held that New Okhla Industrial Development Authority (NOIDA) is not a Financial Creditor and claim of the authority falls under the category of Operational Debt.

Case Title : New Okhla Industrial Development Authority Vs Anand Sonbhadra (2023) 1 SCC 724
Date of Decision : 17.05.2022
Bench : K. M. Joseph, J; Hrishikesh Roy, J

FACTS OF THE CASE

NOIDA (Appellant) acquired land for setting up of an "urban and industrial township". The Appellant entered into lease deed for construction of the residential flats with Shubhkamna Buildtech Pvt. Ltd. (Corporate Debtor) on 30th July, 2010. The Lease Deed provided that the shareholding of lessor will remain unchanged till temporary occupancy/completion of the first phase. Consideration (10% of total amount) of Rs. 46,14, 69,996.40/- stood paid. The lease deed further contemplated moratorium of 24 months from the date of allotment. Only interest of 7% per annum compounded half yearly which accrued during the moratorium period shall be payable in equal half yearly instalments. The Lease Deed provided for payment of balance 90% of amount after expiry of moratorium in 16 half yearly instalments along with interest as specifically set out.

CIRP was initiated against the Corporate Debtor. The Appellant initially filed claim in Form B as Operational Creditor. Subsequently the Appellant filed claim in Form C as Financial Creditor. The Resolution Professional rejected the claim under the category of Financial Creditor. The Appellant approached NCLT which also held that the Appellant is not Financial Creditor. The Appellant preferred appeal before NCLAT which also dismissed the appeal.

FINDINGS OF THE SUPREME COURT

Whether the lease is covered under the definition of "Financial Debt" under Section 5 (8) of IBC ?

The Supreme Court observed that essential requirement to attract Section 5 (8) is that there must be a debt along with interest, if any, which is disbursed against consideration for time value of money. In this matter there is no doubt that a debt exists. Interest is also payable but as held in Orator Marketing Pvt. Ltd. Vs. Samtex Desinz Pvt. Ltd. (2021) SCC Online SC 513 interest is not an essential feature of Financial Debt.

Disbursement is essential requirement of Financial Debt under Section 5 (8) and such disbursement must be from Creditor to Debtor. The Supreme Court observed that there is no disbursement of any debt or any sums by the appellant to the lessee, therefore Appellant cannot be Financial Creditor.

Whether debt is Financial Debt under Section 5 (8) (d) of IBC ?

Under Section 5 (8) (d), Financial Debt includes the amount of any liability in respect of any lease or hire purchase contract which is deemed as a finance or capital lease under Indian Accounting Standards. The Supreme Court noted that under Rule 61 of Indian Accounting Standard , the lessor is obliged to classify each of its leases as operating lease or financial lease. It is not case of Appellant that it has classified lease as Financial Lease.

Rule 62 of Indian Accounting Standards provides that a lease is classified as a financial lease if it transfers, substantially all the risks and rewards incidental to ownership of an underlying asset. The Supreme Court noted that there is no right with the lessee to purchase the leased asset i.e. land. Ownership of land remains with the Appellant.

Rule 63 of Indian Accounting Standards provides that the lease term is for the major part of economic life even if title is not transferred. The Court observed that economic life of land is not limited. Land does not depreciate with passage of time. Ordinarily the price of land will increase with time.

The Supreme Court concluded that the lease does not fall in the category of capital lease.

Whether debt is financial debt under Section 5 (8) (f) ?

Section 5 (8) (f) provides that a financial debt includes any amount raised under any transaction, including any forward sale or purchase agreement, having the commercial effect of a borrowing. The Supreme Court relied on Pioneer Urban Land and observed that the presence of profit motive is essential for the commercial effect of borrowing. The Appellant has not raised any amount from the Corporate Debtor as such the question whether it has commercial effect of borrowing does not arise. Obligation incurred by lessee to pay the rental and the premium cannot be treated as an amount raised by lessee from the appellant.

The Supreme Court observed that concept of disbursement as present in the main provision appears to be mandatory in Section 5 (8) (f).

Whether Appellant is an Operational Creditor ?

The Court noted that in several legislations the Appellant has been treated as Local Authority. The Appellant also provides civil amenities to the local residents as such it is indeed a local authority. There were concurrent findings of NCLT and NCLAT that the Appellant is an Operational Creditor. The Supreme Court held that Appellant is an Operational Creditor.

CONSOLIDATED CONSTRUCTION CONSORTIUM LIMITED VS HITRO ENERGY SOLUTIONS PVT. LTD.

The Supreme Court held in Consolidated Construction Consortium Ltd Vs Hitro Energy Solutions Pvt Ltd (2022) SCC Online SC 142 that Operational Creditors include persons who either provide goods or services to the Corporate Debtor or receive goods or services from the Corporate Debtor, provided the claim has a nexus with the provision of goods or services.

Case Title : M/s Consolidated Construction Consortium Ltd Vs M/s Hitro Energy Solutions Pvt Ltd
Date of Decision : 04.02.2022
Bench : Dr. Dhananjaya Y. Chandrachud, J; Surya Kant, J; Vikram Nath, J

FACTS OF THE CASE

The Appellant was executing a project with Chennai Metro Rail Ltd. An order was placed with the Appellant to supply of light fitting. In turn,Aappellant placed orders with proprietary concern through three purchase orders. Proprietary concern requested for advance payment of Rs. 50,00,000/-. CMRL issued a cheque in favour of the Respondent. In the meantime, CMRL informed the appellant that the project has been terminated. The proprietary concern deposited the cheque and withdrew the amount of Rs. 50,00,000/-.

The Respondent was incorporated as a company and took over the business of the proprietary concern. The Appellant requested the Respondent to return Rs. 50,00,000/- which was refused on one ground or another.

The Appellant sent demand notice under Section 8 of IBC and thereafter filed application under Section 9 of the IBC. The NCLT vide order dated 6th December, 2018 admitted the application under Section 9 of IBC. The order of NCLT was set aside by the NCLAT on the ground that the Appellant has not supplied any goods or services to the Respondent as such Appellant is not covered under the definition of "operational creditor".

Aggrieved by the order of NCLAT, the Appellant approached the Supreme Court.

FINDINGS OF THE SUPREME COURT

Section 5 (21) defines the term operational debt, which is as under:

5 (21) . "Operational Debt" means a claim in respect of the provision of goods and services including employment or a debt in respect of the re-payment of dues arising under any law for the time being in force and payable to the Central Government, State Government or any local authority.

The Supreme Court noted that unlike other jurisdictions which differentiate between secured and unsecured creditors, the IBC is unique to the extent that it provides for two different types of creditors i.e. financial and operational creditor.

Operational creditors are those whose debt arises from operational transactions. These generally include transactions involving goods and services which are considered necessary for the operational functioning of an entity.

The Supreme Court observed that the Respondent's submissions narrowly define Operational Creditors under the IBC to only include those who supply goods and services to the Corporate Debtor and exclude those who receive goods and services from the Corporate Debtor.

The Supreme Court rejected the submission of the Respondent. The Supreme Court observed that Section 5 (21) defines "operational debt" as a claim in respect of the provision of goods and services. The requirement is that the claim must have some nexus with a provision of goods and services, without specifying who is to be the supplier or the receiver.

The Supreme Court also observed that notice under Section 8 of IBC can be issued either through demand notice or an invoice. As such, the presence of an invoice is not sine qua non, since demand notice can also be issued on the basis of other documents which prove existence of debt. Regulation 7 (2) (b) (i) and (ii) of CIRP makes it clearer which provides that an Operational Creditor has an option between relying on a contract of supply of goods and services with the Corporate Debtor or an invoice demanding payment for goods and services supplied to the Corporate Debtor. While the latter indicates that the Operational Creditor should have supplied goods and services to the CD, the former is broad enough to include all forms of contracts for supply of goods and services between the Operational Creditor and Corporate Debtor, including ones where the Operational Creditor may have been the receiver of goods and services from the Corporate Debtor.

The Supreme Court concluded that advance payment made to the Corporate Debtor for supply of goods and services would be considered as an operational debt.

The Supreme Court also concluded that the Respondent took over the proprietary concern and was liable to repay the debt to the appellant. The application under Section 9 IBC was maintainable. The Supreme Court also held that the Application was within limitation. The supreme Court allowed the appeal and set aside the order of the NCLAT.

M/S ORATOR MARKETING PVT. LTD. Vs. M/S SAMTEX DESINZ PVT. LTD.

The Supreme Court in M/s Orator Marketing Pvt. Ltd. Vs. M/s Samtex Desinz Pvt. Ltd. (2023) 3 SCC 753 held that an interest-free loan is covered under the definition of Financial Debt under Section 5(8) of the Insolvency and Bankruptcy Code, 2016

Case Title : M/S Orator Marketing Pvt. Ltd. Vs. M/S Samtex Desinz Pvt. Ltd.
Date of Decision : 26.07.2021
Bench : Indira Banerjee, J; V. Ramasubramanian, J

FACTS OF THE CASE

Sameer Sales Pvt. Ltd. advanced a term loan of Rs. 1.60 Crore to the Corporate Debtor for a period of two years to enable the Corporate Debtor to meet its working capital requirement. Sameer Sales assigned the outstanding loan to the Appellant. The loan was to be repaid by the Corporate Debtor in full within 01.02.2020.

The Appellant filed a Petition under Section 7 IBC for initiation of Corporate Insolvency Resolution Process. The NCLT dismissed the application on the ground that the claim is not covered under "financial debt" as loan was interest free.

An appeal was filed before NCLAT, which was also dismissed.

FINDINGS OF THE SUPREME COURT

The short issue before the Supreme Court in this matter was whether loan advanced to the Corporate Debtor, which was interest-free , will be covered under financial debt or not .

The Supreme Court observed that in construing and/or interpreting any statutory provision, one must look into the legislative intent of the statute.

When a question arises as to the meaning of a certain provision in a statute, the provision has to be read in context.

The Supreme Court noted that in Pioneer Urban Land and Infrastructure Ltd Vs. Union of India (2019) 8 SCC 416 even individuals who were debenture holders and fixed deposit holders were held to be financial creditors.

Section 5 (8) defines "financial debt" Section 5(8) defines "Financial Debt" as a debt, along with interest, if any, which is disbursed against the consideration for the time value of money, and includes the categories specified in clauses (a) to (i).

The NCLT and NCLAT have overlooked the words "if any" which could not have been intended to be otiose. "Financial Debt" means outstanding principal due in respect of loan and would also include interest thereon, if any interest was payable. If there is no interest payable on the loan, only outstanding principal would qualify as financial debt. Both NCLT and NCLAT failed to notice clause (f) of Section 5 (8), in terms whereof "financial debt" includes any amount raised under any transaction having commercial effect of borrowing.

The Court observed that sub-clauses (a) to (i) of Section 5 (8) IBC are apparently illustrative and not exhaustive. Where the word is defined to include something, the definition is prima facie extensive.

The Supreme Court observed that definition of "Financial Debt" in Section 5 (8) IBC does not expressly exclude an interest free loan. "Financial Debt" would have to be construed to include interest free loans advanced to finance the business operations of a corporate body.

The Supreme Court set aside the judgment of NCLAT and allowed the appeal. Section 7 Petition was revived and directed to be decided afresh in accordance with law.

EPC CONSTRUCTIONS INDIA LTD Vs. MATIX FERTILIZERS & CHEMICAL LTD.

The Supreme Court held in EPC Constructions Ltd Vs. Matix Fertilisers & Chemical Ltd. (Civil Appeal 11077/2025) that Cumulative Redeemable Preference Shares (CRPS) are part of the share capital of a company and cannot be treated as "financial debt" under the Insolvency and Bankruptcy Code (IBC).

Case Title : EPC Constructions Ltd Vs. Matix Fertilisers & Chemical Ltd. Date of Decision : 28.10.2025 Bench : J. B. Pardiwala, J; K. V. Viswanathan, J

BRIEF FACTS

EPC Construction India Ltd. (EPCC) entered into an engineering , procurement and construction (EPC) Contract with Matix Fertilizers & Chemicals Ltd. in 2009 for the establishment of a fertilizer complex for Ammonia and Urea production at Panagarh Industrial Park, District Burdwan, West Bengal. Separate on-shore and off-shore supply contracts were executed. Matix became liable to pay Rs. 572.72 crore to EPCC under the contract. Out of this amount, Rs. 400 crore was converted into Cumulative Redeemable Preference Shares (CRPS).

EPCC went into CIRP and, through its Resolution Professional, raised a demand of Rs. 632.71 crore (Rs. 310 crore on account of maturity of CRPS and Rs. 322.71 crore on account of outstanding receivables). EPCC subsequently went into liquidation. The Liquidator initiated CIRP proceedings against Matix under Section 7, which were dismissed by the NCLT. The NCLT rejected the petition on the ground that the balance sheets for 2018-19 to 2020-21 showed continuous losses, and the fourth proviso to Section 123 of the Companies Act, 2013 clearly provides that no dividend is payable out of losses. Unless the CRPS become redeemable, they cannot be regarded a "debt," much less a financial debt. An appeal before the Hon'ble NCLAT was also dismissed.

FINDINGS OF THE SUPREME COURT

The Supreme Court noted that it is well settled under Company Law that preference shares are part of a company's share capital and the amounts paid up on them are not loans. Dividends are payable only when the company earns profits. If dividends were paid without profits or in excess of the profits earned, it would amount to an illegal return of capital. Since the amount paid up on preference shares is not a loan, it does not qualify as a debt.

The Court observed that for maintaining proceedings under Section 7, the application must be filed by a financial creditor and only when a default has occurred. For a default "to kick in," there must be non-payment of debt when the whole or any part of the debt has become due and payable and is not paid. Admittedly, the CRPS had not become due and payable since Matix had not made profits, did not have any reserves from past profits, and did not possess proceeds from a fresh issue of shares for the purpose of redemption. In these admitted circumstances, the question of any default under Section 3(12) IBC does not arise.

The Court further held that the expiry of the redemption period of the CRPS does not strengthen the appellant's case. The holders of CRPS continue to remain preference shareholders, and as preference shareholders they do not enjoy the status of creditors. Hence, they do not fall within the definition of a financial creditor for the purposes of Section 7 IBC.

The Supreme Court also observed that the earlier outstanding amount had stood extinguished upon conversion, and the nature of the relationship between the parties became that of a preference shareholder and company. There was no question of any underlying contrary intent, as the sole intention was conversion of the debt into preference shareholding.

The Court rejected the argument that the financial debt was an admitted liability in the accounts of the respondent. It held that accounting treatment in accordance with accounting rules cannot determine the legal relationship between the parties as reflected in the documents executed by them. The Court concluded that cumulative redeemable preference shares do not satisfy the definition of "debt" under Section 5(8) IBC.

The Supreme Court found no merit in the appeal and dismissed it.

INITIATION OF CIRP

M/S SURENDRA TRADING COMPANY Vs. M/S JUGGILAL KAMLAPAT JUTE MILLS COMPANY LTD AND OTHERS

The Supreme Court held in M/s Surendra Trading Company Vs M/s Juggilal Kamlapat Jute Mills Company Ltd. (2017)16SCC 143 that period of seven days provided under Section 7 (5), Section 9 (5) or Section 10 (4) for removal of defects in an application for initiating CIRP is not mandatory.

Case Title : M/s Surendra Trading Company Vs. M/s Juggilal Kamlapat Jute Mills Company Ltd. Date of Decision : 19.09.2017 Bench : A. K. Sikri, J; Ashok Bhushan, J

FACTS OF THE CASE

Juggilal Kamlapat Jute Mills Company became a sick industrial company and was referred under the Sick Industrial Companies (Special Provisions) Act (SICA). Appellant had supplied raw jute to Respondent No. 1 payment against which was outstanding. After IBC came into force, the Appellant sent a a demand notice under prescribed form on 06.01 .2017. As the dues were not paid the Appellant filed application before the Adjudicating Authority for initiating CIRP against the Respondent on 10.02.2017. The Registry raised certain defects on 14.02.2017. The Adjudicating Authority granted time to remove defects on 16.02.2017. The Appellant removed defects on 28.02.2017. The Appellant filed documents related to BIFR proceedings on 03.03.2017. On 09.03.2017 the Adjudicating Authority directed the Corporate Debtor to maintain status quo in respect of immovable properties. An appeal was filed before the NCLAT wherein order of NCLT was set aside and directed the NCLT to close the application. NCLAT held that period of 14 days prescribed for admitting or rejecting an application is not mandatory but provision of removal of defects within seven days are mandatory.

FINDINGS OF THE SUPREME COURT

The issue before the Supreme Court was whether the period of seven days prescribed under Section 7 (5), Section 9 (5) and Section 10 (4) for removal of defects in an Application for initiating CIRP is mandatory or directory ?

The Supreme Court noted that the timeline for several activities by either creditor or adjudicating authority are mentioned under IBC.

The Supreme Court observed that time consumed in filing of application under Section 7, 9 or 10 and removal of defects do not impact time period for completion of CIRP given under Section 12 IBC. Such period is computed from the date of admission. In fact till the objections are removed it cannot be treated as application validly filed. No purpose is going to be served in making period of seven days mandatory.

The Supreme Court observed that if rejection on account of delay in removing defect is treated as rejection on merits, it will be travesty of justice as even if the case of the Applicant is strong on merits, such applicant will be shown the door. if rejection is treated as administrative order, such application can again be filed afresh. In both scenarios, treating the period of seven days as mandatory will serve no purpose.

The Supreme Court observed that there are three stages in IBC proceedings – (i) In the first stage application is filed. If there is any defect, seven days have to be given for removing defects. If application is defect free it is listed before the Adjudicating Authority. (ii) The Adjudicating Authority has to take a decision within fourteen days to either accept or reject the Application, (iii) After admission of application CIRP commences.

NCLAT has held timeline of fourteen days given in second stage as directory. The Supreme Court reasoned that if timeline provided in second stage is not mandatory then there is no reason to make timeline given in the first stage mandatory.

The Supreme Court held that provision providing for removal of defects within seven days is directory and not mandatory. At the same time, the Supreme Court directed that if defects are not removed within seven days, the Applicant has to file an application explaining reasons why defects could not be removed within seven days.

Accordingly, the Supreme Court allowed the appeal and set aside the order of NCLAT to the extent it has held that provision providing for period of seven days for removal of defect is mandatory.

MACQUARIE BANK LTD. Vs. SHILPI CABLE TECHNOLOGIES LTD.

The Supreme Court in Macquarie Bank Ltd. Vs Shilpi Cable Technologies Ltd. (2018) 2 SCC 674 held that certificate from financial institution under Section 9 (3) (c) is not mandatory for filing Application under Section 9 IBC. It was also held that an Advocate is competent to send demand notice under Section 8 IBC.

Case Title : Macquarie Bank Ltd. Vs Shilpi Cable Technologies Ltd. Date of Decision : 15.12.2017 Bench : R. F. Nariman, J; Navin Sinha, J

FACTS OF THE CASE

Hamera International Pvt. Ltd. executed an agreement with the Appellant Bank on 27.07.2015 by which the Appellant purchased original supplier's rights, title and interest in a supply agreement in favour of the Respondent. The Respondent entered into agreement dated 02.12.2015 for supply of goods worth USD 6, 321,337.11 in accordance with terms and conditions contained in the said sales contract. The supplier issued two invoices dated 21.12.2015 and 31.12.2015. Payment terms under the said invoices were 150 days from the date of the bill. As amounts were not paid , the Appellant issued notices under Sections 433 and 434 of Companies Act, 1956, which was disputed by the Respondent.

After enactment of IBC the Appellant issued demand notice under Section 8 IBC on 14.02.2017 for payment of outstanding amount. The Appellant initiated insolvency proceedings under Section 9 IBC. The NCLT rejected the Petition on the ground that certificate under Section 9 (3)(c) has not been submitted. The NCLT also observed that dispute has been raised in the matter.

An appeal was filed before NCLAT which concurred with NCLT and dismissed the Appeal. The NCLAT also held that an advocate/lawyer cannot send notice on behalf of the Operational Creditor.

Aggrieved by order of the NCLAT, the Appellant preferred appeal before the Supreme Court.

FINDINGS OF THE SUPREME COURT

Two issues were involved in the matter – (i) Whether certificate from a financial institution under Section 9 (3) (c) of IBC is mandatory for filing Application by Operational Creditor ? and (ii) Whether an advocate is ineligible to send demand notice under Section 8 of the Code ?

Whether certificate under Section 9 (1) (c) is mandatory for filing Application by Operational Creditor ?

The Supreme Court observed that Section 9 (1) contains certain conditions precedent for triggering the code on behalf of the Operational Creditor which are – (i) occurrence of default, (ii) delivery of demand notice or invoice demanding payment of operational debt and (iii) non-payment of unpaid operational debt within 10 days of demand notice or reply which does not indicate existence of dispute or repayment of unpaid operational debt. If only these conditions are met, an application can be filed under Section 9 (2) of the Code.

It is mandatory under Section 9 (3) (a) R/w Rule 5 and 6 of Adjudicating Rules and Form 3 and 5 to attach demand notice/invoice with application. If the Applicant does not receive any notice of dispute, an affidavit to that effect has to be attached under Section 9 (3) (b).

The Supreme Court observed that certificate from the financial institution maintaining accounts of the Operational Creditor confirming that there is no payment of unpaid operational debt by the Corporate Debtor is certainly not a condition precedent under Section 9 (3) (c). The expression "confirming" makes it clear that it is only a piece of evidence although certainly an important one. Relevant Form speaks of copies of relevant accounts kept by banks/financial institutions maintaining accounts of the Operational Creditor, confirming that there is no payment of unpaid operational debt only "if available".

Whether an advocate is ineligible to send demand notice under Section 8 of the Code ?

The Supreme Court observed that Section 8 of IBC speaks of an operational creditor "delivering" demand notice. If the Legislature had wished to restrict sending of demand notice by the Operational Creditor only, the Legislature would have used the word "issued". The Court noted that signature of person "authorized to act" has to be appended on both demand notice and application in relevant forms. Both the expressions show that an authorized agent or a lawyer acting on behalf of a client is included within the aforesaid expression.

The Supreme Court observed that the word "practice" used under Section 30 of the Advocates Act, 1961 includes all preparatory steps including filing of an application before a Tribunal. Advocates Act and IBC have to be harmoniously interpreted. Non-obstante clause in Section 238 does not override the Advocates Act, as there is no inconsistency between Section 9 R/w Adjudicating Authority Rules and Forms and Advocates Act. The Supreme Court concluded that a notice sent on behalf of Operational Creditor would be in order.

The Supreme Court set aside the judgment of NCLAT on both counts.

INDUS BIOTECH PVT. LTD. Vs. KOTAK INDIA VENTURE (OFFSHORE) FUND

The Supreme Court held in Indus Biotech Pvt. Ltd. Vs. Kotak India Venture (Offshore Fund) & Ors, AIR 2021 SC 1638 that if Application under Section 8 of Arbitration and Conciliation Act, 1996 is filed before NCLT, the submissions made in Section 7 IBC Application have also to be considered. After considering all the relevant facts NCLT may admit 7 IBC Application or reject it. In case of rejection the parties can approach appropriate forum for appointment of Arbitral Tribunal.

Case Title : Indus Biotech Pvt. Ltd. Vs. Kotak India Venture (Offshore) Fund & Ors Date of Decision : 26.03.2021 Bench : S. A. Bobde, CJI; A. S. Bopanna, J; V. Ramasubramanian

FACTS OF THE CASE

An Arbitration Petition was filed before the Supreme Court under provisions of Arbitration and Conciliation Act, 1996 by Indus Biotech against the Respondent No. 1 to 4 seeking constitution of Arbitral Tribunal. Respondent No. 1 is a Mauritius based company while Respondent No. 2-4 are India based. The disputes arose from several Share Subscription and Shareholders' Agreements. Through these agreements Respondent No. 1 to 4 subscribed equity shares and Optionally Convertible Redeemable Preference Shares (OCRPS) of the Corporate Debtor.

The Corporate Debtor took a decision to issue a Qualified Initial Public Offering (QIPO). However, under SEBI regulations a company which has any outstanding convertible securities or any other right was not entitled to issue QIPO. The Corporate Debtor proposed to Respondent No. 1 to 4 to convert OCRPS into equity shares. Dispute arose between the parties regarding calculation and conversion formula to be applied in conversion of OCRPS to equity shares.

The Respondents No. 1 to 4 claimed amount of Rs. 367,08,56,503/- on redemption of OCRPS. The Respondents demanded the said amount from the Corporate Debtor and as the same was not paid by the Corporate Debtor, a Petition under Section 7 was filed before NCLT by the Respondent No. 2. The Corporate Debtor filed Application under Section 8 of the Arbitration and Conciliation Act, 1996 for referring the matter to arbitration.

NCLT Mumbai rejected the Application under Section 7 and allowed the Application under Section 8 of the Arbitration and Conciliation Act, 1996.

FINDINGS OF THE SUPREME COURT

The Supreme Court observed that it is not in dispute that the share subscription and shareholders' agreements were in existence having arbitration clauses. However, the nature of Arbitration Tribunal has to be considered as one concerns international arbitration while others concern domestic arbitrations.

It was contended before the Supreme Court that Indus Biotech Private Ltd having defaulted and Section 7 IBC Petition has been filed, dispute is no longer arbitrable.

The Supreme Court observed that the test of arbitrability in respect of in rem actions has been laid down in Vidya Drolia & Ors Vs Durga Trading and Ors (2021) 2 SCC 1. The Supreme Court relying on Vidya Drolia held that a proceeding will be non-arbitrable when a proceeding is in rem and proceedings under IBC is considered only in rem after admission.

The Supreme Court after relying on Swiss Ribbon Pvt Ltd Vs Union of India (2019) 4 SCC 17 and Pioneer Urban Land and Infrastructure Limited Vs Union of India AIR (2019) SC 4055 held that to consider Section 7 proceedings as in rem proceedings it is necessary that the Adjudicating Authority has applied its mind, recorded a finding of default and admitted the Petition. Once Section 7 Petition is admitted third party right is created on all the creditors of the Corporate Debtor and will have erga omnes effect. Mere filing of a petition cannot be considered a proceeding in rem.

The Supreme Court observed that if an application under Section 8 of Arbitration and Conciliation Act is filed, the NCLT has a duty to advert to contentions put forth on the application filed under Section 7 of the Code, examine the material placed by the Financial Creditor and record satisfaction whether there is a default. If the Adjudicating Authority reached conclusion that there is default and debt is payable, arbitration should not be allowed to delay the insolvency proceedings.

Once Insolvency Petition under Section 7 is admitted the proceedings will get transformed into in rem proceedings having erga omnes effect.

On the other hand if the Adjudicating Authority concluded that there is no default, the Section 7 Petition will be rejected and parties can approach appropriate authority for appointment of arbitral tribunal.

The Supreme Court affirmed the view taken by NCLT. The Supreme Court also observed that the dispute can be resolved by arbitral tribunals consisting of the same members but constituted separately under each agreement.

DENA BANK (NOW BANK OF BARODA) Vs. C. SHIVAKUMAR REDDY AND ANR.

The Supreme Court in Dena Bank (Now Bank of Baroda) Vs. C. Shivakumar Reddy and Anr. (2021) 10 SCC 330 held that a judgment/decree in favor of Financial Creditor would give rise to fresh cause of action to initiate proceedings under Section 7 IBC.

> Case Status : Dena Bank (Now Bank of Baroda) Vs. C. Shivakumar Reddy and Anr
> Date of Decision : 04.08.2021
> Bench : Indira Banerjee, J; V. Ramasubramanian, J

FACTS OF THE CASE

Appellant Bank has sanctioned term loan and letter of credit cum buyer's credit in favour of the Corporate Debtor with an upper limit of Rs. 45 Crore. The Corporate Debtor defaulted in payment of its dues and the loan amount of Corporate Debtor was declared NPA on 31st December, 2013. On 22nd December, 2014, the Appellant Bank issued legal notice to the Corporate Debtor calling upon them to make payment of Rs. 52.12 Crore. On 1st January, 2015 the Appellant Bank filed an application being O.A. No. 16/2015 under Section 19 of the Recovery of Debts Due to Banks and Financial Institutions Act, 1993 for recovery of Rs. 51.12 Crore.

On 27th March, 2017 the DRT passed final judgment and order against the Corporate Debtor for recovery of Rs. 52.12 Crore with 16.55% interest. On 25th May, 2017, DRT issued a recovery certificate of Rs. 52.12 Crore. The Corporate Debtor in its annual report for FY 2016-17 and 2017-18 acknowledged its liability in respect of the loan taken by it from the Appellant Bank.

On 1st October, 2018, the Appellant Bank issued demand notice and thereafter on 12th October, 2018 filed an Application under Section 7 of IBC. On 2nd January, 2019, Vijaya Bank, Dena Bank and Bank of

Baroda were amalgamated. On 9th January, 2019, the Appellant filed an application for placing on record additional documents including final judgment and order of DRT and Recovery Certificate. By order dated 4th February, 2019 the NCLAT directed Appellant to file amended Application. On 5th March, 2019 the Appellant Bank filed an application to place on record one time settlement and annual statements, which was allowed by the NCLT.

NCLT admitted the application vide order dated 21st March, 2019 and initiated CIRP. An appeal was filed before NCLAT which set aside the order of NCLT.

FINDINGS OF THE SUPREME COURT

Three issues arose for consideration in this matter – (i) Whether the Section 7 Application was barred by limitation ? (ii) Whether final judgment and decree of the DRT will give fresh cause of action to the Financial Creditor to initiate proceedings under Section 7 IBC ? (iii) Whether there is bar on amendment of pleadings or producing additional documents under Section 7 IBC ?

The Supreme Court noted that an Application under Section 7 IBC has to be made in the prescribed form 1 of Application to Adjudicating Authority Rules along with documents and records required therein. The Financial Creditor can only fill in particulars as specified in the various columns of the Form. There is no scope for elaborate pleadings. Application under Section 7 IBC cannot be compared with plaint in a suit. Such application cannot be judged by the same standards as a plaint in the suit.

The Supreme Court observed that IBC is not just another statute for recovery of debts. It is essentially a statute which works towards revival of the Corporate Debtor, which is unable to pay its debts.

IBC has overriding effect on other acts. Unlike coercive recovery litigation, CIRP under IBC is not adversarial to the interests of the Corporate Debtor. Relegation of creditors to the remedy of coercive litigation against the Corporate Debtors could be detrimental to the interests of the Corporate Debtor and its creditors alike. Provisions of IBC and Rules and Regulations made thereunder have to be construed liberally in a purposive manner to further the objects of the statute and not be given a narrow, pedantic interpretation which defeats purposes of the Act.

The Supreme Court held that on careful reading of the provisions of IBC, it is evident that there is no bar to the filing of documents at any time until a final order either admitting or dismissing the application has been passed. The time stipulation of 14 days in Section 7 (4) to ascertain existence of a default is apparently directory and not mandatory. There is no penalty except recording of reasons by the Adjudicating Authority. Section 7 (5) (b) obliges Adjudicating Authority to give notice to the applicant to rectify any defect in application within seven days, but there is no penalty for not curing defects within seven days. Even in case of Section 12 , the Supreme Court in Arcelormittal (India) Pvt. Ltd. Vs. Satish Kumar Gupta & Ors (2019) 2 SCC 1 held that time stipulation was directory. Failure to complete Resolution Process within stipulated time should not result in corporate death by shelving an otherwise good resolution plan.

On aspect of limitation the Supreme Court observed that the view of the NCLAT , that there was nothing on record to show that there was acknowledgment of debt within three years, is not sustainable in view of statement of accounts/balance sheets/Financial Statements for years 2016-17 and 2017-18 and offer of one time settlement.

The Supreme Court observed that in any case, NCLAT overlooked the fact that a Recovery Certificate has been issued in favour of Appellant Bank on 25th May, 2017. The Recovery Certificate itself gives a fresh cause of action to the Appellant Bank to institute a Petition under Section 7 IBC. The petition under Section 7 IBC was well within three years from 28th March, 2014.

The Supreme Court held that final judgment or decree of any Court or Tribunal or Arbitral Award for payment of money, if not satisfied, would fall within ambit of a financial debt, enabling the creditor to initiate proceedings under Section 7 IBC.

The Supreme Court allowed the appeal and set aside judgment of NCLAT.

E. S. KRISHNAMURTHY & ORS. Vs. M/S BHARATH HI TECH BUILDERS PVT. LTD.

The Supreme Court in E. S. Krishnamurthy Vs Bharath Hi Tech Builders Pvt. Ltd, (2022) 3 SCC 161 held that once an application is filed under Section 7 IBC, the NCLT has only jurisdiction to admit the application or reject it. NCLT cannot compel the parties to settle the matter.

Case Title : E. S. Krishnamurthy Vs Bharath Hi Tech Builders Pvt. Ltd Date of Decision : 14.12.2021 Bench : Dr. Dhananjaya Y. Chandrachud, J; A. S. Bopanna, J

FACTS OF THE CASE

A Master Agreement was entered into between Bharathi Hi Tech Builders Pvt. Ltd. (Corporate Debtor), IDBI Trusteeship Ltd (Security Trustee) and Karvy Realty (India) Ltd. (Facility Agent) for raising an amount of Rs. 50 Crores for development of agricultural land.

The Respondent was to convey plots to the investors/allottees against their loan amount. In case of default in conveyance of plot, the Respondent was to repay the loan amount along with interest. The Respondent failed to convey the plots despite several extensions.

Some of the aggrieved allottees filed an Application under Section 7 of the Insolvency and Bankruptcy Code, 2016 for initiating CIRP against the Respondent. The NCLT declined to admit the application and directed the Applicant to settle the matter. An appeal was filed against the same before NCLAT, which dismissed the same.

FINDINGS OF THE SUPREME COURT

The central issue in the appeal was whether the NCLT and NCLAT were correct in their approach of rejecting the appellant's Petition under

Section 7 of IBC at the pre-admission stage and directing them to settle with the Respondent within three months.

The Supreme Court noted that after an application under Section 7 IBC is filed, the Adjudicating Authority may by order admit an application under Section 7 (5) (a) or reject such application under Section 7 (5) (b). Only two courses are open to the Adjudicating Authority. Either it can admit the application or reject the application. The statute does not provide for the Adjudicating Authority to undertake any third action.

The Supreme Court in Innoventive Industries Ltd. Vs ICICI Bank (2018) 1 SCC 407 had observed that the Adjudicating Authority has only to determine whether a "default" has occurred. If Adjudicating Authority is of the opinion that "default" has occurred , it has to admit the application unless it is incomplete.

The Supreme Court noted that settlement has not been arrived at between the Applicants before Adjudicating Authority and the Corporate Debtor. The NCLT disposed of the Petition by directing the Respondent to settle the remaining claims no later than three months and if any of the remaining original petitioners were aggrieved by the settlement process, they would be at liberty to approach the Adjudicating Authority again in accordance with law.

The Supreme Court observed that the Adjudicating Authority has acted outside the scope of its jurisdiction under Section 7 (5) IBC. The Adjudicating authority is only empowered to verify whether a default has occurred or not. Based on the same, the Adjudicating Authority has either to admit or reject an application respectively. The Adjudicating Authority cannot compel a party to settle a dispute.

Undoubtedly, settlement has to be encouraged but in this matter NCLT and NCLAT had abdicated the jurisdiction under Section 7 of the IBC.

NCLT and NCLAT are creatures of statutes. The statutes which confer jurisdiction also structures, channelizes, and circumscribes the ambit of such jurisdiction. While NCLT and NCLAT can encourage settlements, they cannot direct them by acting as Courts of Equity.

The Supreme Court set aside the order of NCLAT and directed the NCLT to determine the Application afresh.

VIDARBHA INDUSTRIES POWER LTD. Vs. AXIS BANK LTD.

The Supreme Court in Vidarbha Industries Power Ltd. Vs Axis Bank Ltd (2022)8SCC352 held that admission of Application under Section 7 of the Insolvency and Bankruptcy Code, 2016 on behalf of the Financial Creditor is discretionary even if Corporate Debtor has defaulted in payment of debt.

Case Title : Vidarbha Industries Power Ltd. Vs Axis Bank Ltd. Date of Decision : 12.07.2022 Bench : Indira Banerjee, J; J. K. Maheshwari, J

FACTS OF THE CASE

The Appellant is an electricity generating company. (MERC) approved a power procurement agreement between Appellant and Reliance Industries Ltd (RIL).

On 19th July, 2013, the Maharashtra Electricity Regulatory Commission (MERC) granted approval to Reliance Industries Limited (RIL) to procure power from Appellant's Unit No. 1. Accordingly, a consolidated Power Purchase Agreement was executed on 14th August between the Appellant and RIL. On 1st April, the Appellant started supply of power to RIL.

In January, 2016 the Appellant filed an application before Maharashtra Electricity Regulatory Commission (MERC) for determination of tariff in view of increase in fuel costs, consequential to the rise in the cost of procuring coal for the purposes of running the power plant. Maharashtra Electricity Regulatory Commission (MERC) disallowed a substantial portion of actual fuel. The Appellant filed appeal before Appellate Tribunal for Electricity (APTEL), which allowed the appeal. The Appellant claims that Rs. 1730 crore is due to the Appellant in terms of said order of APTEL. Maharashtra Electricity Regulatory Commission (MERC) filed appeal before the Supreme Court which is pending for adjudication.

Axis Bank filed an application under Section 7 of the Insolvency and Bankruptcy Code, 2016 for initiation of CIRP against the Appellant. The Appellant filed an application before the NCLT for stay the insolvency proceedings in light of pendency of matter before the Supreme Court. NCLT rejected the Application. An appeal was filed against the same before NCLAT which was also rejected.

FINDINGS OF THE SUPREME COURT

The Supreme Court noted that Financial Creditor has claimed an amount of about Rs. 553 crore, out of which the Principal Amount is around Rs. 499 crore. When an application is filed under Section 7 (2) of the Code, the NCLT is required to ascertain the existence of default from the record of the Information Utility or any other evidence furnished by Financial Creditor under Section 7 (3) IBC within 14 days of receipt. When the NCLT is satisfied that default has occurred, application is complete and no disciplinary proceedings are pending against the proposed Resolution Professional, the NCLT "may" admit the application. If no default has occurred or application is not complete or disciplinary proceedings are pending against the Resolution Professional, the NCLT may reject the Application.

The Supreme Court observed that both NCLT and NCLAT proceeded on premise that an application must be necessarily entertained under Section 7 (5) (a) of the Code if a debt existed and Corporate Debtor was in default of payment of debt. The NCLT and NCLAT interpreted Section 7 (5) (a) of the Code to be mandatory.

The Supreme Court observed that no doubt that a Corporate Debtor, which is in red, should be resolved expeditiously. However overall financial health and viability of the Corporate Debtor are not extraneous factors. The claim of the Appellant that an amount of Rs. 1,730 crore is realizable in terms of award of APTEL cannot be disregarded.

The Supreme Court observed that the NCLT was required to apply its mind to relevant factors including the feasibility of initiation of CIRP, impact of MERC Appeal, order of APTEL, overall financial health and viability of the Corporate Debtor.

The Legislature has used the word "may" in Section 7 (5) (a) of the Code. Ordinarily "may" is directory. In contrast "shall" postulates mandatory requirement. The Supreme Court relied on Lalita Kumari Vs State of Uttar Pradesh (2014) 2 SCC 1 , Hiralal Ratanlal Vs State of Uttar Pradesh (1973) 1 SCC 216, B. Premanand Vs Mohan Koikal , (2011) 4 SCC 266 and observed that It is well settled the first and foremost rule of interpretation is literal interpretation. If Section 7 (5) (a) of IBC is construed literally, the provision confers a discretion on the Adjudicating Authority.

The Supreme Court noted that legislature in its wisdom has used word "may" in Section 7 (5) (a) of IBC while the word "shall" has been used in Section 9 (5) which provides the procedure for initiation of insolvency proceedings on the instance of Operational Creditor. It is evident that the Legislature intended Section 9 (5) (a) IBC to be mandatory while Section 7 (5) (a) to be discretionary.

The Supreme Court observed that there are innate differences between Financial Creditors and Operational Creditors. Financial Strength of Financial Creditor cannot be compared with that of Operational Creditors who supply goods and services. Impact of non-payment of dues can be far more serious on the Operational Creditor in comparison to Financial Creditor.

The Supreme Court observed that the objective of the Code cannot be to penalize solvent companies temporarily in default in payment of debts. NCLT failed to appreciate that time bound initiation and completion of CIRP could only arise if companies were bankrupt or insolvent and not otherwise.

The Supreme Court set aside the order passed by NCLT and NCLAT and directed the NCLT to re-consider the application for stay of further proceedings.

M. SURESH KUMAR REDDY VS. CANARA BANK

Supreme Court in M. Suresh Kumar Reddy Vs. Canara Bank & Ors 2023) 8 SCC 387 has held that once NCLT is satisfied that the default has occurred, there is hardly any discretion left with NCLT to refuse admission of application under Section 7.

Case Title : M. Suresh Kumar Reddy Vs. Canara Bank & Ors Date of Decision : 11.05.2023 Bench : Abhay S. Oka, J; Rajesh Bindal, J

VIDARBHA JUDGMENT

It is pertinent to mention that in Vidarbha Industries Power Ltd. Vs. Axis Bank Ltd. (2022)8SCC352 the Supreme Court has held that if an application has been filed by Financial creditor for initiation of CIRP and Application is complete in all respects including the fact that default has occurred in payment of debt, NCLT has discretion to admit such application or not admit such application. On the other hand if an application is filed under Section 9 by an operational creditor and application is complete in all respects, the NCLT is bound to admit such application. Relevant para is as under:

76. The fact that Legislature used 'may' in Section 7(5)(a) of the IBC but a different word, that is, 'shall' in the otherwise almost identical provision of Section 9(5)(a) shows that 'may' and 'shall' in the two provisions are intended to convey a different meaning. It is apparent that Legislature intended Section 9(5)(a) of the IBC to be mandatory and Section 7(5)(a) of the IBC to be discretionary. An application of an Operational Creditor for initiation of CIRP under Section 9(2) of the IBC is mandatorily required to be admitted if the application is complete in all respects and in compliance of the requisites of the IBC and the rules and regulations thereunder, there is no payment of the unpaid operational debt, if notices for payment or the invoice has been delivered to the Corporate Debtor by the Operational Creditor and no notice of dispute has been received by the Operational Creditor. The IBC does not countenance dishonesty or deliberate failure to repay the dues of an operational creditor.

This judgment has created some confusion and seemed to be going back to earlier regime when "default" was not sufficient for initiating winding up proceedings but the court has discretion to judge whether the company is "insolvent" .before initiating winding up proceedings.

THE FINDINGS OF THE SUPREME COURT

Now the Supreme Court has clarified that the judgment of the Supreme Court in "Vidarbha" was limited to its facts. The Supreme Court relied on judgments in "Innovative Industries Ltd Vs. ICICI Bank & Another" and E. S. Krishnamurthy and Ors. Vs. Bharat Hi Tech builders Pvt. Ltd. (2022) 3 SCC 161 and held that if default has occurred, there is hardly any discretion left with the NCLT to refuse admission of application under Section 7. Relevant para is as under:

10. Thus, once NCLT is satisfied that the default has occurred, there is hardly a discretion left with NCLT to refuse admission of the application under Section 7. Default is defined under sub-section 12 of Section 3 of the IBC which reads thus:

3. Definitions : In this code unless the context otherwise requires -

(12) "default" means non-payment of debt when whole or nay part or instalment of the amount of debt has become due and payable and is not paid by the debtor or the corporate debtor, as the case may be.

Thus, even the non-payment of a part of debt when it becomes due and payable will amount to default on the part of the Corporate Debtor. In such a case, an order of admission under Section 7 of the IBC must follow. If the NCLT finds that there is a debt, but it has not become due and payable, the application under Section 7 can be rejected. Otherwise, there is no ground available to reject the application.

Thus, this judgment has dispelled all the apprehensions regarding admission of an application by Financial Creditors in event of default.

AXIS BANK LTD. Vs. NAREN SHETH & ANR

The Supreme Court in Axis Bank Ltd Vs. Naren Sheth & Anr, (2024) 1 S.C.R. 1183 has reiterated that documents related with acknowledgment of debt can be accepted at the appellate stage.

Case Title : Axis Bank Ltd Vs. Naren Sheth & Anr Date of Decision : 12.09.2023 Bench : Vikram Nath, J; Ahsanuddin Amanullah, J

FACTS OF THE CASE

Axis Bank entered into a leave and license agreement with Universal Premises and Textiles Pvt. Ltd. for premises from ground to 10th floor in a building named Solaris C. Universal Premises executed a sale deed in favour of Rajput Retail Ltd. The Leave and License Agreements in favour of the appellant were duly acknowledged, reserved, and protected under the sale deed. Rajput Retail Ltd. availed credit facilities from State Bank of India and mortgaged land underneath Solaris C to secure credit facilities. Universal Premises and Textiles Pvt. and Rajput Retail Ltd. were merged and renamed Shreem Corporation Ltd. Axis Bank filed summary suits for recovery of security deposit.

The State Bank of India declared the account of the Shreem Corporation Ltd. NPA. State Bank of India filed an Application for initiation of CIRP against Shreem Corporation Ltd. along with Application for condonation of delay of 1392 days. Later, an additional affidavit was filed stating that the delay was only of 662 days in view of acknowledgement of debt. The NCLT condoned the delay of 662 days and passed the order of admission.

Axis Bank filed an appeal against the admission order before the NCLAT which was dismissed. Aggrieved by the same Axis Bank filed an Appeal before the Supreme Court.

FINDINGS OF THE SUPREME COURT

It was contended by the Axis Bank (Appellant) that the Application was barred by Limitation. The loan was declared NPA on 28.06.2013 with effect on 31.03.2013. As such limitation would expire on 31.03.2016. The SBI relied on the balance sheet ending 31.03.2015,which extended the limitation to 31.03.2018. The application would have been barred by limitation on 31.03.2021.

It was argued by the Appellant that from time to time the case has been improved by the SBI abusing the process of law. Two OTS proposals were produced before the Supreme Court for the first time which is not permissible under law. Additional documents submitted by the appellant suffers from various defects.

The SBI submitted that debt has been acknowledged time to time and right to initiate insolvency proceedings was never lost.

The Supreme Court observed that limitation would have expired on 31.03.2016. But there were four major acknowledgments. (i) Balance Sheet ending at 31.03.2015 (ii) First OTS dated 16th March, 2017 (iii) Second OTS dated 1st January, 2018 (iv) Third OTS Proposal dated 16th May, 2019. The petition under Section 7 was filed on 22nd January, 2020 within three years from the date of the first, second and the third OTS proposals.

The issue before the Supreme Court was whether such OTS proposals could be considered which have been produced subsequently before NCLAT or the Supreme Court.

The Supreme Court relied on Dena Bank (Now Bank of Baroda) vs. C. Sivakumar Reddy (2021) 10 SCC 330 and Kotak Mahindra Bank Limited vs. Kew Precision Parts Private Limited and Ors (2022) 9 SCC 364) wherein it has been held that documents acknowledging debt could be accepted even at the appellate stage.

The Supreme Court also held that Section 14 will have no application inasmuch as the proceedings under the SARFAESI Act before the DRT cannot be said to be before a Court or Tribunal having no jurisdiction. State Bank of India, being a Secured Creditor, had a right to invoke the power under the SARFAESI Act and the said proceedings cannot be said to be without jurisdiction. Therefore, no benefit under Section 14 would be admissible to State Bank of India in the present case.

The appeal was dismissed by the Supreme Court.

TOTTEMPUDI SALALITH Vs. STATE BANK OF INDIA & ORS

The Supreme Court in Tottempudi Salalith Vs State Bank of India & Ors (Civil Appeal 2348 of 2021) has held that recovery certificate issued by the DRT creates a fresh cause of action and doctrine of election will not apply in initiating insolvency proceedings. The Supreme Court has also held that specific pleadings are required for acknowledgement or admission of claim in the Application for initiating insolvency proceedings.

> Case Title : Tottempudi Salalith Vs State Bank of India & Ors
> Date of Decision : 18.10.2023
> Bench : Aniruddha Bose, J; Vikram Nath, J

FACTS OF THE CASE

Several banks , namely, the State Bank of Hyderabad, State Bank of Mysore, State Bank of Travancore, State Bank of Bikaner and Jaipur and State Bank of Patiala and other banks had extended credit facilities to the Totem Infrastructures Ltd. The State Bank of Hyderabad, State Bank of Mysore, State Bank of Travancore, State Bank of Bikaner and Jaipur and State Bank of Patiala merged with the State Bank of India on 01.04.2017. State Bank of India initiated proceedings under Section 7 IBC.

Prior to initiating Section 7 proceedings, the SBI issued 13 (2) notices under SARFAESI Act and thereafter filed Original Applications before DRT. Two Applications were filed before DRT Hyderabad and one before DRT Bengaluru. Two recovery certificates were issued by DRT Hyderabad on 08.09.2015 and 17.10.2017. In another application Recovery Certificate was issued on 04.08.2017.

State Bank of India filed an Application under Section 7 IBC based on these three recovery certificates. By order dated 12.01.2021 the Adjudicating Authority admitted the Application. The admission was challenged before the NCLAT, which was dismissed.

Aggrieved by the same, Mr. Tottempudi Salalith, the Managing Director of Totem Infrastructures Ltd filed an Appeal before the Supreme Court of India mainly on procedural grounds.

FINDINGS OF THE SUPREME COURT

Following issues arose for consideration of the Supreme Court.

(1) Whether the SBI having approached DRT was barred under doctrine of election to approach NCLT ?

(2) Whether the Application was barred by limitation before NCLT ?

The Supreme Court findings on the aforesaid issues were as under.

On the aspect of doctrine of election

It was submitted before the Supreme Court that doctrine of election is a doctrine of law of evidence which bars a party from pursuing before two different fora for the same cause of action. SBI had already initiated proceedings before the DRT and as such proceeding under Section 7 IBC was not maintainable before NCLT.

The Supreme Court rejected this argument relying on Kotak Mahindra Bank Limited Vs. A. Balakrishnan and Another (2022) 9 SCC 186. In this judgment the Supreme Court had held that recovery certificate would give a fresh cause of action entitling Financial Creditor to initiate Corporate Insolvency Resolution Process. The enforcement of recovery certificate is an independent cause of action and the Financial Creditor can opt for proceedings under IBC rather than chasing mechanism under 1993 Act. The Supreme Court also observed that IBC is not really a debt recovery mechanism but a mechanism for revival of a company fallen in debt, but the procedure envisaged in the IBC substantially relates to ensuring recovery of debts in the process of applying such mechanism.

On the aspect of Limitation

The Application for initiation of insolvency proceedings had been filed based on three recovery certificates. The Supreme Court relying on Vashdeo R. Bhojwani ¬vs¬ Abhyudaya Co¬operative Bank Limited and Another (2019) 9 SCC 158 has held that limitation would start ticking from date of issuance of recovery certificate.

Relying on Kotak Mahindra (Supra) the Supreme Court held that in case of recovery certificates, the limitation period is guided by Article 137 of the Limitation Act.

Out of three recovery certificates two were within limitation and one was time barred. There were no averments regarding limitation in the Application before NCLT.

State Bank of India had relied on letter dated 29.01.2020 as an acknowledgement of debt. The same has been contested by the Appellant on the ground that any valid acknowledgment must be within period of limitation. State Bank had pressed for treating the letter under Section 25 (3) of the Contract Act.

Supreme Court relying on Reliance Asset Reconstruction Company Limited ¬vs¬ Hotel Poonja International Private Limited (2021) 7 SCC 352 and Babulal Vardharji Gurjar Vs. Veer Gurjar Aluminium Industries Private Ltd (2020) 15 SCC 1 observed that specific pleading regarding facts constituting acknowledgement or admission of claim has to be given.

Finally Supreme Court held that the application in respect of the two recovery certificates issued in the year 2017 is maintainable. In the event the Appellate Tribunal is of the opinion that the CIRP could not lie so far as the recovery certificate that is barred by limitation is concerned, as the decree would still be alive, the claim based on the said recovery certificate could be segregated from the composite claim and the Committee of Creditors shall, in that event, treat the sum reflected in the said recovery certificate as part of the claims made in pursuance of the public announcement. This direction was issued by the Supreme Court under Article 142 of the Constitution.

SATINDER SINGH BHASIN Vs. COL. GAUTAM MULLICK & ORS

The Supreme Court in Satinder Singh Bhasin Vs. Col. Gautam Mullick & Ors (Civil Appeal No 13628 of 2025) held that in cases of intrinsically linked companies it would be in their interest to have a joint insolvency process so as to maximize asset realization.

Case Title : Satinder Singh Bhasin Vs. Col. Gautam Mullick & Ors Date of Decision : 02.01.2026 Bench : Sanjay Kumar, J; K. Vinod Chandran, J

FACTS OF THE CASE

An application was filed by some allottees to initiate CIRP against two interlinked companies - Grand Venezia Ltd. and Bhasin Ltd. which was admitted by NCLT vide order dated 04.12.2023. The admission was challenged before NCLAT by the aggrieved erstwhile directors of both companies on several grounds including the ground that initiation of insolvency process against two separate corporate entities by way of one application was not maintainable. The appeal was dismissed by the NCLAT. Appeals were filed by aggrieved parties before the Supreme Court.

FINDINGS OF THE SUPREME COURT

One of the questions raised before the Supreme Court was whether the threshold limit of 100 allottees prescribed by the second proviso to Section 7(1) of the Code stood fulfilled in the case on hand. It was contended that, out of the 103 allottees who had applied to the NCLT, 28 allottees had taken possession while 13 allottees were refunded their monies by the time of passing of the admission order. It was further claimed that 7 allottees signed settlement deeds but did not take possession due to registration formalities. Therefore, according to the appellants, the petitioning allottees with unsettled claims were only 55 in number. The

Supreme Court observed that in any event, the day of reckoning stands settled by this Court in Manish Kumar Vs Union of India (2021) 5 SCC 1, wherein it was held that the crucial date for ascertaining whether the threshold is adequately met is the date of filing of the petition and not the date of the admission or hearing thereof.

Another contention was submitted that the cause-title with regard to the names of the allottees who appeared as petitioners therein and the refiled petition did not reflect the same names as were there in the petition initially filed on 07.07.2021. The Supreme Court observed that Rule 28(2) makes it clear that if, upon scrutiny, the appeal or petition or application or document is found to be defective, the same should be returned to the party for compliance. However, Rule 28(3) goes further and states that a party may be allowed to not only rectify but also amend such returned appeal or petition or application or document. Rule 28(4) manifests that it is only after the refiling, upon curing of the defects, that the Registrar would register the pleading or document. Rule 29 of the NCLT Rules is titled 'Registration of proceedings admitted' and states that on admission of an appeal or petition or caveat or application, the same shall be numbered and registered in the appropriate register maintained in that behalf and the number shall be entered therein. Mere filing of the company petition on 07.07.2021 did not result in the same being 'registered' on the file of the NCLT and it was only after rectification/amendment of the petition and upon its refiling, with the defects therein cured, that the same would have been registered. The Supreme Court noted that in Surendra Trading Company vs. Juggilal Kamlapat Jute Mills Company Limited and others, (2017) 16 SCC 143 it was held that till the objections in an application filed under Sections 7, 9 or 10 of the Code are removed, it is not to be treated as an application validly filed, as it is only after the application is complete in every respect that it is required to be entertained.

On the aspect of application being filed for initiation of CIRP in respect of two companies, the Supreme Court noted that the letter of allotment, in relation to the leased land, was issued by the UPSIDA on 05.08.2006 in favour of Bhasin Ltd. alone. The project was, therefore, to be undertaken essentially by Bhasin Ltd. It was only thereafter, i.e., on 14.12.2009, that Bhasin Ltd. entered into an agreement with Grand Venezia Ltd., granting it marketing rights in relation to the sale of units in the project. It is a matter of record that the two companies had common directors, including Satinder Singh Bhasin, for some length of time. Further, demand notices and possession letters were issued by Bhasin Ltd. to the allottees of Grand Venezia Ltd. and the correspondence/communications with the allottees were by both the companies interchangeably. Payment receipts also manifested the same. These documents formed part of the company petition. The argument that these were two completely independent and separate companies, therefore, falls to the ground. In any event, as they were jointly answerable to the allottees, the filing of a single company petition against them was justified.

The Supreme Court also negated the contention of the appellants that the construction was completed in all respects and possession was delivered to some of the petitioning allottees. The Supreme Court affirmed the decision of the NCLT and the NCLAT.

MANSI BRAR FERNANDES Vs. SHUBHA SHARMA & ANR

The Supreme Court in Mansi Brar Fernandes Vs Shubha Sharma & Anr (Civil Appeal No. 3826/2020) has reiterated that speculative investors cannot be permitted to misuse IBC as a recovery mechanism. The Supreme Court has also issued several important directions for reforms in Real Estate Sector.

Case Title : Mansi Brar Fernandes Vs Shubha Sharma & Anr Date of Decision : 12.09.2025 Bench : J. B. Pardiwala, J; R. Mahadevan, J

BRIEF FACTS

Mansi Brar Fernandes and Gayatri Infra Planners Pvt. Ltd. (Corporate Debtor) entered into MoU dated 06.04.2016 with a buy back agreement at the discretion of the Corporate Debtor in respect of four flats. She paid a sum of Rs. 35,00,000/- via cheque towards part consideration. The Corporate Debtor could either buy back the units after 12 months for Rs. 1 Crore or hand over possession of the flats to the appellant at no extra cost. MoU was extended twice namely on 07.04.2017 for six months and on 07.10.2017 for twelve months. Cheques provided by the Corporate Debtor bounced. Possession was also not given by the Corporate Debtor.

Mansi Brar initiated proceedings under the IBC and her petition was admitted by NCLT. Admission was reversed by NCLAT on the ground that Mansi Brar was not Financial Creditor but speculative investor.

FINDINGS OF THE SUPREME COURT

The Supreme Court noted that schemes of assured returns, compulsory buybacks, or excessive exit options are in truth financial derivatives masquerading as housing contracts. These arrangements enable developers, on the one hand, to mislead gullible individuals, and seasoned investors, on the other, to 'jump ship' when the market turns or to hold developers to ransom by invoking the IBC as a coercive recovery mechanism, thereby creating a situation of "heads I win, tails you lose".

The Supreme Court noted that it has drawn a crucial distinction between a speculative buyer and a genuine buyer and had observed that speculative investors cannot be permitted to misuse the code as recovery mechanism.

The Supreme Court noted that where there is an actual chain of delivery ending with possession by a genuine buyer, the transaction is not speculative. Conversely, in the present context, where there is no intention to take possession, the onus to find another buyer and effect resale is cast on the developer. Delivery in such cases is more in the nature of a lien or an option. For a genuine allottee, however, delivery and possession are a sine qua non. The determination of whether an allottee is a speculative investor must be holistic, having regard to terms of the agreement, the allotment letter, the payment terms, and the overall conduct of the allottee.

The Supreme Court concluded that in the present case the appellant's true interest lay in assured returns, not possession. The MOU was in substance a buyback contract, not an agreement to sell flats. By the standard in Pioneer Urban, the appellant was a speculative investor, disentitling her from invoking Section 7.

The Supreme Court upheld the judgment of the NCLAT. The Supreme Court also issued several directions for reforms in real estate sector , some of which are - (i) filling of NCLT/NCLAT vacancies on a war footing and upgradation of NCLT/NCLAT infrastructure. (ii) creation of a Committee under chairmanship of retired High Court Judge for suggesting reforms for cleansing and infusing credibility in real estate sector. (iii) IBBI to create Council in consultation with RERA to frame guidelines for insolvency proceedings in real estate. (iv) Real estate insolvency to be resolved on project basis as rule. (v) NCLTs must record a prima facie finding on whether the applicant is a genuine homebuyer or speculative investor.

VISA COKE LTD Vs. M/S MESCO KALINGA STEEL LIMITED

The Supreme Court held in Visa Coke Ltd. Vs. M/s Mesco Kalinga Steel Ltd (Civil Appeal 357/2025) that demand notice sent to the Key Managerial Personnel at the registered office in their official capacities constitutes valid service on the Corporate Debtor

Case Title : Visa Coke Ltd. Vs. M/s Mesco Kalinga Steel Ltd Date of Decision : 29.04.2025 Bench : J. B. Pardiwala, J; R. Mahadevan, J

BRIEF FACTS

Visa Coke Ltd. (Operational Creditor) was engaged in business of manufacturing and selling of Low Ash Metallurgical Coke. The Operational Creditor supplied LAM Coke to the Respondent. The Corporate Debtor failed to pay the outstanding amount as such the Operational Creditor sent legal notice demanding the outstanding payment for supply of 1700 MT of LAM Coke amounting to INR 3,34,16,661.60 along with penal interest at 15% per annum. As amount was not paid the Operational Creditor sent demand notice under Form 3 on 31.03.2021 in compliance with section 8 of the IBC, to the Corporate Debtor at its registered address through its Key Managerial Personnel , namely, Director, Chief Financial Officer and Manager, Commercial. As outstanding amount was not paid, Section 9 IBC petition was filed before NCLT for initiation of CIRP process. NCLT dismissed the Petition on the ground that service has not been effected on the Corporate Debtor but only on key managerial personnel. An appeal was filed before NCLAT, which was also dismissed.

FINDINGS OF THE SUPREME COURT

The Supreme Court observed that section 9 petition can be filed only against the corporate debtor after giving a prior notice under section 8 of the IBC to the corporate debtor and the key requirements for filing the same are - (i) demand notice under section 8 must be served on the corporate debtor; (ii) after 10 days, if the payment is not made or if there is no valid dispute, the application can be filed; (iii) application must be filed in Form 5 as prescribed by the Adjudicating Authority Rules, 2016; and (iv) supporting evidence such as invoices, bank statements, or written contracts must be attached. Further, a conjoint reading of section 8 of the IBC r/w Rule 5(2)(a) and (b) of the Adjudicating Authority Rules, 2016 would reveal that a demand notice under section 8 can be addressed and delivered to the corporate debtor through its KMP.

The Supreme Court observed that on a perusal of Form 3 notice dated 31 .03.2021 issued by the appellant, it is revealed that the same was addressed to Key Managerial Personnel and delivered to the registered office of the respondent - Corporate Debtor viz., MESCO Kalinga Steel Limited. Even the 'subject' and paragraph 1 of the notice clearly demonstrate that as per the IBC, demand notice / invoice demanding payment in respect of unpaid operational debt due from the corporate debtor was issued and thereby, the appellant called upon the Corporate Debtor to pay the operational debt within a period of ten days from the date of receipt of the notice, failing which, CIRP be initiated in respect of the Corporate Debtor. Notably, the said notice dated 31.03.2021 was served on the KMP in their official capacities at the registered office address of the corporate debtor. The contents of the notice clearly establish that the same was issued to the Corporate Debtor in respect of the operational debt due and payable by them. As such, it cannot be said that the appellant did not comply with the statutory requirement of sending demand notice in Form 3 to the respondent - Corporate Debtor as provided under section 8 of the IBC, before filing the section 9 petition seeking initiation of CIRP against the respondent in respect of the unpaid operational debt.

The Supreme Court observed that the purpose of sending a demand notice is to give the corporate debtor an opportunity to either repay the outstanding debt, or dispute the debt if there are genuine reasons. In the present case, the notice dated 31.03.2021 sent by the appellant to the KMP of the corporate debtor at the registered office address in their official capacities, explicitly demonstrates that the same was issued to the corporate debtor demanding payment of the operational debt due and payable by them. However, it is not the case of the respondent that no notice was sent by the appellant calling upon the respondent - Corporate Debtor to pay the operational debt. Further, it is pertinent to point out that during the pendency of the section 9 petition, the Corporate Debtor approached the Operational Creditor for settlement, which did not materialise.

The Supreme Court concluded that the approach of the NCLT and the NCLAT rejecting the section 9 petition on the technical ground that no notice was sent to the corporate debtor and the notice sent by the appellant to the KMP of the corporate debtor cannot be taken to be a notice issued under section 8 of the IBC, is incorrect and is unsustainable in law.

The Supreme Court allowed the appeal and remanded the matter to NCLT for determination on merits.

DISPUTE

MOBILOX INNOVATIONS PVT. LTD. Vs. KIRUSA SOFTWARE PVT. LTD.

The Supreme Court in Mobilox Innovations Pvt. Ltd. Vs. Kirusa Software Pvt. Ltd. (2018) 1 SCC 353 interpreted the term "dispute". The Supreme Court held that at the admission stage all that the Adjudicating Authority has to see is whether there is a plausible contention which requires further investigation and that the "dispute" is not a patently feeble legal argument or an assertion of fact unsupported by evidence.

Case Title : Mobilox Innovations Pvt. Ltd. Vs. Kirusa Software Pvt. Ltd.
Date of Decision : 21.09.2017
Bench : R. F. Nariman, J; Sanjay Kishan Kaul, J

FACTS OF THE CASE

Mobilox Innovations Pvt. Ltd. was engaged by the Star TV for conducting tele-voting for programme "Nach Baliye". Mobilox Innovations subcontracted work to Kirusa Software Pvt. Ltd. and issued purchase orders between October and December, 2013. The requisite services were provided by Kirusa Software and invoices were raised between December 2013 and November, 2014, which were payable within 30 days. A non-disclosure agreement was also executed between Mobilox Innovations and Kirusa Software. Mobilox Innovations vide letter dated 30th January, 2015 wrote to Kirusa Software that they are withholding payment as Kirusa Software had disclosed on the webpage that it has worked for "Nach Baliye" programme. Kirusa Software sent demand notice under Section 8 of the Insolvency and Bankruptcy Code, 2016. Mobilox Innovations replied vide letter dated 27th December, 2016 that there exists serious and bonafide dispute between the parties and nothing was payable in light of breach of Non Disclosure Agreement. On 30th December, 2016, an application was filed under Section 9 of the Code. NCLT dismissed the application vide order dated 27.01.2017 in light of dispute regarding default.

An appeal was filed before the NCLAT which was allowed by the NCLAT. Aggrieved by order of the NCLAT Mobilox Innovations preferred appeal before the Supreme Court.

FINDINGS OF THE SUPREME COURT

The Supreme Court held that before admitting the application under Section 9 of the Code three things have to be checked by the Adjudicating Authority:

(i) Whether there is an operational debt exceeding the limit prescribed under the Code?

(ii) Whether the documentary evidence furnished with the application shows that the aforesaid debt is due and payable and has not been paid?

(iii) Whether there is existence of dispute between the parties or record of pendency of a suit or arbitration proceedings filed before the receipt of the demand notice of the unpaid operational debt in relation to such dispute?

Notice under Section 8

The Supreme Court noted that a demand notice of an unpaid operational debt or copy of an invoice demanding payment of the amount involved must be delivered in the prescribed form. The corporate debtor is then given a period of 10 days from the receipt of the demand notice or copy of the invoice to bring to the notice of the operational creditor the existence of a dispute, if any. At that time Section 8 (2) (a) used term "existence of a dispute if any, and record of the pendency of the suit or arbitration proceedings" . The Court said that "and" should be read as "or". After this judgment vide 2018 amendment of IBC "and" has been substituted with "or".

Interpretation of Dispute

The Supreme Court observed that the winding up on the ground of inability of payment of debt under Section 271 of the Companies Act, 2013 is no longer a ground for winding up in light of enactment of Insolvency and Bankruptcy Code, 2016. With the omission of the said ground principle enunciated by the Supreme Court regarding "bonafide dispute" in Madhusudan Gordhandas Vs Madhu Wollen Industries Pvt. Ltd. (1972) 2 SCR 201 is no longer applicable. All that the Adjudicating

Authority is to see at this stage is whether there is a plausible contention which requires further investigation and that the "dispute" is not a patently feeble legal argument or an assertion of fact unsupported by evidence. It is important to separate the grain from the chaff and to reject a spurious defence which is mere bluster. The relevant para is as under:

40. It is clear, therefore, that once the operational creditor has filed an application, which is otherwise complete, the adjudicating authority must reject the application under Section 9(5)(2)(d) if notice of dispute has been received by the operational creditor or there is a record of dispute in the information utility. It is clear that such notice must bring to the notice of the operational creditor the "existence" of a dispute or the fact that a suit or arbitration proceeding relating to a dispute is pending between the parties. Therefore, all that the adjudicating authority is to see at this stage is whether there is a plausible contention which requires further investigation and that the "dispute" is not a patently feeble legal argument or an assertion of fact unsupported by evidence. It is important to separate the grain from the chaff and to reject a spurious defence which is mere bluster. However, in doing so, the Court does not need to be satisfied that the defence is likely to succeed. The Court does not at this stage examine the merits of the dispute except to the extent indicated above. So long as a dispute truly exists in fact and is not spurious, hypothetical or illusory, the adjudicating authority has to reject the application.

In light of aforesaid interpretation, the Hon'ble Supreme Court allowed appeal filed by Mobilox Innovation Pvt. Ltd.

K. KISHAN Vs. M/S VIJAY NIRMAN COMPANY PVT LTD

The Supreme Court in K. Kishan Vs M/s Vijay Nirman Company Pvt Ltd (2018) 17 SCC 662 held that if a petition under Section 34 of the Arbitration and Conciliation Act has been filed challenging an Arbitral Award, the same constitutes a pre-existing dispute.

Case Title : K. Kishan Vs M/s Vijay Nirman Company Pvt Ltd Date of Decision : 14.08.2018 Bench : R. F. Nariman, J; Indu Malhotra, J

FACTS OF THE CASE

Vijay Nirman Company Pvt. Ltd. (Respondent) entered into sub-contract Agreement with one M/s Ksheerbad Construction Pvt. Ltd. (KCPL) for construction and widening of certain section of existing two lane highway to four lane highway on NH67. KCPL and SDM Projects Pvt. Ltd. also entered into a separate agreement. A tripartite agreement was also entered among Respondent, KCPL and SDM Projects Pvt. Ltd. During course of project, dispute and differences arose between the parties and the same was referred to Arbitral Tribunal, which delivered award on 21.01.2017. Claim was allowed in favour of the Respondent.

A notice under Section 8 of the Code dated 06.02.2017 was sent by the Respondent to KCPL to pay an amount of Rs. 1,79,00,166/-. In its reply KCPL disputed the invoice. KCPL also filed Petition under Section 34 of the Arbitration and Conciliation Act, 1996 challenging the aforesaid award.

Thereafter a petition was filed under Section 9 of the Code on 14.07.201 7. NCLT admitted the Petition vide order dated 29.08.2017 and observed that a Section 34 Petition pending was irrelevant for the reason that the claims stood admitted and there was no stay on the award. NCLAT concurred with NCLT.

FINDINGS OF THE SUPREME COURT

The Supreme Court observed that Section 9 (5) (ii) (d) shows that an application must be rejected if notice of a dispute has been received by the Operational Creditor. In this case entire basis for the notice under Section 8 is the fact that an Arbitral Award was passed on 21.07.2017 against the Appellant. Reply to Section 8 notice was filed within 10 days as provided under the Code.

The Court noted that Counter Claim No. 1 and 2 were rejected for lack of evidence, Counter claim no. 3 was rejected on the basis of price adjustment clause on merits.

The Supreme Court held in Mobilox Innovations Pvt. Ltd. Vs. Kirusa Software Pvt. Ltd. (2018) 1 SCC 353 that what is important is the existence of the dispute and/or a suit or arbitration proceedings must be pre-existing i.e. it must exist before the receipt of the demand notice or invoice, as the case may be.

Operational Creditors cannot use the Code either prematurely or for extraneous considerations or as a substitute for debt enforcement procedures. If an Arbitral Award is challenged it is sufficient to be covered under "dispute". An alarming result of an operational debt contained in Arbitral Award for a small amount will jeopardize an otherwise solvent company. The Code cannot be used in terrorem to extract money although adjudication proceedings for the same is still pending.

The Supreme Court held that Judgment of Australian High Court in Ramsay Health Care Australia Pty Ltd Vs Adrian John Compton (2017) HCA 28 is not applicable in Indian insolvency regime. In this judgment it has been held that where judgment debt has been obtained after testing of merits in adversarial litigation, then in absence of fraud, collusion, or miscarriage of justice, bankruptcy court will rarely have substantial reasons to investigate regarding the debt.

The Supreme Court in Mobilox Innovations has made it clear that the insolvency process, particularly in relation to operational creditors, cannot be used to bypass the adjudicatory and enforcement process of a debt contained in other statutes.

The Supreme Court held that filing of Section 34 Petition against an Arbitral Award shows that a pre-existing dispute which culminates at the first stage of the proceedings in an award, continues even after the award , at least till the final adjudicatory process under Section 34 & 37 has taken place. If Section 34 petition is barred by limitation and period of 90 days and the additional condonable period of 30 days have expired, Insolvency proceedings may thereafter be initiated.

M/S JAI BALA JI INDUSTRIES Vs. D. K. MOHANTY & ANR

The Supreme Court in M/s Jai Balaji Industries Vs D. K. Mohanty & Anr (2021) SCC Online SC 3104 reiterated that in case of an Application under Section 9 IBC , the Adjudicating Authority is supposed to examine prima facie if dispute truly existed between thethethe parties and the same was not patently feeble or imaginary. The Supreme Court also held that when a suit or appeal is dismissed in default and restored , such restoration would revive the proceedings to their status before dismissal and doctrine of relation back would come into play.

Case Title : M/s Jai Balaji Industries Vs D. K. Mohanty & Anr. Date of Decision : 01.10.2021 Bench : Dinesh Maheshwari, J; Vikram Nath, J

FACTS OF THE CASE

Jai Balaji Industries (Appellant) is engaged in the business of manufacturing sand supply of iron and steel products, having its plants in the States of West Bengal and Chhattishgarh. Orissa Minerals Development Company Ltd (Respondent Company) agreed to supply 1 lakh and 7 lakh metric tons of iron ore per month vide two MoUs dated 13.08.2003 and 11.03.2004.

Dispute ensued between the parties and appellant invoked the arbitration clause. Two arbitral awards dated 22.02.2010 and 15.02.2010 were passed in relation to respective MOUs and Respondent Company was held liable to make payment of Rs. 4.44 Crores and 2.79 Crores respectively.

Respondent Company challenged the award under Section 34 of Arbitration and Conciliation Act, 1996 which was dismissed. An appeal was filed under Section 37 of the Arbitration Act, which was dismissed in default. An application for restoration application was filed which was allowed by High Court. Both appeals were pending before the High Court.

In the meantime the Appellant sent two demand notices under Section 8 of IBC claiming operational debts of Rs. 7,75,13, 684 and Rs. 5,62,01,258/- under respective arbitral awards. The Respondent Company replied that the matter of debt owed is sub judice and no operational debt was payable to the appellant. Subsequently, the Appellant filed two applications under Section 9 of IBC for initiating CIRP. NCLT admitted the application on the ground that no appeal under Section 37 of the Arbitration and Conciliation Act was pending before High Court. The NCLT also observed that after receipt of demand notice, the Respondent No. 2 filed restoration application before High Court only to delay the legitimate dues of the Corporate Debtor.

The Respondent No. 2 filed appeals before NCLAT wherein NCLAT observed that once appeal is restored to its original number, the interlocutory orders stood revived. Once appeal under Section 37 was restored, it related back to the original date. NCLAT held that it is a clear case of pre-existing dispute and set aside the orders of NCLAT.

FINDINGS OF THE SUPREME COURT

The Supreme Court observed that the entire approach of the appellant seems to be based on misconception that IBC has provided another avenue for recovery of money. IBC is a beneficial legislation to put the Corporate Debtor on its feet and not merely a recovery legislation for the creditors.

The Supreme Court relying on Mobilox Innovations Pvt. Ltd. V. Kirusha Software Pvt. Ltd. (2018) 1 SCC 353 observed that adjudicating authority was not required to examine the merit of the dispute but it was supposed to examine only prima facie if a dispute truly existed between the parties and the same was not patently feeble or arbitrary. If the answer to the aforesaid was in the affirmative, the Adjudicating Authority was required to reject the Application.

The Supreme Court also relied on K. Kishan Vs Vijay Nirman Company Pvt. Ltd. (2018) 17 SCC 662 wherein it has been held that challenge to the arbitral award shows a pre-existing dispute which continues at least until final adjudicatory process has concluded in terms of Section 34 and 37 of the Arbitration and Conciliation Act, 1996.

The Supreme Court noted that in the instant case Appellant chose to serve notices under Section 8 of Code on 14.02.2020, arbitration award has not attained finality. Even appeals before the High Court had been dismissed in default, the Respondent Company has moved restoration with advance notice to the Appellant. On the date of issuance of demand notice, the appellant was aware that Appeal under Section 37 has not been decided and application for restoration has been moved.

The Supreme Court also observed that when a suit or appeal is dismissed in default and is restored and Court is satisfied on the cause shown for default, such restoration will revive the proceedings to their status before default dismissal, and doctrine of relation back will come into play in the manner that proceedings shall continue in their original status, unless otherwise stated in the order of restoration or coming out by necessary implication.

The real issue in the case is about 'pre-existing" dispute as regards money claimed by Operational Creditor. The default dismissal of appeals could only be regarded as partial eclipse, which momentarily puts the dispute in hibernation. There can be a case where restoration is declined , which might put an effective end to the dispute but when restoration of the appeal is granted , it re-activates the dispute. Even pendency of an application for restoration is sufficient to bring the matter within the four corners of "pre-existing dispute".

The NCLAT took note of the fact that Section 9 Applications, though sworn on 29.02.2020 were filed only on 02.03.2020. The NCLT failed to appreciate that on the date of filing application, appeals stood restored.

The Supreme Court affirmed the view of the NCLAT and dismissed the appeals.

KAY BOUVET ENGINEERING LTD Vs. OVERSEAS INFRASTRUCTURE PVT. LTD.

The Supreme Court in Kay Bouvet Engineering Ltd. Vs. Overseas Infrastructure Alliance (India) Pvt. Ltd. (2021) 10 SCC 483 reiterated that Section 9 IBC Application has to be rejected where dispute exists in fact and is not spurious, hypothetical or illusory.

Case Title : Kay Bouvet Engineering Ltd. Vs. Overseas Infrastructure Alliance (India) Pvt. Ltd. Date of Decision : 10.08.2021 Bench : R. F. Nariman, J; B. R. Gavai, J

FACTS OF THE CASE

The Government of India extended Dollar Line of Credit of USD 150 Million to the Republic of Sudan through Exim Bank of India for carrying out Mashkour Sugar Project in Sudan. This was in two tranches of USD 25 Million and USD 125 million. Mashkour Sugar Company Ltd, Sudan entered into an agreement with the Respondent for USD 149,975,000 to be financed by Exim Bank. As per the said agreement, Mashkour was to nominate a sub-contractor. A subsequent agreement was entered into between Mashkour and the Respondent for payment of USD 25 Million to Respondent towards "design and engineering package and plant civil package including site mobilization".

The Appellant submitted its bid as a sub-contractor for supply, erection and completion of sugar plant at Sudan which was accepted by Mashkour. On 18th December, 2010 a MoU was entered into Mashkour, the Respondent , and the Appellant at Khartoum Sudan. A Tripartite Agreement was also executed between all the parties whereby Appellant was appointed as sub-contractor for executing the whole work of designing, engineering, supply , installation, erection, testing and completion of Factory Plant for Mashkour Sugar Company for an amount of USD 106.200 Million.

Mashkour was to release payment of first tranche of LoC to Respondent and the Respondent in turn was to release payment of USD 10.62 Million to Appellant on submission of Advance Bank Guarantee and Performance Bank Guarantee by Appellant to Mashkour. Vide letter dated 21st April , 2011 Exim Bank informed the Respondent that an amount of Rs. 46.58 Crore had been remitted to its bank account. The Respondent paid the appellant Rs. 47,12,10,000/-.

After execution of the second tranche, on 30th October, 2014 , Respondent informed Exim Bank to transfer partial amount of USD 95,580,000 in favour of Appellant.

On 15th June 2017, Mashkour terminated the contract with Respondent for failure on its part to perform the duties.

Mashkour informed Appellant about the developments and termination of contract and further informed that advance payment of Rs. 47,12,10,000/- received by Appellant from Respondent was to be adjusted against supplies to be made to Mashkour for completion of the project. It was further informed that Respondent will not claim back the said amount from Appellant. An agreement to that effect was executed between Mashkour and Appellant.

A demand notice was issued by the Respondent under Section 8 IBC claiming default of the tri-partite agreement and claiming an amount of USD 10.62 million. The Appellant denied the claim. It was pointed out by the Appellant that amount which was paid by the Respondent was only routed through the Respondent. The Respondent filed an Application under Section 9 IBC before NCLT which was dismissed. An appeal was filed before NCLAT , which allowed the appeal.

FINDINGS OF THE SUPREME COURT

The Supreme Court relied on Mobilox Innovations Private Ltd Vs. Kirusa Software private Ltd (2018) 1 SCC 353 wherein it has been held that one of the objects of IBC qua operational debts is to ensure that the amount of such debts, which is usually smaller than that of financial debts, does not enable operational creditors to put the corporate debtor into the insolvency resolution process prematurely or initiate the process for extraneous considerations. It is enough that a dispute exists between the parties.

The Adjudicating Authority has to reject the application of the Operational Creditor under Section 9 , if a notice has been received by the

Operational Creditor or if there is a record of dispute in the information utility. Notice by the "Corporate Debtor" must bring to the notice of "Operational Creditor" the existence of a dispute or the fact that a suit or arbitration proceedings relating to a dispute is pending between the parties. All that the adjudicating authority is required to see at this stage is a plausible contention which requires further investigation and that the dispute is not a patently feeble legal argument or an assertion of fact unsupported by evidence. It is important to separate the grain from the chaff and to reject a spurious defense which is a mere bluster. The Court is not required to be satisfied as to whether the defense is likely to succeed or not. So long as a dispute truly exists in fact is not spurious, hypothetical or illusory, the adjudicating authority has no other option but to reject the application.

The Supreme Court noted that It had been clearly stated by the Appellant that the amount of Rs. 47,12,10,000/- was received as advance money on behalf of Mashkour. Execution of fresh contract in favour of Appellant in no manner creates an automatic liability on Appellant.

The Supreme Court noted that Respondent was to release payment of USD 10.62 Million to the Appellant on submission of Advance Bank Guarantee and Performance Bank Guarantee to Mashkour and its confirmation and acceptance by Mashkour.

The Appellant vide communication dated 21st September, 2011 has requested Mashkour to advise the Respondent to release amount of Rs. 1,99,98,012 /- .

Thus, the case of the Appellant that the amount of Rs. 47,12,10,000/- which was paid to it by the Respondent , was paid on behalf of Mashkour from the funds released to Respondent from Exim Bank on behalf of Mashkour cannot be said to be a dispute which is spurious, illusory or not supported by evidence placed on record.

The Supreme Court concluded that NCLT has rightly rejected the application of Respondent after finding that there existed a dispute between Appellant and the Respondent , as order under Section 9 could not be passed.

The Supreme Court quashed and set aside order of the NCLAT and affirmed the order passed by NCLT

LIABILITY OF CORPORATE GUARANTOR

LAXMIPAT SURANA Vs. UNION OF INDIA

The Supreme Court held in Laxmipat Surana Vs. Union Bank of India & Anr. (Civil Appeal No. 2734 of 2020) that status of guarantor, who is a Corporate Person, metamorphoses into Corporate Debtor, the moment principal borrower (regardless of not being a Corporate Person) commits default in payment of debt which had become due and payable. As such insolvency proceedings can be initiated against Corporate Guarantor. The Supreme Court has also reiterated that Section 18 of Limitation will be applicable to the proceedings under the Insolvency and Bankruptcy Code, 2016.

Case Title : Laxmipat Surana Vs. Union Bank of India & Anr. Date of Decision : 26.03.2021 Bench : A. M. Khanwilkar, J; B. R. Gavai, J; Krishna Murari, J

FACTS OF THE CASE

Union Bank of India has extended credit facility to M/s Mahaveer Construction a proprietary firm through two loan agreements in years 2007 and 2008 for a term loan of Rs. 9,60,00,000/- and an additional amount of Rs. 2,45,00,000/- was disbursed to Mahaveer Construction. M/s Surana Metals Ltd. had offered guarantee to the two loan accounts of the principal borrower. The loan account was declared NPA on 30.01.2010. The Financial Creditor issued recall notice on 19.02.2010 to the principal borrower as well as Corporate Guarantor.

FINDINGS OF THE SUPREME COURT

The issues before the Supreme Court were as under:

(i) Whether an action under Section 7 of the Insolvency and Bankruptcy Code, 2016 can be initiated by the Financial Creditor (Bank) against a Corporate Person (being a Corporate Debtor) concerning guarantee offered by it in respect of loan account of the principal borrower, who had committed default and is not a "Corporate Person".

(ii) Whether an application under Section 7 of the Code filed after three years from the date of declaration of the loan account as Non performing Asset, being the date of default is not barred by limitation?

The Supreme Court held that a right or cause of action would enure to the lender (financial creditor) to proceed against the principal borrower, as well as guarantor in equal measure in case they commit default in repayment of amount of debt acting jointly and severally. It would still be case of default committed by the guarantor itself, if and when the principal borrower fails to discharge his obligation in respect of amount of debt. For, the obligation of the guarantor is coextensive and coterminous with that of principal borrower to defray the debt, as predicated in Section 128 of the Contract Act.

The Supreme Court held that if a guarantor is a Corporate Person, it would come within purview of the Corporate debtor. The relevant para is as under:

20. A priori, in the context of the provisions of the Code, if the guarantor is a Corporate Person (as defined in Section 3 (7) of the Code), it would come within the purview of expression "Corporate Debtor" within the meaning of Section 3(8) of the Code.

The Hon'ble Supreme Court finally held as under:

27. In law, status of guarantor , who is a Corporate Person, metamorphoses into Corporate Debtor, the moment principal borrower (regardless of not being a corporate person) commits default in payment of debt which had become due and payable. Thus, action under Section 7 of the Code could be legitimately invoked even against a (corporate) guarantor being a Corporate Debtor. The definition of "corporate guarantor" in Section 5 (5A) of the Code need to be understood.

28. A priori, we find no substance in the argument advanced before us that since the loan was offered to a proprietary firm (not a Corporate Person) , action under Section 7 of the Code can not be initiated against the Corporate Person even though it had offered guarantee in respect of that transaction. Whereas , upon default committed by the principal borrower, the liability of the company (Corporate Person) , being the guarantor, instantly triggers the right of the financial creditor to proceed against the corporate person (being a Corporate Debtor). Hence the first question stands answered against the appellant.

Hon'ble Supreme Court held that Section 18 of Limitation will be applicable to the proceedings under the Insolvency and Bankruptcy Code, 2016. Section 18 of the Limitation Act gets attracted the moment acknowledgment in writing signed by the party against whom such right to initiate resolution process under Section 7 of the Code enures. Section 18 of the Limitation Act would come into play every time when the principal borrower and/or the Corporate Guarantor (Corporate Debtor), as the case may be, acknowledge their liability to pay the debt. Such acknowledgment, however, must be before the expiration of the prescribed period of limitation including the fresh period of limitation due to acknowledgment of the debt, from time to time, for institution of the proceedings under Section 7 of the Code. Further, the acknowledgment must be of a liability in respect of which the financial creditor can initiate action under Section 7 of the Code .

K. PARAMASIVAM VS THE KARUR VYSYA BANK LTD

The Supreme Court in K. Paramasivam Vs. the Karur Vysya Bank Ltd. AIR (2022) SC 4184 held that a financial creditor may initiate proceedings against a Corporate Guarantor without first proceeding against the Principal Borrower.

Case Title : K. Paramasivam Vs. the Karur Vysya Bank Ltd. Date of Decision : 06.09.2022 Bench : Indira Banerjee, J; J. K. Maheshwari, J

FACTS OF THE CASE

Karur Vysya Bank Ltd (Financial Creditor) has advanced credit facility to Maharaja Refineries (A Partnership Firm), Sri Maharaja Industries (a proprietary concern of K. Paramasivam) , and Sri Maharaja Industries (a proprietary concern of P. Sathiyamoorthy) . Maharaja Theme Parks and Resorts Pvt. Ltd. stood as guarantor for loans availed by three borrowers. Borrowers failed to repay the debt.

The Financial Creditor filed Petition under Section 7 of the Insolvency and Bankruptcy Code, 2016 seeking initiation of corporate insolvency resolution process against the Corporate Guarantor. It was contended by the Financial Creditor that Maharaja Theme Parks and Resorts Pvt. Ltd. was not a Corporate Debtor. Maharaja Theme Parks and Resorts Pvt. Ltd. did not owe any Financial Debt to the Financial Creditor. The NCLT admitted the Application under Section 7 vide order dated 8th April, 2019.

Being aggrieved by the order dated 8th April, 2019 , the Appellant filed an appeal before the NCLAT , which was also dismissed.

FINDINGS OF THE SUPREME COURT

The Supreme Court observed that under Section 7 of the IBC, CIRP can be initiated against corporate entity who has furnished a guarantee to secure the dues of non-corporate entity, in case such non-corporate entity defaults in making payment of debt.

The Supreme Court relied on Laxmipat Surana Vs. Union Bank of India & Ors (2021) 8 SCC 481 wherein it was held that Corporate Person can also become Corporate Debtor having offered guarantee, if and when the Principal Borrower (be it a Corporate Person or otherwise) commits default in payment of its debt. The cause of action would enure to the Financial Creditor to proceed against the principal borrower, as well as the guarantor in equal measure in case of commission of default in repayment of debt acting jointly and severally.

The Supreme Court reiterated as held in Laxmipat Surana that liability of the guarantor is co-extensive with that of the Principal Borrower. The Supreme Court observed that Judgment in Laxmipat Surana rendered by three judge bench is binding on this Bench. It was open for the Financial Creditor to proceed against the guarantor without first suing the Principal Borrower.

The Supreme Court did not find any ground to interfere in the concurrent findings of the Adjudicating Authority and NCLAT and dismissed the Appeal.

BRS VENTURES INVESTMENT LTD. VS SREI INFRASTRUCTURE FINANCE LTD.

The Supreme Court in BRS Ventures Investment Ltd. Vs SREI Infrastructure Finance Ltd. (Civil Appeal No. 4565 /2021) has reiterated that CIRP can be initiated simultaneously against Corporate Debtor as well as Corporate Guarantor. The Supreme Court also held that assets of Subsidiary Company cannot be included in Resolution Plan of the Holding Company.

Case Title : BRS Ventures Investment Ltd. Vs SREI Infrastructure Finance Ltd.
Date of Decision : 23.07.2024
Bench : Abhay S. Oka, J; Pankaj Mithal, J

FACTS OF THE CASE

Gujarat Hydrocarbon and Power SEZ Ltd. (GHPSL) approached SREI Infrastructure Finance Ltd. (Financial Creditor) for grant of loan. SREI granted loan of 100 Crore for setting up SEZ project. GHPSL is a subsidiary of Assam Company India Ltd (ACIL). The loan granted by SREI was secured by mortgage of leasehold land of GHPSL and pledge of shares of GHPSL and ACIL. The loan was also secured by Corporate Guarantee furnished by ACIL.

Financial Creditor initiated recovery proceedings before DRT. The Financial Creditor also invoked Corporate Guarantee given by ACIL. The Financial Creditor filed Application under Section 7 of IBC against ACIL for initiating CIRP which was admitted on 26th October, 2017.

During CIRP, the Appellant emerged as Successful Resolution Applicant and its Resolution Plan was approved on 13th August, 2018. The Resolution Plan was approved by NCLT on 20.09.2018. Appeal filed before NCLAT was dismissed. Under Resolution Plan the Financial Creditor got 38.87 Crore against its claim of 241.27 Crore.

The Financial Creditor filed Application under Section 7 against GHPSL for initiating CIRP in respect of balance amount. NCLT admitted the application vide order dated 18th November, 2020. Appeals were filed before NCLAT, which were dismissed.

FINDINGS OF THE SUPREME COURT

The Supreme Court was dealing with the issue whether Application was maintainable against the Corporate Debtor for same debt and default when the Financial Creditor has accepted its dues in CIRP of Corporate Guarantor.

The Supreme Court observed that the law is well settled. The liability of principal debtor and surety is co-extensive. The Creditor has remedies available to recover amount payable by principal borrower by proceeding against both or any of them. The Creditor can also proceed against the Guarantor first.

If a Creditor recovers a part of guaranteed amount from the surety and agrees not to proceed against surety for balance amount, that will not extinguish remaining debt payable by the borrower. In such a case the Creditor can proceed against the principal borrower to recover the balance amount. If there is a compromise between the creditor and the surety to which the principal borrower is not a party, the liability of the borrower qua the creditor will remain unaffected.

The Supreme Court relied on Lalit Kumar Jain Vs Union of India (2021) 9 SCC 321 wherein it has been held that the contract between creditor and surety is independent, therefore, the approval of the Resolution Plan of the Principal Borrower will not amount to discharge of surety. The Same principle will apply when the Resolution Plan of surety is approved. In such a case surety gets a discharge by operation of law or by involuntary process, it will not amount to discharge of the Principal Borrower.

The Supreme Court observed that Section 60 (2) contemplates separate or simultaneous insolvency proceedings against Corporate Debtor and the Guarantor. Section 60 (3) provides that if CIRP in respect of Guarantor is pending before another Adjudicating Authority and CIRP against the Corporate Debtor is pending before another Adjudicating Authority, CIRP proceedings against the Corporate Guarantor has to be transferred to Adjudicating Authority before whom CIRP proceedings against the Corporate Debtor is pending.

It was contended before Supreme Court that assets of the Second Respondent was part of Resolution Plan in the matter of ACIL. The Supreme Court concurred with NCLAT view that Resolution Plan of ACIL takes care of investment in subsidiaries and not the assets of subsidiaries. Supreme Court observed that assets of subsidiaries cannot be part of Resolution Plan of Holding Company.

The Supreme Court noted that Section 36 (4) (d) provides that the assets of Indian Subsidiary of the Corporate Debtor will not be included in Liquidation Estate assets and shall not be used for recovery in liquidation. Similarly, explanation 2 to Section 18 (1) provides that the term "assets" used in Section 18 shall not include the assets of the Indian Subsidiary of the Corporate Debtor.

A holding company and a subsidiary company are distinct legal identities. The holding company owns shares of its subsidiary but that does not make holding company the owner of subsidiary assets.

The Supreme Court observed that if the surety pays the entirety of the amount payable under the guarantee to the creditor, Section 140 of Contract Act provides a remedy to the surety to recover the entire amount paid by him in the discharge of his obligations. The Surety gets invested with the rights of the creditor to recover from the principal debtor the amount which was paid as per guarantee. If the surety pays only a part of the amount payable to the creditor, the equitable right the surety gets under Section 140 will be confined to the debt cleared. In the instant case only liability of the ACIL has extinguished after payment of Rs. 38.87 Crore. The right of the Financial Creditor to recover balance debt is not extinguished.

The Supreme Court concluded that view of the NCLAT cannot be faulted with and dismissed the appeal.

WITHDRAWAL OF CIRP

VALLAL RCK Vs. M/S SIVA INDUSTRIES AND HOLDINGS LTD

The Supreme Court in Vallal RCK Vs M/s Siva Industries and Holding Ltd. (2022) SCC Online SC 717 held that if 90% or more of members of CoC in their wisdom have permitted settlement and withdrawal of Corporate Insolvency Resolution Process (CIRP), the Adjudicating Authority cannot sit in appeal over it.

Case Title : Vallal RCK Vs M/s Siva Industries and Holdings Ltd. Date of Decision : 03.06.2022 Bench : B. R. Gavai, J; Hima Kohli, J

FACTS OF THE CASE

IDBI Bank Ltd filed Application under Section 7 IBC for initiation of insolvency proceedings against the Corporate Debtor, which was admitted by NCLT vide order dated 4th July, 2019. The Resolution Professional submitted plan before the CoC but the same was not approved. The Resolution Professional filed application for initiation of liquidation proceedings on 8th May, 2020.

In the meantime the Promoter filed an application before NCLT for one time settlement. Settlement Plan was approved by the Committee of Creditors with more than 90% voting share.

RP filed an application before the Hon'ble NCLT for withdrawal of CIRP. NCLT held that it was not a Settlement Plan simpliciter but a "business restructuring plan" and rejected the application for withdrawal of the CIRP and passed order for liquidation of the Corporate Debtor. Appeal against the same was filed before the NCLAT which was dismissed.

FINDINGS OF THE SUPREME COURT

It was contended before the Supreme Court that NCLT cannot sit in appeal over commercial wisdom of the Committee of Creditors. When Committee of Creditors has approved the Settlement Plan with the voting majority of 94.23%, the NCLT and NCLAT have erred in rejecting the settlement plan.

The Supreme Court noted that Section 12A has been introduced vide Insolvency and Bankruptcy Code (Second Amendment) Act, 2018 on the recommendation of the Insolvency Law Committee which was of the view that in exceptional circumstances, withdrawal of CIRP in post-admission stage should be allowed with at least 90% voting share of CoC.

The Court noted that Section 12 A requires 90% voting share of CoC for withdrawal of CIRP on account of settlement. Such application has to be made through the Resolution Professional if the CoC has been constituted. If such application is made after publication of Expression of Interest, reasons have to be given for withdrawal of Application. RP is required to place such Application before the CoC for approval. If CoC approves the Application with at least 90% majority, the same has to be filed with NCLT for approval.

The Supreme Court noted that in Swiss Ribbons Pvt. Ltd Vs. Union of India (2019) 4 SCC 17 validity of Section 12 A was challenged on the ground that figure of 90% voting share was arbitrary. The Supreme Court rejected this contention and held Section 12 A valid.

The Supreme Court observed that commercial wisdom of the Committee of Creditors has been given paramount status in several judgments. There is an intrinsic presumption that Financial Creditors are fully informed about the viability of the Corporate Debtor and feasibility of the proposed Resolution Plan.

When 90% or more of the CoC Members in their wisdom after due deliberation permit settlement and withdrawal of the CIRP, NCLT cannot sit in appeal over the same. Interference could be only warranted in case the decision of the CoC is capricious, arbitrary, irrational and de hors the provisions of statutes or rules.

The Supreme Court noted that in the instant case there were wide deliberations among members of CoC on the Settlement Plan. NCLT or NCLAT was not justified in not respecting the commercial wisdom of the Committee of Creditors.

The Supreme Court noted that it has time and again emphasized the need for minimal judicial interference by NCLT and NCLAT.

The Supreme Court allowed the appeal and permitted withdrawal of Corporate Insolvency Resolution Process (CIRP).

GLAS TRUST COMPANY LLC VS BYJU RAVEENDRAN

The Supreme Court in Glas Trust Company LLC Vs. Byju Raveendran (Civil Appeal No. 9986 of 2024) held that inherent powers under Rule 11 of NCLAT Rules cannot be invoked for withdrawal of CIRP proceedings, as a detailed procedure for withdrawal has been provided under IBC and regulations made thereunder.

Case Title : Glas Trust Company LLC Vs. Byju Raveendran & Ors Date of Decision : 23.10.2024 Bench : Dr. Dhananjaya Y. Chandrachud, J; J. B. Pardiwala, J; Manoj Mishra, J

BRIEF FACTS

Think and Learn Pvt Ltd, (Corporate Debtor) is a company engaged in the business of providing online educational services of which Byju's Alpha Inc. was a 100% subsidiary company. Byju's Alpha Inc availed a loan facility aggregating to approximately USD 1,200,000,000 under a credit and guarantee agreement dated 24 November 2021. GLAS Trust Company LLC (Appellant) was the 'Administrative Agent' of all the lenders under this agreement and the 'Collateral Agent' for the secured parties. Under the terms of the Credit Agreement, the Corporate Debtor acted as a guarantor and issued a guarantee deed dated 24 November 2021 in favour of the appellant. The appellant, acting as the Administrative Agent of the lenders, issued a notice of demand dated 6 December 2023 to the Corporate Debtor, invoking the guarantee deed and demanding that the Corporate Debtor pay the requisite amount, but payment was not made.

It was alleged that Byju's Alpha Inc. transferred USD 533 million to a hedge fund based in the United States. United States Bankruptcy Court,

District of Delaware issued injunctive orders in respect of transferred USD 533 million.

On 23rd September, 2023, the Board of Control for Cricket in India (BCCI) filed Section 9 IBC Petition for initiating Insolvency Proceedings against Corporate Debtor, which was admitted by NCLT. Appellant also filed Section 7 application, wherein it was directed to file claim in the admitted Petition.

Glas Trust Company LLC filed appeal before NCLAT against disposal of Section 7 Petition. Think and Learn Pvt. Ltd. (Corporate Debtor) also filed appeal against admission of Section 9 Petition. During pendency of appeal before NCLAT, Think and Learn Pvt. Ltd. settled the matter with BCCI and paid the operational debt. The NCLAT invoking powers under Rule 11 of NCLAT Rules approved the settlement and set aside Section 9 proceedings.

Appeal was filed before the Supreme Court wherein the Supreme Court granted stay on order of the NCLAT and directed for deposit of Rs. 158 Crore in Escrow account. CIRP against Corporate Debtor was also revived.

FINDINGS OF THE SUPREME COURT

The Supreme Court observed that the framework created by Rule 8 of the NCLT Rules and Section 12A of the IBC read with Rule 30A of the CIRP Regulations lays down an exhaustive procedure for the withdrawal of an application filed by creditors under Sections 7, 9, or 10 of the IBC. Withdrawal may be sought at four stages, all of which have a procedure prescribed under the existing framework.

In cases where application under Section 7, 9 or 10 has not been admitted, application can be filed directly before the NCLT for withdrawal. At this stage the case is *in personam* between the Applicant and Respondent.

In cases where application has been admitted but CoC has not been constituted, application has to be filed through IRP. At this stage, the proceedings become *in rem* and NCLT has to hear all the relevant parties.

In cases where CoC has been constituted, Application has to be filed through IRP/RP after CoC approves withdrawal application with 90 % voting share.

In cases where expression of interest has been invited, in addition to approval of CoC with 90% majority, the applicant must state the reasons for withdrawal at this belated stage.

The Supreme Court observed that inherent powers' may be exercised in cases where there is no express provision under the legal framework. However, such powers cannot be exercised in contravention of, conflict with or in ignorance of express provisions of law.

The Supreme Court was of the view that recourse to Rule 11 of the NCLAT Rules was not warranted in the present circumstances. As noted above, 'inherent powers' cannot be used to subvert legal provisions, which exhaustively provide for a procedure. To permit the NCLAT to circumvent this detailed procedure by invoking its inherent powers under Rule 11 would run contrary to the carefully crafted procedure for withdrawal. In the Impugned Judgment, the NCLAT does not provide any reasons for deviating from this procedure or the urgency to approve the settlement without following the procedure. The correct course of action by the NCLAT would have been to stay the constitution of the CoC and direct the parties to follow the course of action in Section 12A read with Regulation 30A of the CIRP Regulations 2016. This legal framework for such withdrawal was formulated after giving due consideration to the appropriate procedure for withdrawal and balancing it with the objectives of the IBC.

The Supreme Court observed that even if the procedural infirmity is kept aside, once the CIRP was admitted, the proceedings became collective, and all creditors of the Corporate Debtor became stakeholders and should have been heard.

The Supreme Court set aside the order of the NCLAT.

MORATORIUM

P. MOHANRAJ & ORS Vs. M/S SHAH BROTHERS ISPAT PVT. LTD.

The Supreme Court in P. Mohanraj Vs Shah Brothers Ispat Pvt Ltd (2021) 6 SCC 258 held that proceedings under Section 138 of Negotiable Instruments Act, 1881 will be covered under Section 14 (1) (a) IBC. The Supreme Court also held that such proceedings can be initiated against persons mentioned under Section 141 (1) and (2) of the Negotiable Instruments Act.

Case Title : P. Mohanraj & Ors. Vs M/s Shah Brothers Ispat Pvt. Ltd.
Date of Decision : 01.03.2021
Bench : R. F. Nariman, J; Navin Sinha, J; K. M. Joseph, J

FACTS OF THE CASE

Shah Brothers Ispat Pvt. Ltd. (Operational Creditor/Respondent) supplied steel products to Diamond Engineering Pvt. Ltd. (Corporate Debtor) as a result of which Rs. 24, 20, 91, 054/- was due and payable by the company. 51 cheques issued by the Corporate Debtor were returned dishonored for the reason "fund insufficient" on 03.03.2017. As a result the Respondent issued statutory demand notice under provisions of Negotiable Instruments Act. On 28.04.2017 two more cheques were dishonored for which demand notice was sent. As payment was not made, two Criminal complaints were filed under Section 138 R/w 141 of Negotiable Instruments Act, 1881.

Meanwhile, the NCLT admitted an application under Section 9 IBC filed by Shah Brothers Ispat Pvt. Ltd. on 06.06.2017 and moratorium was declared under Section 14 IBC. The NCLT also stayed proceedings in two criminal complaints. On appeal, the NCLAT set aside the order holding that Section 138, being criminal proceedings , cannot be held to be proceedings within the meaning of Section 14 IBC.

FINDINGS OF THE SUPREME COURT

The issue before the Supreme Court was whether the institution or continuation of proceedings under Section 138/141 of the Negotiable Instruments Act, 1881 can be said to be covered by the moratorium under Section 14.

Under Section 14 (1) the Adjudicating Authority prohibits what follows in clauses (a) to (d). Certain exceptions have been provided under sub-sections (2) and (3). Under sub-section 2 , the supply of essential goods and services to the Corporate Debtor during this period cannot be terminated or suspended or even interrupted. Sub-section 3 (a) refers to transactions as may be notified by the Central Government in consultation with experts in finance.

The sweep of Section 14 (1) (a) is very wide indeed as it includes institution, continuation, judgment and execution of suits and proceedings. Award of an arbitration panel or an order of authority is also included. Expression "institution of suits or continuing of pending suits" is to be read as one category and proceedings against the Corporate Debtor would be a separate category. The expression "any judgment, decree or order" and "any court of law, tribunal, arbitration panel or other authority" throws light on the width of expression "proceedings". Section 138 proceedings conducted before a Court of Law will certainly be covered under Section 14 (1) (a).

The principles of ejusdem generis and noscitur a sociis, being rules of construction of statutes, cannot be exalted to nullify the plain meaning of words used in statute if they are designedly used in a wide sense.

A quasi-criminal proceeding like Section 138, which would lead to depletion of assets in form of compensation, would directly impact the Corporate Insolvency Resolution Process (CIRP) in the same manner as a decree in a suit in civil court.

When the language of Section 14 and Section 85 are contrasted it becomes clear that Section 85 is only in respect of debts while Section 14 is not subject specific. Section 95 and 101 also use the word "debt" as used in Section 85. A Legal action or proceedings in respect of any debt would on its plain meaning include Section 138 proceedings. The Scope of Section 14 is even greater than the scope of Sections 85, 95, and 101.

Section 14 and Section 32A

Section 32 A cannot possibly throw light on true interpretation of Section 14 (1) (a) as reason for introducing Section 32A has nothing to do whatsoever with any moratorium provision. Heart of Section 32 A is extinguishment of criminal liability of the Corporate Debtor from the date of approval of Resolution plan. On the other hand moratorium does not extinguish any liability, civil or criminal. If there is a clash between Section 14 and Section 32 A (1), this has to be best resolved by harmonious construction. The Expression "prosecution" in the first proviso of Section 32 A (1) refers to criminal proceedings either through First Information Report or complaint but not to quasi-criminal proceedings instituted under Section 138/141 of Negotiable Instrument Act.

The nature of proceedings under Chapter XVII of Negotiable Instrument Act

Civil proceedings are not necessarily a proceedings which begins with filing of suit and ends with execution. It includes revenue proceedings as well as Writ Petition filed under Article 226. Criminal proceedings are such proceedings wherein interest of state is involved. It is clear that a Section 138 proceedings can be said to be "civil sheep" in a "criminal wolf's" clothing.

The gravamen of a proceedings under Section 138 is to get back the amount contained in dishonoured cheque together with interest and costs, expeditiously and cheaply.

Quasi Criminal Proceedings

It was contended before the Supreme Court that Section 138 proceedings are criminal proceedings rather than quasi-criminal proceedings as these proceedings result in imprisonment, fine or both. The Supreme Court rejected this argument. The Supreme Court observed that there are many instances wherein there are provisions for punishment of imprisonment or fine or both in quasi-criminal proceedings. Such instances are Section 630 of Companies Act, 1956, contempt of court proceedings etc.

Section 14 IBC and SICA

The Supreme Court observed that as the language, object , and context of Section 22 (1) of the SICA and Section 446 (2) of the Companies Act are far removed from Section 14 (1) of the IBC, none of the aforesaid judgments have any application to Section 14 of the IBC and are therefore distinguishable.

Whether natural person is covered under Section 14 ?

In Aneeta Hada Godfather Travels & Tours (P) Ltd (2012) 5 SCC661 it has been held that Section 138/141 proceedings cannot be initiated without impleading the Corporate Debtor. Legal impediment under Section 14 makes it impossible to initiate proceedings against the Corporate Debtor as such Section 138/141 proceedings can be initiated against persons mentioned under Section 141 (1) and (2) of the Negotiable Instruments Act.

SUNDARESH BHATT VS. CENTRAL BOARD OF INDIRECT TAXES AND CUSTOMS

The Supreme Court in Sundaresh Bhatt, Liquidator of ABG Shipyard Vs. Central Board of Indirect Taxes and Customs (Civil Appeal No. 7667/2021) held that after initiation of moratorium, the Custom Authorities had only limited jurisdiction to assess/determine the quantum of customs duty and other levies and after such assessment can file claim. Further, IRP/RP/Liquidator can immediately secure goods to be dealt with appropriately in terms of IBC.

Case Title : Sundaresh Bhatt, Liquidator of ABG Shipyard Vs. Central Board of Indirect Taxes and Customs
Date of Decision : 26.08.2022
Bench : N. V. Ramana, CJI; J. K. Maheshwari, J; Hima Kohli, J

FACTS OF THE CASE

Liquidation Proceedings were initiated against ABG Shipyard (Corporate Debtor) vide order dated April 25, 2019.

Certain materials imported by the Corporate Debtor were lying in customs bonded warehouses. These materials were to be used for construction and building of ships, which were to be exported after manufacturing was complete. The Corporate Debtor availed the benefits available to it under the Export Promotion Capital Goods Scheme (EPCG Scheme) with respect to the said materials. Since the Corporate Debtor failed to submit an Export Obligation Discharge Certificate (EODC) and thereby comply with its obligations in respect of the EPCG License, Custom Authorities had issued various notices to the Corporate Debtor, *interalia* directing the Corporate Debtor to pay the applicable customs duty failing which proceeding for recovery of the customs duty would be initiated under Section 142 of the Customs Act.

The Liquidator filed an IA No. 474/2019 in CP (IB)No. 53/NCLT/AHM/2017 before NCLT, Ahmadabad Bench seeking direction to the Custom Authority to allow removal of material which was lying in the custom Bonded warehouses, which was allowed. The Custom Authorities aggrieved by the said order filed an appeal before the NCLAT, which was allowed by the NCLAT and order of the NCLT was set aside. The Liquidator filed an appeal before the Supreme Court, which was allowed by the Supreme Court.

FINDINGS OF THE SURPEME COURT

The Supreme Court observed that IBC being more recent statute overrides the Customs Act. This is clearly made out by reading of Section 142 A of the Customs Act. The aforesaid provisions note that the Customs Authority could have first charge on the assets of an assessee under the Customs Act, except with respect to cases under Section 529A of the Companies Act, 1956, Recovery of Debts Due to Banks and Financial Institutions Act, 1993, Securitisation and Reconstruction of Financial Assets and Enforcement of Security Interest Act, 2002 and the IBC, 2016.

Custom Act and IBC act in their own spheres. In case of any conflict, the IBC overrides the Customs Act.

The Supreme Court held that demand notices to seek enforcement of custom duties during the moratorium period would clearly violate the provisions of Section 14 or 33 (5) of the IBC. Demand Notices are initiation of legal proceedings against the Corporate Debtor and the same are not permissible under Section 14 of the Code.

The Supreme Court relying upon S. V. Kondaskar Vs. V. M. Deshpande (AIR 1972 SC 878) held that the authorities can only take steps to determine the tax, interest, fines or any penalty which is due. However, the authority cannot enforce a claim for recovery or levy of interest on the tax due during the period of moratorium.

The Supreme Court held that Custom Act and IBC can be read in harmonious manner wherein authorities under the Customs Act have a limited jurisdiction to determine the quantum of operational debt in order to stake claim in terms of Section 53 of the IBC before the Liquidator. However, Custom Authorities do not have the power to execute its claim beyond the ambit of Section 53 of IBC. The Supreme Court also held that there has not been any abandonment of goods which would authorize the Customs Authorities to initiate the adjudicatory process to transfer the title to themselves. Before any goods can be declared to have been "abandoned" the same must be adjudged by some authority after due notice. The position cannot be assumed or deemed.

SARANGA ANILKUMAR AGGARWAL VS BHAVESH DHIRAJ LAL SHETH & ORS

The Supreme Court in Saranga Anilkumar Aggarwal Vs. Bhavesh Dhirajlal Sheth & Ors (2025 INSC 314) has held that the penalties imposed by the NCDRC are regulatory in nature and do not constitute "debt" under IBC. Moratorium under Section 96 of the IBC does not extend to regulatory penalties imposed for non-compliance with consumer protection laws.

> Case Title : Saranga Anilkumar Aggarwal Vs. Bhavesh Dhirajlal Sheth & Ors
> Date of Decision : 04.03.2025
> Bench : Vikram Nath, J; Prasanna B. Varale, J

FACTS OF THE CASE

The appellant was engaged in development of real estate development. Several complaints were filed before the NCDRC alleging delay in possession, deficiency of service and breach of contractual obligations. NCDRC issued directions for obtaining occupancy certificates, handover of possession and imposed penalties. The Respondents filed application for execution of orders of NCDRC. The Appellant took several defences including the defense that an interim moratorium was triggered against the Appellant as per Section 96 of IBC, which the appellant claimed barred further legal proceedings, including ongoing execution proceedings before the NCDRC.

NCDRC held that consumer claim and penalty imposed did not fall within moratorium imposed under IBC. The NCDRC relied on judgment of the Supreme Court on State Bank of India Vs. Ramakrishnan & Anr, (2018) 17 SCC 394 which clarified that Section 95 and 101 of the IBC provide a distinct moratorium applicable to personal guarantors, separate from the moratorium under Section 14 applicable to Corporate Debtors. The NCDRC emphasized that the stay under Section 96 and 101 extends only to proceedings concerning the debt and does not necessarily shield the guarantor from all legal actions. The NCDRC also relied on the judgment of the Supreme Court in Ajay Kumar Radheshyam Goenka Vs. Tourism Finance Corporation of India Ltd., (2023)10SCC545 wherein it was held that criminal proceedings against directors or signatories of a company do not abate merely because the corporate debtor is undergoing insolvency resolution.

FINDINGS OF THE SUPREME COURT

The Supreme Court observed that there is a fundamental distinction between civil and criminal proceedings concerning debt moratorium. While civil proceedings are generally stayed under IBC provisions, criminal proceedings including penalty enforcement, do not automatically fall within its ambit unless explicitly stated by law. The penalties imposed by the NCDRC are regulatory in nature and arise due to non-compliance with consumer protection laws, they are distinct from "debt recovery proceedings" under the IBC.

The Supreme Court further observed that moratorium under Section 96 IBC is distinct from a corporate moratorium under Section 14 IBC. Section 96 IBC applies to individuals and personal guarantors and provides that during the interim moratorium period "any legal action or proceedings relating to any debt shall be deemed to have been stayed". However, it is pertinent to note that this provision applied only to "debt" as defined under the IBC and not to regulatory penalties imposed for non-compliance with consumer protection laws. A careful reading of the statutory scheme of the IBC suggests that penalties arising from regulatory infractions are not covered under the ambit of "debt" as envisioned under the Code.

The Supreme Court further observed that there exists a distinction between punitive actions and criminal proceedings. While a criminal proceeding is initiated by the State against an accused to determine guilt and impose penal consequences, punitive actions in the regulatory sphere, such as those imposed by the NCDRC are meant to ensure compliance with the law and to act as a deterrent against future violations. Section 27 of the Consumer Protection Act empowers consumer fora to impose penalties to ensure adherence to consumer protection norms. These penalties do not arise from any "debt" owed to a creditor but rather from the failure to comply with the remedial mechanisms established under consumer law. Unlike a criminal prosecution, which requires the establishment of mens rea, the penalties imposed by NCDRC are regulatory in nature and aim to protect the public interest rather than to punish criminal behavior.

The Supreme Court further observed that a distinction must be drawn between the moratorium applicable to a corporate debtor under Section 14 of IBC and the interim moratorium applicable to individuals and personal guarantors under Section 96 of IBC. The former is much broader in scope and stays all proceedings against the Corporate Debtor including execution and enforcement actions. However, Section 96 is more limited in its scope, staying only "legal actions or proceedings in respect of any debt". Unlike corporate insolvency proceedings, where the goal is a comprehensive resolution of the company's liabilities, individual insolvency proceedings are designed primarily for restructuring personal debts and providing relief to the debtor. The legislative intent behind limiting the scope of the interim moratorium under Section 96 of the IBC must be respected and a blanket stay on all regulatory penalties would result in defeating the objective of consumer protection laws. The moratorium under Section 96 IBC is intended to provide temporary relief to debtors by preventing certain proceedings against them during the resolution process. However, this protection is not absolute and does not extend to all categories of debts. The legislative intent behind the moratorium is to ensure that the debtor's assets are preserved for an efficient resolution process and to prevent creditors from taking unilateral actions that may frustrate the objective of insolvency proceedings. The statutory scheme of IBC makes it clear that the protection under the moratorium does not cover all forms of liabilities, particularly those classified as "excluded debts" under Section 79 (15) of IBC. Section 94 (3) of the IBC explicitly limits the scope of the moratorium by carving out exceptions for certain categories of debts. Section 79 (15) of the IBC defines "excluded debts" to include liabilities arising from fines imposed by courts or tribunals, damages for negligence or breach of obligation, maintenance liabilities, student loans and other prescribed debts. This classification is based on the nature of such obligations, which are either statutory, penal or personal in nature, and therefore, they do not form part of the insolvency estate that can be discharged under the resolution process.

The Supreme Court held that the damages awarded by the NCDRC arise from a consumer dispute, where the appellant has been held liable for deficiency in service. Such damages are not in the nature of ordinary contractual debts but rather serve to compensate the consumers for loss suffered and to deter unethical business practices. Courts and tribunals, including the NCDRC, exercise their statutory jurisdiction to award such damages, and these are distinct from purely financial debts that may be subject to restructuring under the IBC. Since such damages are covered under “excluded debts” as per Section 79(15) of the IBC, they do not get the benefit of the moratorium under Section 96 of the IBC and their enforcement remains unaffected by the initiation of insolvency proceedings.

The Appeal was dismissed by the Supreme Court.

RAKESH BHANOT VS M/S GURDAS AGRO PVT. LTD

The Supreme Court in Rakesh Bhanot Vs. M/S Gurdas Agro Pvt. Ltd. (2025 INSC 445) held that Interim Moratorium under Section 96 or 101 IBC does not stall criminal prosecution under Section 138 of the Negotiable Instruments Act, 1881.

Case Title : Rakesh Bhanot Vs. M/S Gurdas Agro Pvt. Ltd. Date of Decision : 01.04.2025 Bench : J. B. Pardiwala, J; R. Mahadevan, J

FACTS OF THE CASE

Several petitions were filed before the Supreme Court against the refusal of the High Courts to stay the proceedings *sine die* under Section 138 R/w Section 142 of Negotiable Instruments Act, 1881 till conclusion of insolvency proceedings under Section 94 IBC.

The common legal question before the Supreme Court was whether Section 138 NI proceedings should be stayed in view of interim moratorium under Section 96 IBC coming into effect after filing of applications under Section 94 IBC.

FINDINGS OF THE SUPREME COURT

The Supreme Court after surveying Section 14,94,96 and 101 IBC observed as under :

10.1. Form the above provisions, it is clear that the term "Corporate Person" includes a company as defined under Section 2 (2)) of the Companies Act, 2013 and a Limited Liability Partnership. However, there is a subtle difference in the protection available to the Directors and the Partners. In case of a Partnership firm, the interim moratorium protects not only the firm, but also the partners. But in case of a company, such protection is available only to the company and not to its directors. That apart, the object of interim moratorium can be no different from that of the moratorium specified under Section 14. It is also clear form Section 14 that the protection from legal action during the period of moratorium is not available to the surety or in other words, to a personal guarantor. The use of the words "all the debts" and "in respect of any debt" in sub-section (1) of Section 96 is not without a purpose, as the moratorium is intended to offer protection only against civil claim to recover the debt. Hence, such period of moratorium prescribed under Section 14 or 96 is restricted in its applicability only to the protection against civil claims which are directed towards recovery and not from criminal action.

The Supreme Court observed that upon filing of the Application under Section 94 IBC, a moratorium comes into effect, designed to protect the debtors from any legal actions concerning their debts. Specifically, Section 96 IBC provides that any legal proceedings pending against the debtor concerning any debt shall be deemed to have been stayed. The term "any legal action or proceedings" does not mean "every legal action or proceeding". In sub-clause 96 (b) (i) and (ii), the term "legal action or proceedings" would have to be understood to include such legal action or proceedings relating to recovery of debt by invoking the principles of *Noscitur a sociius*. The purpose of interim moratorium contemplated under Section 96 is to be derived from the object of the act, which is not to stall the proceedings unrelated to the recovery of the debt. The protection is not available against penal actions, the object of which is to not recover any debt. This moratorium serves as a critical mechanism, allowing the debtor to reorganize their financial affairs without the immediate threat of creditor actions. The clear and unequivocal language of this provision reflects the legislative intent to provide a protective shield for debtors during the insolvency process.

The Supreme Court observed that the object of the moratorium or for that purpose, the provision enabling the debtor to approach the Tribunal under Section 94 is not to stall the criminal prosecution, but to only postpone any civil actions to recover any debt. The deterrent effect of the Section 138 of Negotiable Instruments Act, 1881 is essential for maintaining trust in negotiable instruments.

A A ESTATES PVT LTD, THROUGH RP Vs. KHER NAGAR SUKHSADAN CO-OPERATIVE HOUSING SOCIETY LTD. & ORS.

The Supreme Court in A A Estates Ltd, through RP Vs Kher Nagar Sukhsadan Co-operative Society Ltd. (2025 INSC 1366) held that the moratorium under Section 14 does not revive terminated contracts or protect rights that have ceased to exist prior to insolvency.

Case Title : A A Estates Pvt. Ltd, through RP Vs Kher Nagar Sukhsadan Co-operative Society Ltd. Date of Decision : 28.11.2025 Bench : J. B. Pardiwala, J; R. Mahadevan, J

FACTS OF THE CASE

A A Estates Pvt. Ltd (Appellant) and Maharashtra Housing & Area Development Authority entered into a Lease Deed dated 12.02.1996 in respect of land admeasuring 1890.31 sq.m. On 16.10.2005, Appellant entered into development agreement with Kher Nagar Sukhsadan Co-operative Housing Society Ltd. for redevelopment of the property. Redevelopment process was halted as several members refused to vacate the premises. On the application of SBI, CIRP was initiated in respect of the Appellant vide order dated 06.12.2022. After initiation of CIRP, the Respondent No. 1 Society terminated the Development Agreement with Appellant and appointed Respondent No. 8 as new developer. Respondent No. 1 Society filed Writ Petition before the Hon'ble High Court seeking *interalia* directions to Respondent 1 and 8 to grant permission for redevelopment of project.

FINDINGS OF THE SUPREME COURT

The Supreme Court framed the following issues.

(i) Whether the termination of the Development Agreement dated 16.1 0.2005 and Supplementary Agreements dated 23.12.2005 and 09.04.2014 by Respondent No. 1 Society prior to the initiation of the second CIRP was valid and effective in law.

The Supreme Court observed that in contract law, time is of the essence in a redevelopment agreement, whose object is timely rehabilitation of displaced members. Prolonged delay defeats the foundation of the contract and constitutes a material breach entitling the owner to terminate. The right to terminate for default was expressly reserved in the Development Agreement and the Supplementary Agreements. The termination was thus effected after due notice and prolonged default, and cannot be termed arbitrary or mala fide. The Society, being the owner of the property and guardian of the members' welfare, cannot be compelled to indefinitely await performance from a defaulting developer. The IBC is not intended to freeze urban welfare projects or protect commercial indolence at the cost of citizens awaiting rehabilitation.

Relying on Gujarat Urja Vikas Nigam Ltd v. Amit Gupta and others, the Supreme Court observed that NCLT under Section 60 (5) jurisdiction can only set aside termination of contracts when termination is only on account of insolvency and such termination would inevitably result in the corporate death of the corporate debtor by depriving it of its sole or central contract essential to the success of the CIRP.

The termination in the present case was not occasioned by the insolvency of the corporate debtor but by its persistent non-performance. Letters issued by the Society, including one dated 31.05.2019, record that continuation of the agreement was conditional upon compliance by the developer, failing which the contract would stand cancelled. These defaults occurred well before initiation of the CIRP. Thus, the termination was based on legitimate grounds unrelated to insolvency. The Supreme Court further noted that the Appellant had several other contracts. The Supreme Court concluded that No subsisting contractual or proprietary right survived in favour of the corporate debtor on the date of initiation of the second CIRP. Consequently, the NCLT lacked jurisdiction under Section 60(5)(c) of the IBC to interfere with such termination.

(ii) Whether the aforesaid Development Agreement and the Supplementary Agreements constitute "assets" or "property" of the corporate debtor so as to attract the protection of moratorium under Section 14 of the IBC.

The Supreme Court observed that Development Agreement dated 1 6.10.2005 and the Supplementary Agreements dated 23.12.2005 and 09.04.2014 stood terminated by Respondent No. 1 Society on account of persistent default and failure of the developer to commence or complete the project. The termination was duly communicated through letters dated 09.06.2019, 02.12.2019 and 06.11.2021 – each preceding the initiation of the second CIRP on 06.12.2022. No subsisting challenge to such termination was pending when CIRP commenced. The Supreme Court observed that the moratorium under Section 14 does not revive terminated contracts or protect rights that have ceased to exist prior to insolvency. The protection is intended to preserve the existing value of the corporate debtor's estate, not to resurrect lapsed or extinguished interests. Extending moratorium to such non-existent rights would defeat commercial certainty and the sanctity of lawful termination under general law. The Supreme Court concluded that the Development Agreement dated 16.10.2005 and the Supplementary Agreements dated 23.12.2005 and 09.04.2014 do not constitute "assets" or "property" of the corporate debtor within the meaning of Section 14 of the IBC, as the same stood terminated prior to initiation of the second CIRP.

(iii) Whether the High Court was justified in allowing the writ petition filed by Respondent No. 1 Society and directing the statutory authorities to process and grant approvals in favour of Respondent No.8 for redevelopment of the subject project.

The Supreme Court observed that the jurisdiction under Article 226 is wide enough to ensure that statutory authorities perform their public duties and do not withhold approvals without legal justification. The High Court did not usurp the jurisdiction of the NCLT or interfere with any matter directly arising from the insolvency process. Its directions were confined to ensuring that the Society's rights as the owner of the land were not indefinitely suspended due to the pendency of CIRP proceedings against a developer who no longer had any subsisting contractual or proprietary interest in the project. The Supreme Court observed that the IBC does not oust the constitutional jurisdiction of the High Courts, particularly where intervention is sought against administrative or statutory inaction in the public law domain, provided such intervention does not obstruct or undermine the insolvency process.

(iv) Whether the proceedings before the High Court stood vitiated by violation of the principles of natural justice, as alleged by the appellants

The Supreme Court observed that the writ petition filed by Respondent No. 1 Society was pending before the High Court for a considerable period prior to its final hearing. The record shows that the appellants were duly represented by counsel throughout and were aware of the proceedings. No application seeking an adjournment or extension of time to file a reply was made. The proceedings on 03.09.2024 were conducted in the presence of the counsel for the Resolution Professional, whose submissions were duly recorded in the impugned judgment. In these circumstances, it cannot be said that the High Court acted in undue haste or deprived the appellants of a reasonable opportunity of being heard.

The Supreme Court noted that the questions before the High Court were essentially legal in nature – relating to the applicability of the moratorium under Section 14 of the IBC and the validity of termination of the redevelopment agreement – both turning upon undisputed documents. No complex factual adjudication was required. Even before this Court, the appellants have failed to point out any specific prejudice or material that they were prevented from placing before the High Court.

The Supreme Court held that the proceedings before the High Court were conducted in substantial compliance with the principles of natural justice. The appellants were duly represented, were not denied any reasonable opportunity of hearing, and have failed to establish any demonstrable prejudice.

The appeal was dismissed by the Hon'ble Supreme Court. The IBC was never designed to serve as a refuge for corporate debtors who, by their conduct, display no bona fide intention to fulfil contractual or statutory obligations. Its purpose is to revive viable entities and ensure equitable resolution of insolvency – not to extend protection to those who have persistently defaulted, abandoned performance, or frustrated projects of public significance.

TREATMENT OF SECURED CREDITORS

INDIA RESURGENCE ARC PVT. LTD. VS M/S AMIT METALIKS LTD

The Supreme Court in India Resurgence Arc Pvt. Ltd. Vs M/s Amit Metaliks Ltd ,2021 SCC online 409 held that dissenting Secured Creditor cannot insist on a higher amount to be paid to it with reference to the value of the security interest during Corporate Insolvency Resolution Process.

Case Title : India Resurgence Arc Pvt. Ltd. Vs M/s Amit Metaliks Ltd Date of Decision : 13.05.2021 Bench : Vineet Saran,J; Dinesh Maheshwari, J

FACTS OF THE CASE

The appellant is the assignee of the rights, title and interest carried by Religare Fivnest Ltd. It was a secured Financial Creditor having 3.94 % voting share in Committee of Creditors. Substantial majority consisting of 95.35 % voting share approved the Resolution Plan. The Appellant was dissenting Financial Creditor. The Resolution Plan was approved by the NCLT.

The Appellant preferred an appeal before NCLAT, which was dismissed. Aggrieved by the same, the Appellant filed appeal before the Supreme Court.

FINDINGS OF THE SUPREME COURT

The Supreme Court observed that it is beyond a shadow of doubt that the matter is essentially that of the commercial wisdom of the Committee of Creditors and scope of judicial review remains limited within four corners of Section 30 (2) of the Insolvency and Bankruptcy Code, 2016 for the Adjudicating Authority and Section 30 (2) read with Section 61 (3) for the Appellate Authority.

The Supreme Court observed that Financial Proposal in the Resolution Plan forms the core decision of Committee of Creditors. Once it is found that all the mandatory requirements have been duly complied with, the judicial review cannot be stretched to do quantitative analysis qua a particular creditor or any stakeholder who may carry dissatisfaction.

The Supreme Court also refused to interfere on the newly amended clause (4) of the Section 30. The Supreme Court agreed with the observation that Clause (4) of Section 30 only amplified the consideration for the Committee of Creditors while exercising commercial wisdom so as to take informed decision in regard to viability and feasibility of the Resolution Plan with fairness in distribution amongst similarly situated creditors. No interference can be made unless a similarly situated class has been denied fair and equitable treatment.

The Court noted that proposal for payment to all secured creditors is equitable. Payment to the appellant is at par with other Secured Financial Creditors.

The Supreme Court observed that value of security interest neither carry any meaning or any substance. Dissenting Financial Creditors are only entitled to minimum amount as mentioned in Section 30 (2) (b). The Supreme Court observed as under :

13.1 Thus, what amount is to be paid to different classes or subclasses of creditors in accordance with provisions of the Code and the related Regulations, is essentially the commercial wisdom of the Committee of Creditors ; and a dissenting secured creditor like the appellant cannot suggest a higher amount to be paid to it with reference to the value of he security interest.

The Supreme Court observed that in Jaypee Kensington Boulevard Apartments Welfare Association Vs NBCC (India) Ltd (2021) 1 SCC 401 it was made clear that dissenting Financial Creditor would be receiving payment as per his entitlement and that entitlement could be satisfied by allowing him to enforce security interest. Jaypee Kensington never laid down that dissenting Financial Creditor would be entitled to enforce the whole secured interest or to receive the entire value of security available with him.

The Supreme Court observed that if submissions on behalf of the Appellant is accepted, result would be more liquidations rather than resolution of Corporate Debtors, with every secured Financial Creditor opting to stand on dissent. Such a result would be defeating the very purpose envisaged by the Code and cannot be countenanced.

STATE TAX OFFICER Vs. RAINBOW PAPERS LTD.

The Supreme Court in State Tax Officer Vs Rainbow Papers Ltd (2022) SCC Online SC 1162 held that Section 53 IBC does not override Section 48 of Gujarat Value Added Tax Act, 2003 (GVAT Act) and State is a secured creditor under the GVAT Act. Time period of filing claims is directory. The Supreme Court also held that if the Resolution Plan ignores statutory dues, the Resolution Plan is bound to be rejected.

Case Title : State Tax Officer Vs Rainbow Papers Ltd. Date of Decision : 06.09.2022 Bench : Indira Banerjee, J ; A. S. Bopanna, J

FACTS OF THE CASE

Insolvency proceedings were initiated against the Respondent under Section 9 of the Insolvency and Bankruptcy Code, 2016, which was admitted by the NCLT vide order dated 12th September, 2017. Public announcement was made and claims were invited by the Interim Resolution Professional. The last date of filing the claim was 5th October, 2017. The Appellant filed a claim of Rs. 47.36 Crore beyond the last date mentioned in the public announcement. By a letter dated 22nd October, 2018 the entire claim of the appellant was waived off.

The Appellant challenged the Resolution Plan before the NCLT on the ground that it was a secured creditor and it should be paid Rs. 47. 36 Crore towards VAT/CST. The NCLT rejected the Application. An appeal was filed against the same before NCLAT which was also rejected.

FINDINGS OF THE SUPREME COURT

The Supreme Court observed that Regulation 12 of IBBI (Insolvency Resolution Process) Regulations, 2016 deals with the time period of filing of claim along with proof. The time period is, however, directory and not mandatory.

The Supreme Court observed that there was no obligation on the part of the State to lodge a claim in respect of dues for which recovery proceedings have also been initiated. Appellants were never told to produce materials in respect of claim.

The Supreme Court observed that in view of the statutory charge in terms of Section 48 of the GVAT Act, claim of the Tax Department of the State squarely falls within definition of "security interest" under Section 3 (31) of the IBC and the State becomes secured creditor under Section 3 (30) of the Code.

Section 31 of IBC provides that NCLT can approve the Resolution Plan only upon satisfaction that the Resolution Plan, as approved by CoC, meets requirements of Section 30 (2) IBC. When Resolution Plan does not meet the requirements of Section 30 (2), the same cannot be approved.

Once grievance is made to the Adjudicating Authority with regard to Resolution Plan, the NCLT is required to examine whether the Resolution Plan met requirements of Section 30 (2) of IBC. The word "satisfied" used in Section 31 (1) imposes a duty on the NCLT to examine the Resolution Plan. The Resolution Plan cannot be approved by an empty formality.

A Resolution Plan which does not meet the requirements of Sub-section (2) of Section 30 IBC would be invalid and not binding on the Central Government, any state government, any statutory or other authority, any financial creditor, or other creditor to whom a debt in respect of dues arising under any law for the time being in force is owed. Such a Resolution Plan would not bind the State when there are outstanding statutory dues of a Corporate Debtor.

Even if Section 31 (2) is construed to confer discretionary power on the adjudicating authority to reject a Resolution Plan, it has to be kept in mind that discretionary power cannot be exercised arbitrarily, whimsically, or without proper application of mind to the facts and circumstances which require discretion to be used one way or the other. If the Resolution Plan is not in conformity with law or provisions of IBC or rules and regulations framed thereunder, the Resolution Plan has to be rejected.

If the Resolution Plan ignores the statutory demands payable to the State Government or a legal authority , the Adjudicating Authority is bound to reject the Resolution Plan.

The Supreme Court observed that the NCLAT erred in observing that Section 53 overrides Section 48 of the GVAT Act. Section 48 of the GVAT Act is not inconsistent with Section 53 of the Code. State is a secured creditor under the GVAT Act . Section 3 (30) IBC defines secured creditor to mean a creditor in favour of whom security interest is created. Such security interest can be created by operation of law. The definition of secured creditor does not exclude any Government authority.

The Supreme Court held that NCLT and NCLAT erred in law in rejecting the Application on the sole ground of delay in filing claim and set aside the Resolution Plan.

DBS BANK LTD SINGAPORE Vs. RUCHI SOYA INDUSTRIES LTD & ANR

The Supreme Court in DBS Bank Ltd Singapore Vs. Ruchi Soya Industries Ltd (Civil Appeal 9133 of 2019) has referred the issu in respect of treatment of dissenting secured creditors during CIRP to a larger bench.

Case Title : DBS Bank Ltd Singapore Vs. Ruchi Soya Industries Ltd & Anr
Date of Decision : 03.01.2024
Bench : Sanjiv Khanna, J; S. V. N. Bhatti, J

FACTS OF THE CASE

DBS Bank Limited has advanced loan of Rs. 243 Crore to Ruchi Soya Industries. This loan was secured by first charge over various assets. Ruchi Soya Industries went into CIRP. DBS Bank filed a claim of Rs. 242.96 Crore, which was admitted by the Resolution Professional. Patanjali Ayurved Ltd submitted Resolution Plan of Rs. 4134 Crore against admitted claims of Rs. 8398 Crore. DBS Bank requested that liquidation value of security be considered, which was not considered by Committee of Creditors. Resolution Plan was approved on 30.04.2019 by the CoC. DBS Bank voted against the Resolution Plan and as such became dissenting financial creditor. Resolution Plan was conditionally approved by NCLT on 24.07.2019. The Application of DBS Bank challenging the distribution mechanism was also dismissed by the NCLT. An appeal was filed by the DBS Bank before NCLAT.

During the Pendency of the Appeal Section 30 (2) (b) was amended to the effect that the dissenting Financial Creditor will not be paid an amount lessh than the amount paid to the creditor in the event of liquidation of the Corporate Debtor under Section 53 (1) of the Code.

NCLT finally approved the Resolution Plan on 04.09.2019. The DBS Bank also filed an appeal against order granting approval to the Resolution Plan. Both appeals were dismissed by NCLAT.

These dismissal orders were challenged before the Supreme Court. By the order of the Supreme Court an amount of Rs. 99.74 Crore was deposited in the escrow account.

FINDINGS OF THE SUPREME COURT

The first issue which the Supreme Court considered was whether amendment to Section 30 (2) (b) which has come into effect during pendency of appeal before NCLAT is applicable. The Supreme Court held that the amendment has itself provided that it will be applicable to an appeal preferred under Section 61 or 62, when it is not barred by time under any provision of law, shall be heard and decided after considering the amended Section 30(2)(b) under the Amendment Act. Further, an appellate proceeding is a continuation of the original proceeding. A change in law can always be applied to original or appellate proceedings. The Supreme Court upheld the applicability of amendment during appellate proceedings.

The second issue was related to the interpretation of the amendment. The Court noted that there are contradictions between finding of Supreme Court in India Resurgence ARC Pvt Ltd and findings of the Supreme Court in Committee of Creditors of Essar India Ltd and Jaypee Kensington.

The Court was of the opinion that dissenting creditors have to be paid the value of their security interest during CIRP. The Court relied on judgments of the Supreme Court in Committee of Creditors of Essar Steel India Limited v. Satish Kumar Gupta & Ors. (2020) 8 SCC 531, Jaypee Kensington Boulevard Apartments Welfare Association & Others. v. NBCC (India) Limited & Others (2022) 1 SCC 401).

The Court differed from view in India Resurgence ARC Private Limited v. Amit Metaliks Limited & Another (2021 SCC Online SC 409) that the dissenting financial creditor would not be entitled to receive the liquidation value, the amount payable to him in terms of Section 53(1) of the Code.

In light of differing opinion expressed in India Resurgence Ltd matter was referred to a larger bench.

TREATMENT OF CLAIMS

RPS INFRASTRUCTURE Vs. MUKUL KUMAR

The Supreme Court in RPS Infrastructure Vs. Mukul Kumar & Anr (2023 INSC816) has held that once the Resolution Plan has been submitted, a fresh claim cannot be admitted and hydra-headed monster of undecided claims cannot be unleashed on the Resolution Applicant.

Case Title : RPS Infrastructure Vs. Mukul Kumar & Anr Date of Decision : 11.09.2023 Bench : Sanjay Kishan Kaul, J; Sudhanshu Dhulia, J

FACTS OF THE CASE

RPS Infrastructure and KST Infrastructure Pvt. Ltd. (Corporate Debtor) entered into an agreement for development of land licensed to the appellant. There were disputes regarding advertising of project and arbitration proceedings were initiated. An award was passed in favour of the RPS Infrastructure. An appeal was filed against the award. During the pendency of the Appeal, KST Infrastructure Pvt. Ltd. was admitted to insolvency. RPS Infrastructure filed claim with delay of 289 days. At the time of filing of claim, Resolution Plan had already been approved and submitted to the NCLT for approval. The claim was rejected by the RP on ground of delay.

The RPS Infrastructure filed an Application before NCLT seeking direction for admission of its claim. NCLT allowed the application on the ground that the claim would have appeared in the books of account. If claim has not appeared in books of account the RP had a duty to obtain them and verify the financial position. The Public Announcement may have been missed by RPS Infrastructure.

Appeal was filed against the order of NCLT before NCLAT. The NCLAT reversed the order. Aggrieved by the same, the Appellant preferred Appeal before the Supreme Court.

FINDINGS OF THE SUPREME COURT

The Supreme Court observed that there was no fault on the part of the Respondent. The Respondent did all that could be done to procure the Corporate Debtor's records by even moving an application under Section 19 of the IBC. The Supreme Court further observed that public announcement would constitute deemed knowledge on the part of Appellant. The Adjudicating Authority has not approved the plan, it does not mean that the plan can go back and forth.

The relevant paragraphs are reproduced as under:

20. Section 15 of the IBC and Regulation 6 of the IBBI Regulations mandate a public announcement of the CIRP through newspapers. This would constitute deemed knowledge on the appellant. In any case, their plea of not being aware of newspaper pronouncements is not one which should be available to a commercial party.

21. The mere fact that the Adjudicating Authority has yet not approved the plan does not imply that the plan can go back and forth, thereby making the CIRP an endless process. This would result in the reopening of the whole issue, particularly as there may be other similar persons who may jump onto the bandwagon. As described above, in Essar Steel, the Court cautioned against allowing claims after the resolution plan has been accepted by the COC.

BHARTI AIRTEL LTD & ANR Vs. VIJAYKUMAR V. IYER & ORS

The Supreme Court has held in Bharti Airtel Ltd. & Anr Vs. Vijaykumar V. Iyer & Ors (2024 INSC 15) that set-off is not permissible under CIRP except involving certain contractual and equitable circumstances.

Case Title : Bharti Airtel Ltd. & Anr Vs. Vijaykumar V. Iyer & Ors Date of Decision : 03.01.2024 Bench : Sanjiv Khanna, J ; S. V. N. Bhatti, J

FACTS OF THE CASE

Bharti Airtel Ltd and Bharti Hexacom Ltd (" Airtel entities") entered into spectrum agreements with Aircel Ltd and Dishnet Wires ("Aircel entities) to purchase spectrum in 2300 MHZ band. The Agreement was contingent on approval of the Department of Telecommunications. DoT directed Aircel entities for deposit of Bank Guarantees against spectrum dues. The same was challenged by Aircel entities before the TDSAT which directed for deposit of bank guarantee of around Rs. 453 Crore. Aircel entities did not have the means to deposit such Bank Guarantee as such they approached Airtel entities.

Airtel Entities were to pay Rs. 4022.75/- to Aircel Entities against spectrum purchase. Airtel entities entered into understanding for depositing of Bank Guarantee on behalf of Aircel Entities and to deduct 587.37 Crore from outstanding payment. In case of replacement of Bank Guarantee by Aircel with DoT, Aircel was to receive Rs. 411.22 Crore.

TDSAT vide order dated 9th January 2018 ordered for return of Bank Guarantee of Rs. 298 Crore. As DoT was not returning the Bank Guarantee, the same was cancelled by the Supreme Court. Airtel entities made a payment of Rs. 341.80 Crore to Aircel and an amount of Rs. 145.20 Crore was set- off against certain pending dues.

In the meantime CIRP was initiated against Aircel Ltd and Dishnet Wireless Ltd. Claims were filed by Bharti Airtel Ltd for itself and on behalf of Telenor Ltd, which has merged with Bharti Airtel Ltd. Claims were also filed by Bharti Hexacom Ltd. Total claims filed by Bharti entities were Rs. 203.46 Crore. Airtel entities also owed 64.11 Crore towards Corporate Debtor against interconnect charges. The RP admitted claim to the extent of 112 Crore of Airtel entities and rejected claim of 5.85 crore.

The RP of Aircel entities wrote to Airtel Entities that Airtel Entities had wrongly set-off Rs. 112.87 Crore and called for payment of balance amount.

Airtel entities approached NCLT seeking set-off which was allowed. RP made an appeal before the NCLAT which reversed the decision of NCLT. Bharti Airtel approached the Supreme Court.

FINDINGS OF THE SUPREME COURT

The Supreme Court noted that "set-off" has five different connotations ie. (i) statutory and legal Set-off (ii) common law set-off (iii) equitable set-off (iv) contractual set-off and (v) insolvency set-off. Contractual set-off is a matter of agreement between parties subject to legality and public policy. Statutory set-off is created by statute as in the case of Order VIII Rule 6 of CPC. Equitable set-off can be claimed in case of unascertained sum of money. The claim for an equitable set-off must have a connection between the plaintiff's claim for the debt and the defendant's claim to set-off, which would make it inequitable to drive the defendant to a separate suit. Insolvency set-off under the law of the United Kingdom is permitted when there are mutual debts, mutual credits and other mutual dealings between the parties at the relevant cut-off time, which is essentially the stage of commencement of the liquidation process.

Set-off under IBC

The Court noted there is a difference of treatment of set-off under CIRP and Liquidation. CIRP focuses on revival and rehabilitation while the liquidation process focuses on distribution and payment out of sale of assets. IBC like Companies Act, 1956 or 2013 does not give a right to a debtor to set-off. But under Liquidation process, Section 36(4) permits the Insolvency and Bankruptcy Board of India to specify assets which could be subject to set-off on account of mutual dealings between the corporate debtor and the creditor. IBBI has framed IBBI (Liquidation

Process) Regulations which permit set=off during liquidation under Regulation 29. In the case of partnerships and individual bankruptcies also, Section 173 of the IBC permits set-off.

After discussing various judgments, the Supreme Court noted that set-off under mutual dealings is wider in comparison to statutory set-off under Order VIII Rule 6 CPC or equitable set-off. Relevant para is as under:

22. In light of the aforesaid discussion, the expression 'mutual dealings' for the purpose of Regulation 29 of the Liquidation Regulations, is wider than the statutory set-off postulated under Order VIII Rule 6 of CPC, as well as, equitable set-off under the common law as applicable in India. Insolvency set-off applies when demands are between the same parties. There must be commonality of identity between the person who has made the claim and the person against whom the claim exists. Even when there are several distinct and independent transactions, mutuality can exist between the same parties functioning in the same right or capacity. Mutual dealings are not so much concerned with the nature of the claims, but with the relationship and apposite identity of the parties giving rise to the respective claims, such that it would offend one's sense of fairness or justice to allow one to be enforced without regard to the other.

The Supreme Court observed that set-off of dues payable by the Corporate Debtor for a period prior to the commencement of the Corporate Insolvency Resolution Process cannot be made and is not permitted in law from the dues payable to the Corporate Debtor post the commencement of the Corporate Insolvency Resolution Process. Further, a debtor cannot, after notice of assignment of his debt by the creditor, improve his position as regards set-off by acquiring debts incurred by the assignor creditor which are payable to a third party. This will not meet the mandate of mutual dealing. This will be contrary to equity and would amount to misuse of the provision for insolvency set-off.

The Supreme Court held that the provisions of statutory set-off in terms of Order VIII Rule 6 of CPC or insolvency set-off under Regulation 29 of the Liquidation Regulations cannot be applied to the Corporate Insolvency Resolution Process. The court noted two exceptions to this rule. Firstly, Contractual set-off which is effective before or on the date the Corporate Insolvency Resolution Process is put into motion or commences. Secondly 'equitable set-off' when the claim and counterclaim in the form of set-off are linked and connected on account of one or more transactions that can be treated as single transaction.

Dispelling the arguments of Airtel entities, the Hon'ble Supreme Court reiterated that CIRP does not recognise concept of insolvency set-off.

41. There are several reasons why in our opinion clause (ii) to subsection (2)(b) of Section 30 does not support the plea of insolvency set-off. The section does not make Chapter III Part II, that is, Section 36(4)(e) or Regulation 29, applicable to the Corporate Insolvency Resolution Process under Chapter II Part II of the IBC. Secondly, clause (ii) to Section 30(2)(b) deals with the amounts to be paid to the creditors and not the amount payable by the creditors to the corporate debtor. Thirdly, clause (ii) to Section 30(2)(b) has appliance when the resolution plan is being considered for approval. Fourthly, and for the reasons elaborated earlier, and in view of the specific legislative mandate as incorporated and reflected in Chapter II Part II of the IBC, we should hold that the provisions of the IBC relating to Corporate Insolvency Resolution Process do not recognise the principle of insolvency set-off. We would not extend it by implication, when the legislature has not accepted applicability of mutual set-off at the initial stage, that is, the Corporate Insolvency Resolution Process stage.

The Supreme Court also rejected the argument that insolvency set-off is automatic and self- executing.

The Supreme Court held that set-off regarding inter-connect charges was permissible as same was subject of separate and distinct agreement. Such set-off can be treated as contractual as well as equitable set-off. But the transaction for purchase of spectrum was an entirely different and unconnected transaction as such set-off was not permissible. Relevant para is as under:

On the aspect of mutual dealings and also equity, it is to be noted that adjustment of the inter-connect charges are under a separate and distinct agreement. The telephone service providers use each other's facilities as the caller or the receiver may be using a different service provider. Accordingly, adjustments of set-off are made on the basis of contractual set-off. These are also justified on the ground of equitable set-off. The set-off to this extent has been permitted and allowed by the Resolution Professional. The transaction for purchase of the right to use the spectrum is an entirely different and unconnected transaction. The agreement to purchase the spectrum encountered obstacles because the DoT had required bank guarantees to be furnished. Accordingly, Airtel entities, on the request of Aircel entities had furnished bank guarantees on their behalf. The bank guarantees were returned and accordingly Airtel entities became liable to pay the balance amount in terms of the letters of understanding. The amounts have become payable post the commencement of the Corporate Insolvency Resolution Process. For the same reason, we will also reject the argument that by not allowing set-off, new rights are being created and, therefore, Section 14 of the IBC will not be operative and applicable. Moratorium under Section 14 is to grant protection and prevent a scramble and dissipation of the assets of the corporate debtor. The contention that the "amount" to be set-off is not part of the corporate debtor's assets in the present facts is misconceived and must be rejected.

The Supreme Court did not find merit in the appeal and dismissed the same.

AMIT NEHRA & ANR Vs. PAWAN KUMAR GARG & ORS

The Supreme Court in Amit Nehra & Anr vs. Pawan Kumar Garg & Ors (2025INSC1086) held that once a claim is verified and incorporated in the list of creditors, it gets full legal recognition.

FACTS OF THE CASE

Case Title : Amit Nehra & Anr vs. Pawan Kumar Garg & Ors Date of Decision : 09.09.2025 Bench : Sanjay Kumar, J; Satish Chandra Sharma, J

Puma Realtors Pvt. Ltd. undertook development of integrated residential townships in Punjab, including IREO Rise situated in Sector 99, SAS Nagar, Mohali. The Appellants booked a flat and paid Rs. 57,56,684/- out of the full consideration of Rs. 60,06,368/-. As the flat was not handed over within the stipulated time, the Appellants filed a consumer complaint before the State Consumer Disputes Redressal Commission. During the pendency of the matter, Puma Realtors Pvt. Ltd. was admitted to insolvency. The consumer case was disposed of with liberty to pursue the claim before the competent authority in the CIRP proceedings.

The Appellants filed a claim before the Resolution Professional, which was admitted to the extent of Rs. 57,56,684/-. Despite inclusion of the Appellants' claim, possession of the flat was not given. Instead, the Appellants were offered 50% refund as per Clause 18.4(xi) and 18.4(xix) on the ground that they had filed the claim after approval of the Resolution Plan by the CoC, while other claimants were handed over possession of flats.

The Appellants filed an application before the NCLT seeking directions to execute the conveyance deed and hand over possession, which was dismissed. The appeal before the NCLAT was also dismissed.

FINDINGS OF THE SUPREME COURT

The issue before the Court was whether the Appellants were to be paid 50% of their claim amount on account of belated filing of the claim under the residual category of the Resolution Plan, or whether they were entitled to possession of the flat.

The case of the Appellants was that they filed their claim on 11.01.2019 physically at the project office and again on 07.02.2020 in response to the email of the RP dated 31.01.2020. Their name also appeared in the List of Financial Creditors dated 30.04.2020. The Respondent disputed filing of the claim on 11.01.2019 and contended that the Appellants filed their claim only on 07.02.2020, after the Resolution Plan was approved by the Committee of Creditors on 23.08.2019, and thus they were entitled only to 50% refund.

The Supreme Court observed that once verification and incorporation of a claim occurs, it acquires full legal recognition within the CIRP process.

The Court noted that the Respondent's reliance on Clause 18.4(xi) was misconceived. That clause is intended to apply only to allottees who had defaulted in filing or pursuing their claims. The Appellants could not be so characterized, having paid nearly the entire consideration, submitted their claim, and had it duly verified and admitted by the Resolution Professional.

The Court further observed that this was not a case of entertaining a fresh claim beyond the Resolution Plan. It concerned an allottee whose claim was verified and admitted by the Resolution Professional and reflected in the list of financial creditors well before approval of the plan by the adjudicating authority. To disregard such an admitted claim and confine the Appellants to the limited benefit under Clause 18.4(xi) of the Resolution Plan would not preserve the binding effect of the plan but would misapply it.

The Supreme Court set aside the order of the NCLAT and directed the Respondent to execute the conveyance deed and hand over possession.

CHINA DEVELOPMENT BANK Vs. DOHA BANK Q.P.S.C.

The Supreme Court in China Development Bank v. Doha Bank Q.P .S.C. (2024 INSC 1029) held that the Appellants, in whose favour the Corporate Debtor had executed a guarantee, were Financial Creditors. The Court further held that an actual default is not a prerequisite for submission of a claim by a Financial Creditor.

Case Title : China Development Bank Vs Doha Bank Q.P.S.C. Date of Decision : 20.12.2024 Bench : Abhay S Oka, J; Pankaj Mithal, J

FACTS OF THE CASE

Doha Bank was the lender and secured creditor of Reliance Infratel Ltd (RITL). CIRP was initiated against RITL. Deed of Hypothecation (DOH) was executed between the Appellants and each of R Com entities (Reliance Communications Infrastructure Ltd (RCIL)., Reliance Communications Ltd (RCL), Reliance Telecom Ltd. (RTL) and Reliance Infratel Ltd (RITL) whereby a charge was created by RCom entities over their property for securing repayment of the facilities advanced by Appellants. RCom entities agreed to provide their assets as security and further undertook to pay any shortfall of debts owed by each of the RCom entities. All the RCom entities pooled their resources to provide security for the facilities availed by any of the entities ensuring that each entity was individually liable to pay the debt of all the entities. In terms of DOH, if there was any default by any entity, all the R Com entities were liable to make good the shortfall in recovery of the amounts after realization of hypothecated assets.

Appellants filed their claims in the category of Financial Creditors, which were admitted. Appellants were made part of CoC.

Doha Bank challenged before the NCLT treatment of Appellants as Financial Creditors as they were not direct lenders but only a Deed of hypothecation has been executed by them.

During the pendency of the Application, Resolution Plan was approved without determining the application of Doha Bank. Resolution Plan was challenged before the NCLAT wherein the NCLAT directed the NCLT to determine the Application of Doha Bank. NCLT held them as Financial Creditors. NCLAT reversed the order of the NCLT and held that they are not Financial Creditors as the only object of DOH was to create a charge on property of the Appellants and they cannot be treated as Financial Creditors.

The Appellants filed appeal before the Supreme Court.

FINDINGS OF THE SUPREME COURT

The Supreme Court observed that Appellants had vested authority in Security Trustee by executing Master Security Trustee Agreement (MSTA) to execute hypothecation deed with Appellants. Under the MSTA, Appellants were original lenders, who were also treated as secured lenders. R. Com entities are shown as chargors. The Chargors executed Deed of Hypothecation in favour of Secured Trustee.

The issue before the Supreme Court was whether Corporate Debtor was a guarantor who had guaranteed the repayment of loan amount by the borrowers of the appellant.

Appellants had advanced credit facility to other R Com entities (R Com and RTL) but no credit facility had been advanced to the RTIL (Corporate Debtor).

The Supreme Court observed that the Appellants claimed their case of being Financial Creditor under Section 5 (8) (i) IBC which provides that the amount of any liability in respect of any guarantee of the items referred to in clauses (a) to (h) becomes financial debt. It was contended that when Section 5 (8) (i) is applicable, it is not necessary that the Financial Creditor tenders any amount to the Corporate Debtor. It was contended that the amount of liability covered by clause (i) is in respect of money borrowed by the RCom. entities (excluding Corporate Debtor) against payment of interest under facility agreements. There is no dispute that facilities were granted by the appellants to RCom entities. The amount of any liability in respect of any of the guarantees for money borrowed against the payment of interest is a financial debt under Section 5 (8) of IBC.

The Supreme Court observed that the name of the document is not a decisive factor. Only because the title of the document contains the word hypothecation, it cannot be concluded that the guarantee is not a part of this document. The Security Trustee has been appointed to act as trustee for the benefit of secured parties which included Secured Lenders. The Secured Lenders have authorized and directed the Security Trustee to execute and deliver security documents to which the Security Trustee is to be a party and to accept the security, all related deeds and documents as may be required to be submitted by the Obligors for the benefit of secured parties. It was the duty of the Security Trustee to enforce the security in accordance with the provisions of the agreement and to receive and apply all money in accordance with the security documents. Therefore, the Secured Lenders have authorized the Security Trustee to accept the security on their behalf.

The Supreme Court noted that under deed of hypothecation all four RCom entities, including Corporate Debtor, hypothecated assets by way of first ranking pari passu charge to Security Trustee, who was in trust and for the benefit of the secured parties for the purpose of securing due discharge of the Obligor's obligations in connection with secured facilities. The Security Trustee acted on behalf of the appellants by accepting the security of hypothecation. Therefore, the DOH is a document on behalf of the appellants. The effect of DOH is that for the discharge of liabilities of the R Com entities, all four R Com entities hypothecated their properties for securing repayment of the facilities extended by the appellants to RCom and RTL.

Deed of Hypothecation provides that in the event of default committed by the borrowers (in the case of the appellants, the borrowers are R Com and RTL), the Security Trustee is entitled to take charge and/or possession of, seize, recover, receive and remove the hypothecated goods and/or sell by public auction or private contract, dispatch or consign for realization or otherwise dispose of or deal with any part of the hypothecated property. The security of hypothecation can be enforced by the Security Trustee on behalf of the appellants. The DOH further provided that each of the Chargors agree to accept the Security Trustee's account of sales and realization as sufficient proof of the amount realized and relative expenses and to pay on demand by the Security Trustee and/or receiver any shortfall or deficiency thereby shown. Under the DOH, even the Corporate Debtor hypothecated its goods. If after the sale of hypothecated assets, there is any shortfall in discharge of the liabilities of R Com or RTL, the Corporate Debtor is under an obligation to pay the shortfall or deficiency. It is indicated that RITL (Corporate Debtor), who is not the borrower of the appellants, agreed to discharge the liability of the third parties (R Com and RTL) to the appellants in the case of the default of R Com and RTL, which amounts to a guarantee provided by the Corporate Debtor to the appellants in terms of Section 126 of the Contract Act.

The Supreme Court observed that the definition of "default" becomes relevant only while invoking the provisions of Section 7 (1) of the IBC when the CIRP is sought to be initiated by the Financial Creditor. For submitting a claim by a Financial Creditor, there is no requirement of actual default.

The Supreme Court observed that although no creditor can recover any dues from the Corporate Debtor during moratorium, but still a creditor can file its claim.

The Supreme Court set aside the judgment of NCLAT and affirmed the judgment of NCLT.

INELIGIBILITY UNDER SECTION 29A

ARCELORMITTAL INDIA PVT LTD Vs. SATISH KUMAR GUPTA

The Supreme Court in ArcelorMittal India Pvt Ltd. Vs Satish Kumar Gupta (2019) 2 SCC 1 held that the stage of ineligibility under Section 29A attaches when the Resolution Plan is submitted, though antecedent facts that are reasonably proximate to the date of submission may also be taken into consideration .

Case Title : ArcelorMittal India Pvt Ltd. Vs Satish Kumar Gupta
Date of Decision : 04.10.2018
Bench : R. F. Nariman, J; Indu Malhotra, J

FACTS OF THE CASE

The NCLT, Ahmedabad Bench admitted Section 7 Petition against Essar Steels India Ltd on 02.08.2017 and Sh. Satish Kumar Gupta was appointed as Interim Resolution Professional. Resolution Professional invited expression of interest from prospective Resolution Applicants. Pursuant to EOI, Arcelor Mittal India Pvt. Ltd. and Numetal Ltd. submitted expression of interest. Arcelor Mittal Indian Pvt. Ltd. (AMIPL) and Numetal also submitted their Resolution Plans. The Resolution Professional found both AMIPL and Numetal to be ineligible under Section 29A.

AMIPL was disqualified under Section 29A (c). Numetal was also disqualified under Section 29 A (c) and (h).

AMIPL and Numetal challenged disqualification before the NCLT. The NCLT remanded to RP and CoC as Resolution Plans had not been considered by the CoC.

Appeals were filed before NCLAT wherein NCLAT held that Numetal was held eligible while AMIPL was held ineligible under Section 29A.

FINDINGS OF THE SUPREME COURT

The issue before the Supreme Court was whether AMIPL and Numetal were ineligible under Section 29 A.

The Scope of 29A IBC

The Supreme Court observed that opening lines of Section 29A of the Amendment Act refer to de facto as opposed to a de jure position of the persons mentioned therein. This is a typical instance of see through provision so that one is able to arrive at persons who are actually "in control" whether jointly, or in concert, with other persons.

The expression "acting jointly" cannot be confused with "joint venture agreements". All that is to be seen by the expression "acting jointly" is whether certain persons have got together and are acting jointly in the sense of acting together.

Other important phrase has been "in concert". Regulation 2(1)(q) of the SEBI (Substantial Acquisition of Shares and Takeovers) Regulations defines "persons acting in concert , Under the said definition any understanding, even if it is informal and even if it is to indirectly cooperate to exercise control over a target company is included. Immediate relatives have also been covered which will include father and son.

Wherever persons act jointly or in concert with the person who submits Resolution Plan is covered under Section 29A.

The Supreme Court held that stage of ineligibility attaches when the Resolution Plan is submitted by a Resolution Applicant. Ineligibility does not attach at the time of commencement of CIRP.

In respect of Section 29 A (c), the Supreme Court noted that any one of three disjunctive things need to be established – (i) the Corporate Debtor may be under the management of a person referred to under Section 29A (ii) the Corporate Debtor may be under control of such person (iii) Corporate Debtor may be a person for whom such person is a promoter.

The term "management" refers to de jure management of the Corporate Debtor. De jure management would vest in the Board of Directors and would include manager, managing director and officer in Section 2 (53), 2 (54) and 2 (59) respectively of the Companies Act, 2013.

Section 2 (27) of the Companies Act, 2013 defines "control". Control is defined in two parts. The first part refers to de jure control which includes the right to appoint majority of directors of the company. The second part is de facto control. So long a person or persons acting in concert, directly or indirectly, can positively influence, in any manner, management of policy decisions, they could be said to be in "control". Section 29A (c) speaks of Corporate Debtor under the management of control of such person. The expression "under" would seem to suggest positive or proactive control rather than mere negative or reactive control. What is referred in 29A (c) and (g) is de jure and de facto proactive or positive control and not mere negative control which may flow from an expansive reading of definition of the word "control" contained in Section 2 (27) of Companies Act, 2013, which is inclusive and not exhaustive in nature.

Promoter is defined by Section 2 (69) of the Companies Act, 2013. Sub-clause (a) refers to de jure position, where a person is expressly named in prospectus or identified by company in an annual return as a promoter. Sub clause (b) and (c) speaks of de facto position. Under sub-clause (b) as long a person has control over the affairs of the company, directly or indirectly, he can be said to be promoter of the company. Under sub-clause (c) such person need not be a member of Board of Directors but can be a person who in fact advises, directs or instructs the Board to act.

Since 29A (c) is a see through provision, great care must be taken to ensure that persons who are in charge of the Corporate Debtor for whom such resolution plan is made do not come back in some other form to regain control of the Company without first paying off its debts. The Code has bifurcated persons in two groups for this purpose as is evident from clauses (c) and (g) of Section 29A. If a person has been promoter or in the management, or control of the Corporate Debtor in which a preferential transaction, undervalued transaction, extortionate credit transaction or fraudulent transaction has taken place in respect of which an order has been made by the Adjudicating Authority, such person is ineligible to present Resolution Plan under 29 A (g). This ineligibility cannot be cured by paying off debts of the Corporate Debtor.

Despite the fact that relevant time for the ineligibility under sub-clause (c) to attach is the time of submission of the Resolution Plan, antecedent facts reasonably proximate to this point of time can always be seen, to determine whether the persons referred to in Section 29A are, in substance, seeking to avoid the consequences of the proviso to sub-clause (c). If it is shown that at a reasonable proximate point of time before the submission of Resolution Plan, the affairs of the persons referred to in Section 29A are so arranged as to avoid paying off debts of non-performing assets, such persons must be held to be ineligible to submit a Resolution Plan.

The power of Resolution Professional

The Supreme Court after surveying all the relevant provisions observed that the Resolution Professional is required to examine whether Resolution Plans submitted by the various applicants are complete in all respects before submitting them to the Committee of Creditors. The Resolution Professional is not required to take any decision, but merely to ensure that Resolution Plans submitted are complete in all respects before they are placed before the Committee of Creditors. Resolution Professional has only to give prima facie opinion to CoC whether a law has or has not been contravened. Resolution Professional himself cannot adjudicate upon eligibility.

Exclusion of litigation period

The Supreme Court observed that a large volume of litigation has to be handled by the NCLT and NCLAT. Even if NCLT or NCLAT decide a matter after 180 days or 270 days, such litigation should be excluded. A balance has to be maintained between timely completion of CIRP and the Corporate Debtor otherwise pushed into liquidation.

The case of Numetal

Numetal was incorporated in Mauritius on 13.10.2017 expressly for the purpose of submission of Resolution Plan.. Two other companies AHL and AEL were also incorporated on the same day in Mauritius. Shri Rewant Ruia , son of Shri Ravi Ruia , who was promoter of the Corporate Debtor, held entire share capital of AHL , which in turn held entire share capital of AEL, which in turn held entire share capital of Numetal. On 18.10.2017, AEL transferred its shareholding of 26.1% in Numetal to a group company , viz, ECL. This group company is ultimately owned by Virgo Trust and Triton Trust, the beneficiaries of which are companies owned by Ravi Ruia and his immediate family members. Shri Rewant Ruia settled an irrevocable and discretionary trust, viz, the Crescent Trust and settled the entire share capital of AHL into the trust at a par value of USD 10,000. The beneficiaries of these trusts were general charities as well as entities owned by Shashikant Ruia and entities owned by Shri Rewant Ruia. On 20.11.2017 , Sh. Rewant Ruia settled Prisma Trust whose beneficiaries are general charities and Solis Enterprises Ltd whose share capital is held by Rewant Ruia. Shri Rewant Ruia was the ultimate person who held beneficial interest in AEL.

The trustees of Plasma Trust acquired 100% of shareholding of AHL for a par value of approximately USD 10,000 from the trustees of the Crescent Trust. Merely one day before promulgation of Section 29A, ECL transferred its shareholding of 26.1 % of the share capital of Numetal to Crinium Bay, indirect wholly owned subsidiary of VTB Bank. AEL transferred 25.1 % of share capital of Numetal to Indo, 9.9% of shares of Numetal to TPE.

The earnest money of 500 Crore deposited by Numetal has been provided by AEL. This amount remained with the Resolution Professional despite AEL exiting shareholding of Numetal.

On 29.03.2018 AEL transferred its 25% share in Numetal to its three other constituents.

The Supreme Court observed that Shri Rewant Ruia is a person deemed to be acting in concert with his father Shri Ravi Ruia (Promoter of ESIL) there is no doubt that Section 29 A (c) was attracted as on the date of submission of First Resolution Plan i.e. 12.02.2018, as AEL was held by Prisma Trust, whose ultimate beneficiary is Shri Rewant Ruia himself.

The case of AMIPL

AMSA is a listed company in Luxembourg. This company is ultimate parent company of the AMIPL (Resolution Applicant) through its wholly owned subsidiary AMBD, which in turn holds 100% of the shares in Oakey Holding BV , a company incorporated in Netherlands , which in turn holds 99.99% shares in AMIPL a company incorporated in India.

AMSA has another 100% subsidiary AMNLBV incorporated in the Netherlands. It is this group company of Sh. L. N. Mittal that held 29.05% of shareholding in Uttam Galva as on 07.02.2018. On 04.09.2009, a co-promotion agreement was signed between AMNLBW and Indian Promoters of Uttam Galva. As per the agreement foreign promoters were to nominate one half of the non-independent directors on the Board and other half was to be nominated by Indian Promoters. Co-promotion agreement not only disclosed that AMNLBV was foreign promoter but also jointly managing Uttam Galva.

Account of Uttam Galva was declared NPA on 31.03.2016. All annual returns of Uttam Galva showed AMNLBV as promoters. All annual reports showed AMNLBV as promoter. That no control was actually exercised by AMNLBV or AMNLBV never appointed any directors or exercised its voting rights cannot be accepted as that makes no difference to the "de jure" position of AMNLBV being promoter. On 07.02.2018, a few days before AMIPL submitted its first Resolution Plan, AMNLBV sold its entire shareholding in Uttam Galva by was of an off-market sale to Srinath Trading Company Ltd. Shares that were purchased at price of Rs. 120 each was sold at Rs 1 each when market value of share was Rs. 19.50 each.

The Court observed that Sh. L. N. Mittal is the ultimate shareholder of Resolution Applicant as well as AMNLBV. AMNLBV shares were only sold to get out of ineligibility mentioned in 29A (c) .

Fraseli an entity registered and incorporated in Luxemburg and managed and controlled by L. N. Mittal held 32.22 % shareholding of KSS Global a company domiciled in Netherlands. By shareholders agreement entered into between KSS holdings, KSS Infra EALQ, Fraseli and KSS Global, the first three companies each were given a right to appoint an equal number of directors on the board of directors of KSS Global. KSS Global held 100% share capital of KSS petron. KSS Petron was declared NPA on 09.02.2018. As in case of Uttam Galva, Fraseli divested its shareholding in KSS Petron on 9.2.2018 only three days before AMIPL submitted its Resolution Plan.

The Supreme Court found AMIPL ineligible on both counts.

ARUN KUMAR JAGATRAMKA Vs. JINDAL STEEL & POWER LTD

The Supreme Court in Arun Kumar Jagatramka Vs Jindal Steel & Power Ltd (2021) 7 SCC 474 held that Regulation 2B of IBBI (Liquidation Process) Regulations is valid. A person who is ineligible under Section 29A of IBC to submit a Resolution Plan will also be ineligible to submit a scheme for compromise or arrangement under Section 230 of the Companies Act, 2013.

Case Title : Arun Kumar Jagatramka Vs Jindal Steel & Power Ltd Date of Decision : 15.03.2021 Bench : Dr. Dhananjaya Y. Chandrachud, j; M. R. Shah, J

FACTS OF THE CASE

The Supreme Court was considering two appeals and one Writ Petition in this matter.

Civil Appeal 9664 of 2019

An Application under Section 10 IBC was moved by GNCL (Corporate Debtor) for initiating CIRP, which was admitted on 7th April, 2017. Mr. Arun Kumar Jagatramka submitted a Resolution Plan. In the meanwhile, Section 29A was introduced vide the Insolvency and Bankruptcy Code (Amendment) Act , 2018 which excluded certain categories of persons from submitting Resolution Plan. Due to insertion of Section 29A, Arun Kumar Jagatramka became ineligible to submit Resolution Plan. CIRP was not successful and Liquidation Order was passed by the NCLT. Liquidation Order was challenged before NCLAT which was dismissed.

Arun Kumar Jagatramka also moved an application under Sections 230 to 232 of the Companies Act, 2013 before NCLT proposing scheme of compromise and arrangement. This application was allowed by NCLT. JSPL , an operational Creditor, preferred an appeal before NCLAT , which was allowed on the ground that promoters who are ineligible to submit Resolution Plan under Section 29A of IBC are not entitled to file an application for compromise and arrangement under Section 230-232 of the Companies Act, 2013. The order of the NCLAT was challenged before the Supreme Court.

Civil Appeal 2719 of 2020

CIRP was initiated against Su-Kam Power Systems Ltd. vide order dated 5th April, 2018 by NCLT. Mr Kunwar Sachdev submitted Resolution Plan along with Phoenix ARC Pvt. Ltd. which was rejected by RP as Mr Kunwar Sachdev was ineligible under Section 29 A IBC. CIRP was not successful and Liquidation Order was passed by the NCLT. Mr Kunwar Sachdev expressed interest in submitting scheme of compromise and arrangement which was rejected by the Liquidator in light of Section 29 A (h). Mr. Kunwar Sachdev challenged the decision before NCLT which was dismissed. Mr. Kunwar Sachdev approached NCLAT which also dismissed the appeals.

Writ Petition

Arun Kumar Jagatramka also filed Writ Petition under Article 32 of the Constitution for seeking declaration that Regulation 2B of IBBI (Liquidation Process) are ultra vires IBC and in violation of Article 14, 19 and 21.

FINDINGS OF THE SUPREME COURT

The Supreme Court noted that Parliament vide the same amendment introduced Section 29A and Section 35 (1) (f) in the Code. While 29A bars certain categories of persons from submitting Resolution Plan while Section 35 (1) (f) prevents the Liquidator from selling the immovable and movable property or actionable claim of the Corporate Debtor in liquidation to any person who is not eligible to be a Resolution Applicant.

The Supreme Court in Chitra Sharma Vs Union of India (2018) 18 SCC 575 observed that Section 29A has been enacted in larger public interest and to facilitate effective good governance. Parliament rectified loophole in the Act, which allowed backdoor entry to erstwhile managements in CIRP.

The Supreme Court in Swiss Ribbons Pvt. Ltd. Vs Union of India (2019) 4 SCC 17 observed that the norms underlying Section 29A continues to permeate Section 35 (1) (f) when it not merely applies to resolution process but to liquidation also.

The Supreme Court noted that purposive interpretation of Section 29A has been adopted in Chitra Sharma, Arcelor Mittal and Swiss Ribbons. Section 29A ensures that the objects of IBC is not defeated by allowing ineligible persons to return in a new avatar of resolution applicants. Section 35 (1) (f) is kept in same continuum.

The Supreme Court noted that Compromise or Arrangement under Section 230 (1) of the Companies Act, 2013 may take place between a company and its creditors or any subset of creditors; or between a company and its members or subset of members. The compromise or arrangement has to be agreed by majority of persons representing 3/4th of value of the creditors, members or class of them. Upon sanctioning of the compromise or arrangement by the NCLT it binds the company, all the creditors, members or a class of them. Liquidation is one of the instances wherein Section 230 can be invoked.

The Supreme Court in Meghal Homes Pvt. Ltd. Vs. Shree Nivas Girni K. K. Samiti (2007) 7 SCC 753 has observed that when a company is in liquidation, its assets are custodia legis, the Liquidator being the custodian for the distribution of the liquidation estate. A compromise or arrangement in respect of company in liquidation must foster revival of a company, this being the clear statutory intention behind entertaining a proposal under Section 391 of the Companies Act, 1956 in respect of company in liquidation.

Section 230 of the Companies Act, 2013 and IBC

It was argued before the Supreme Court that Section 230 of the Companies Act, 2013 is an independent provision and is not regulated by IBC. The Supreme Court observed that Liquidation of Company under IBC is a matter of last resort. There are three modes through which revival is contemplated under IBC. First mode is through CIRP. Second mode is selling as going concern under Liquidation Process Regulation 32 (e) and (f). Third mode is through compromise or arrangement under Section 230 of the Companies Act, 2013. A harmonious construction of the two statutes i.e. Section 230 of the Companies Act, 2013 and provisions of IBC has to be done. Company has to be protected from its management and corporate death. It would lead to absurdity if persons ineligible to submit Resolution Plan or participating in sale of assets are allowed to submit scheme of compromise or arrangement.

Section 12A IBC and Section 230 of the Companies Act, 2013

It was argued before the Supreme Court that Section 12 A of IBC and Section 230 of the Companies Act, 2013 are "settlement mechanism" rather than "resolution mechanism" as such there is no reason to prevent a person ineligible under Section 29A from submitting scheme of compromise or arrangement. This argument was rejected by the Supreme Court. The Supreme Court observed that Section 12 A is not intended to be a culmination of the resolution process. Section 12A is applicable at inception of the process. A scheme of compromise or arrangement represents culmination of the process. A scheme of compromise or arrangement binds the company, its creditors, and members or class of persons or creditors as well as the liquidator.

Constitutional Validity of Regulation 2B

The Supreme Court noted that power of IBBI to frame regulations under Section 240 (1) is conditioned by two requirements- (i) Regulations have to be consistent with the provisions of IBC and rules framed by the Central Government. (ii) the regulations must be to carry out the provisions of IBC. The Court observed that Regulation 2B meets both the requirements of being consistent with the provisions of IBC and of being made in order to carry out the provisions of the Code. There cannot be any doubt that proviso to Regulation 2B is clarificatory in nature. Even in absence of this provision, a person who is ineligible under Section 29A would not be permitted to propose a compromise or arrangement under Section 230 of the Companies Act, 2013. The Supreme Court did not find any merit in challenge to validity of Regulation 2B.

The Supreme Court dismissed the Appeals as well as the Writ Petition.

BANK OF BARODA & ANR Vs. MBL INFRASTRUCTURES LTD.

The Supreme Court in Bank of Baroda Vs MBL Infrastructure Ltd (2022) SCC Online SC 48 held that what is required under Section 29 A (h) is mere existence of personal guarantee that stands invoked by a single creditor, notwithstanding the application seeking initiation of insolvency proceedings filed by another creditor. The Supreme Court found that Resolution Plan submitted by Respondent No. 3 is not maintainable but in light of peculiar facts of the case refused to disturb the Resolution Plan.

Case Title : Bank of Baroda Vs MBL Infrastructure Ltd Date of Decision : 18.01.2022 Bench : Sanjay Kishan Kaul, J; M. M. Sundresh, J

FACTS OF THE CASE

MBL Infrastructure was set up by one Mr. Anjani Kumar Lakhotiya (Respondent No. 3). MBL Infrastructure obtained loan facility from consortium of banks. MBL Infrastructure defaulted in repayment of loan facilities as such personal guarantee given by Respondent No.3 was invoked. RBL Bank and Allahabad Bank initiated proceedings under Section 13 (2) of SARFAESI Act.

RBL also filed an Application under Section 7 of Insolvency and Bankruptcy Code, 2015 against MBL Infrastructures Ltd. (Corporate Debtor) which was admitted vide order dated 30.03. 2017.

Respondent No. 3 submitted Resolution Plan. A modified Resolution Plan was submitted by the Respondent No. 3 on 22.11.2017 which was under consideration by CoC.

In the meantime vide Insolvency and Bankruptcy Code (Amendment) Ordinance , 2017, Section 29 A was introduced. Section 29 A (h) read as under:

"has executed an enforceable guarantee in favour of a creditor, in respect of corporate debtor under insolvency resolution process or liquidation under this code."

The CoC deliberated impact of amendment. Respondent No. 3 filed an application before the NCLT for declaration that he is not disqualified from submitting Resolution Plan. The NCLT declared Respondent No. 3 eligible. Against the same appeal was filed before the NCLAT wherein the NCLAT directed that the NCLT will not accept or reject the Resolution Plan without prior approval of appellate authority.

The Resolution Plan submitted by Respondent No. 3 was approved with the CoC by 78.50% CoC voting share.

Section 29A (h) further went through amendment which came into effect from 18.01.2018. Now Section 29 A (h) reads as under:

(h) has executed an enforceable guarantee in favour of a creditor, in respect of a corporate debtor against which an application for insolvency resolution made by such creditor has been admitted under this code.

On 23.03.2018, the appeal before the NCLAT was withdrawn. The NCLT approved the Resolution Plan vide order dated 18.04.2018, which was challenged before the NCLAT by the Appellant. The said appeal was dismissed by the NCLAT.

In the meanwhile Section 29 (h) was again amended which came into effect from 06.06.2018, which reads as under:

(h) has executed a guarantee in favour of a creditor, in respect of a corporate debtor against which an application for insolvency resolution made by such creditor has been admitted under this code and such guarantee has been invoked by the creditor and remains unpaid in full or part"

FINDINGS OF THE SUPREME COURT

The Supreme Court observed that the objective of Section 29A of the Code is to avoid unwarranted and unscrupulous elements to get into the resolution process while preventing their personal interests to step in. It also consciously seeks to prevent certain categories of persons who may not be in a position to lend credence to the resolution process by virtue of their disqualification.

Section 29 A (h) creates one more category of persons who are ineligible to become Resolution Applicant.

Once a person executes a guarantee in favour of a creditor with respect to credit facilities availed by Corporate Debtor, and CIRP has been admitted and guarantee has been invoked, eligibility of such persons under Section 29 A (h) will become ineligible.

Once an application for CIRP is admitted, the process becomes in rem and all creditors of same class have rights at par with each other. Thus what is required under Section 29 A (h) is mere existence of personal guarantee that stands invoked by a single creditor, notwithstanding the application being filed by another creditor seeking initiation of insolvency process.

The Supreme Court observed that there is bar at the time of submission of the Resolution Plan. But if thereafter by operation of law, a person becomes ineligible, which continues till approval by the CoC or adjudication by the Adjudicating Authority, the subsequent amended provision would govern the question of eligibility of Resolution Applicant to submit a Resolution Plan.

In the instant case Respondent No. 3 has executed personal guarantees which were invoked by three of financial creditors even prior to the application filed, as such Section 29 A (h) gets attracted. The Supreme Court held that plan submitted by Respondent No. 3 should not have been entertained.

The Supreme Court observed that although Resolution Plan submitted by the Respondent No. 3 is non-maintainable, much water has flown under the bridge. The requisite percentage of voting share has been achieved. Resolution Plan is put into operation since 18.04.2018 and Corporate Debtor is a going concern. Interest of 23,000 shareholders and thousands of employees are involved. The Corporate Debtor is in the process of implementing several projects of public importance. In peculiar facts of the case the Supreme Court refused to disturb the Resolution Plan.

HARI BHAI THOTHA

The Supreme Court in Hari Bhai Thota (2023INSC 1056) held that the view of the NCLAT in Digambar Anand Rao Pigle Vs Shrikant Madanlal Zawar & Ors in respect of Micro , Small and Medium Enterprises (MSME) that Section 240A will be applicable from initiation of CIRP is not correct view. Relevant date is the date of submission of Resolution Plan.

Case Title : Hari Bhai Thota Date of Decision : 29.11.2023 Bench : Sanjay Kishan Kaul, J; Sudhanshu Dhulia, J

BRIEF FACTS OF THE CASE

The NCLT rejected the resolution plan submitted by Resolution Professional in the matter of Shree Aashrya Infra Con Limited by the NCLT on the ground that exemption under Section 240 A was not available to Resolution Applicant as MSME certificate has been obtained after initiation of CIRP. The Resolution Professional filed an Appeal before the Supreme Court.

Section 29A provides for ineligibilities of Resolution Applicants to submit Resolution Plan in certain circumstances. Section 240A exempts Micro, Small and Medium Enterprises from ineligibilities under Section 29A (c) and (h). Section 29 A (c) makes promoters, managers etc. of the Corporate Debtor ineligible to submit Resolution Plan. As such promoters, managers etc. of the Corporate Debtor are eligible to submit Resolution Plan in respect of resolution of a MSME even if such persons are ineligible to submit Resolution Plan under 29 A (c).

The Supreme Court in this case framed the following two issues:

Whether the Resolution Applicant was disqualified under the primary conditions as specified under Section 29 A of the Code ?

Whether the corporate debtor not having an MSME status at the time of commencement of CIRP proceedings would disqualify the Resolution Applicant under Section 29A of the Code as benefit of Section 240A would not be available ?

FINDINGS OF THE SUPREME COURT

Regarding the first issue the Supreme Court noted that Section 29 A (c) was not applicable in this case as the account of the Corporate Debtor has not been declared NPA.

On the second issue the Supreme Court gave its opinion on applicability of 240 A , although it was not necessary in light of determination of first issue, as a number of cases of similar nature were pending before Tribunals.

The Supreme Court relied on judgment of Arcelor Mittal India Pvt. Ltd. Vs. Satish Kumar Gupta & Ors which says that the stage of ineligibility attaches when the resolution plan is submitted by a resolution applicant.

The Supreme Court relying on Swiss Ribbons Pvt. Ltd. Vs. Union of India and rationale for introducing Section 240A noted that excluding MSMEs from disqualification under 29A (c) and (h) is because qua such industries other resolution applicants may not be forthcoming which thus would inevitably lead not to resolution but to liquidation.

The Supreme Court relied on Swiss Ribbons and held that exemption to MSME under Section 240A will be on date of making of the bid and not on the date on which CIRP is being initiated. The Supreme Court held that law laid down in Digambar Anand Rao Pigle is not correct law and the cut-off date will be the date of submission of resolution plan.

DISABILITIY OF RELATED PARTIES

PHOENIX ARC PVT. LTD. Vs. SPADE FINANCIAL SERVICES LTD.

The Supreme Court in Phoenix Arc Pvt Ltd Vs Spade Financial Services Ltd AIR 2021 SC 776 held that Financial Creditors, who are related party in praesenti, are barred from becoming member of the CoC under first proviso of Section 21 (2) of IBC. Such Financial Creditors are also barred from becoming members of the CoC, who have ceased to be related parties only to circumvent the exclusion under first proviso of Section 21 (2) of IBC.

Case Title : Phoenix Arc Pvt Ltd Vs Spade Financial Services Ltd Date of Decision : 01.02.2021 Bench : Dr. Dhananjaya Y. Chandrachud, J ; Indu Malhotra, J; Indira Banerjee, J

FACTS OF THE CASE

CIRP was initiated against the Corporate Debtor on an application filed by an Operational Creditor under Section 9 of the Insolvency and Bankruptcy Code, 2016. During CIRP, Spade Financial Services Ltd filed its claim. AAA also filed its claim. IRP rejected the claim of Spade on the ground that the claim does not fall under Financial Debt. IRP also rejected the claim of Spade on the ground that it has been filed after expiry of the period for filing claim. Aggrieved by the same Spade as well as Phoenix approached NCLT which allowed their application and directed the Resolution Professional to admit them in the category of Financial Creditors.

Yes Bank and Phoenix filed an Application before NCLT for exclusion of Spade and AAA from CoC claiming that they are related parties. NCLT held that transactions of Spade and AAA with Corporate Debtor are collusive and they do not qualify to be considered as Financial Creditors. NCLAT also affirmed the findings of the NCLT.

FINDINGS OF THE SUPREME COURT

Spade had entered into MoU with the Corporate Debtor dated 12th August, 2011 through which Spade provided the Corporate Debtor ICD worth a net amount of Rs. 66 Crore from 1st June 2009 till January 2013 which carried 24 % interest. Spade secured these ICD through 37 flats worth 39.825 Crores in their real estate project Akme Raaga through 11 plots worth Rs. 3 Crore. Out of ICD provided to the Corporate Debtor by Spade Rs. 43.06 Crore worth was credited to the Account of Mr. Arun Anand.

AAA has entered into Development Agreements on 1st March, 2012 through which the Corporate Debtor sold 38.3% of its development rights in real estate project AKME RAAGA to AAA for a consideration of Rs. 32.80 Crore. AAA also entered into an Agreement of Sale dated 25th October, 2012 which superseded Development Agreement through which AAA bought a saleable area of 313,928 square feet in AKME RAGA at a price of 43.06 Crore.

Mr Anil Nanda is major shareholder of JIPL which holds 80% of shares of Corporate Debtor. Arun Anand was also director of the Corporate Debtor up to 31st March, 2002. Mr. Arun Anand and his son Mr. Aditya Anand sold their shareholding in Corporate Debtor in 2004/2005. Mr Arun Anand was also brother-in-law of Sonal Anand who was director of the Corporate Debtor from November 2007 to 2013. Mr. Arun Anand has worked in different capacities for Anil Nanda for about 25 years.

The Supreme Court held that order dated 31st May, 2018 whereby the NCLT directed the RP to consider the claim of AAA and Spade as Financial Creditor will not act as res judicata as Phoenix and Yes Bank were not parties in that application.

Whether Spade and AAA are Financial Creditors ?

The Supreme Court analysed the nature of "financial debt" and observed that money advanced as debt should be in possession of the borrower. The borrower is obligated to return the money or its equivalent along with consideration for time value of money. A transaction which is sham or collusive would only create an illusion that money has been disbursed to the borrower but in fact parties have entered into transaction with ulterior motive.

The Supreme Court in respect of transaction with Spade noted that Rate of interest actually charged on ICD was 12% while interest rate stipulated in MoU was 24%. MoU is unregistered and unstamped. No interest has been paid on the alleged loan. MoU does not stipulate period of repayment. The entirety of ICDs were not disbursed to Spade. No Board Resolution was passed by Spade approving the grant of ICDs and the charge created on the loan was not registered with the Registrar of Companies. MoU was nothing but an eyewash and collusive.

AAA and Corporate Debtor entered into multiple agreements in respect of the same property without giving any explanation about or rationale regarding variation in consideration. These transactions were collusive with the purpose of diverting the properties of the Corporate Debtor to AAA.

The Supreme Court concluded that since commercial arrangements between the Corporate Debtor and Spade and AAA were collusive, they would not constitute a financial debt. As such Spade and AAA will not be Financial Creditors.

Whether Spade and AAA are related Parties ?

The Supreme Court noted that Section 5 (24) defines related parties. The definition of related party is very broad. The intention of the legislature is to capture all kinds of interrelationship between the Financial Creditor and the Corporate Debtor.

Mr. Arun Anand was in control of Spade and AAA during relevant period. He held positions in Corporate Debtor or the Anil Nanda Group of companies, which included the Corporate Debtor. Mr. Anil Nanda and Mr. Sonal Anand also held positions in the Corporate Debtor and JIPL during this period. There was deep entanglement between entities of Mr. Arun Anand and Mr. Anil Nanda. Mr. Arun Anand did hold positions during this period which could have been used by him to guide the Corporate Debtor.

The Supreme Court concluded that Corporate Debtor, AAA and Spade were related parties.

Whether Spade and AAA can be excluded from CoC ?

Section 21 (1) requires the IRP to constitute CoC after collating claims. The CoC consists of Financial Creditors. Proviso to Section 21 (2) bars such Financial Creditor to become a member of CoC which are the related parties of Corporate Debtor. The controversy in this case was in respect of word "is" as Spade and AAA were no longer related parties.

The Supreme Court observed that objects and purposes of the Code are best served when CIRP is driven by external creditors so as to ensure that the CoC is not sabotaged by related parties of the Corporate Debtor.

Prima facie it would appear that use of simple present tense in the first proviso to Section 21 (2) indicates that the disqualification applies in praesenti. But the first proviso has to be interpreted in light of context, object and purpose for which it was enacted. The purpose of excluding a related party is to obviate conflict of interest that is likely to arise in the event related party is allowed to become member of CoC.

The Supreme Court held that only those financial creditors who are related parties in praesenti would be debarred from CoC. Those related parties are also barred from CoC, who cease to be related parties in order to circumvent the exclusion under the first proviso of Section 21 (2).

The Supreme Court held that Spade and AAA had been correctly excluded from CoC.

RESOLUTION PLAN

K SASHIDHAR Vs. INDIAN OVERSEAS BANK

The Supreme Court in K. Sashidhar Vs Indian Overseas Bank (2019) 12 SCC 150 held that commercial wisdom of the financial creditors, whether exercised individually or collectively, is non-justiciable. The Adjudicating authority can only interfere with the Resolution Plan on the grounds specified under Section 30 (2) of the Insolvency and Bankruptcy Code, 2016.

> Case Title : K. Sashidhar Vs Indian Overseas Bank
> Date of Decision : 05.02.2019
> Bench : A. M. Khanwilkar, J; Ajay Rastogi, J

FACTS OF THE CASE

The Supreme Court was determining two separate appeals in this matter.

Kamineni Steel & Power India Pvt. Ltd. (KS & PIPL) was facing operational and financial issues. The Company had filed an application before BIFR. After coming into force of Insolvency and Bankruptcy Code, 2016, the Company filed an application under Section 10 IBC. The Petition was admitted on 10th February, 2017. Resolution Plan submitted was approved by only 66.67% voting share of CoC. Bank of Maharashtra having 6.36% of voting share had not either approved, rejected or abstained from voting. The proposed Resolution Plan did not garner approval of 75% of voting share as was then required. The NCLT approved the Resolution Plan. The NCLAT reversed the order of the NCLT and held that approval of resolution plan by a vote of not less than 75% of voting share of the Financial Creditors was mandatory and it was not open to the Adjudicating Authority to disregard the mandate of CoC.

Insolvency proceedings have been initiated by NCLT Mumbai vide order dated 17th January, 2017 in the matter of Innoventive Industries Ltd. Resolution Plan submitted by the Resolution Applicant garnered 66.57%

voting share while 33.43% voted against Resolution Plan. The Resolution Professional filed Application for initiating liquidation proceedings as Resolution Plan did not get approval of 75 % voting share as required under the Code. The NCLT passed Liquidation Order.

An appeal was preferred before NCLAT, which concurred with NCLT. Aggrieved by the same, the Appellant preferred an appeal before the Supreme Court.

FINDINGS OF THE SUPREME COURT

The Supreme Court noted that the CoC is called upon to consider the Resolution Plan under Section 30 (4) of the Code after it is verified and vetted by the Resolution Professional as being compliant with the statutory requirements specified in Section 30 (2).

The Court observed that if the CoC had approved the Resolution Plan by requisite percentage of voting share, the Resolution Professional is required to submit the same to the Adjudicating Authority. On receipt of the Resolution Plan, the Adjudicating Authority is required to satisfy itself that the Resolution Plan as approved by the CoC meets requirement specified under Section 30 (2).

The Supreme Court observed that on a conjoint reading of these provisions it is clear that the stipulation is to reckon the percent of "voting share of the financial creditors" for the purposes of determining as to whether the proposed resolution plan has been approved by CoC or otherwise. The "percent of voting share of the financial creditors" approving vis-à-vis dissenting is required to be reckoned. It is not on the basis of members present and voting. The approving votes must fulfill the threshold percentage of voting share.

The Supreme Court observed that commercial wisdom has been given paramount status without any judicial intervention. There is presumption that financial creditors are fully informed of viability and feasibility of Resolution Plan. The decision of CoC is collective decision. The Legislature has consciously not provided any ground for challenging "commercial wisdom" of individual financial creditor or their collective decision making before the Adjudicating Authority. That has been made non-justiciable.

The Court noted that Report of the Bankruptcy Law Reforms Committee gives primacy to the CoC to evaluate the various possibilities and make a decision.

Adjudicating Authority has been empowered only to make inquiries regarding provision under Section 30 (2).

The Jurisdiction of NCLAT will also be circumscribed being a proceeding in continuity. Further Section 61 (3) provides that an appeal against order approving Resolution Plan can only be filed on ground specified therein.

The Supreme Court also dispelled the argument that decreasing the threshold from 75% to 66% voting share of CoC for passing of Resolution Plan vide the Insolvency and Bankruptcy Code (Second Amendment) Act, 2018 should be applied with retrospective effect. The Supreme Court was of the view that a new norm and qualified standard for approval of Resolution Plan has been introduced. That cannot be treated as a declaratory /clarificatory or stricto sensu procedural matter as such.

The Supreme Court relied on Thirumalai Chemicals Limited Vs Union of India (2011) 6 SCC 739 and Purbanchal Cables & Conductors (P) Ltd. (2012) 7 SCC 462 and held that it is trite law that every statute is prospective unless it is expressly or by necessary implication made to have retrospective operation.

The Supreme Court affirmed the view of the NCLAT that Resolution Plans have not been approved by requisite percent of voting share of Financial Creditors and in absence of alternate Resolution Plan, the only course available is to initiate liquidation proceedings under Section 33 of the Code.

COMMITTEE OF CREDITORS OF ESSAR STEEL INDIA LTD Vs. SATISH KUMAR GUPTA

The Supreme Court in Committee of Creditors of Essar Steel India Ltd vs Satish Kumar Gupta (2020) 8 SCC 531 struck down word "mandatorily" in Section 12 IBC, which made it compulsory to complete CIRP in 330 days. The Supreme Court also held that CoC is not required to treat all creditors equally. The Supreme Court also reiterated that NCLAT cannot substitute its own wisdom with commercial wisdom of Committee of Creditors.

Case Title : Committee of Creditors of Essar Steel India Ltd vs Satish Kumar Gupta Date of Decision : 15.11.2019 Bench : R. F. Nariman, J; Surya Kant, J; V. Ramasubramanian, J

FACTS OF THE CASE

The NCLT, Ahmedabad admitted the Petition under Section 7 of IBC filed by Standard Chartered Bank and State Bank of India. Satish Kumar Gupta was appointed as Interim Resolution Professional who was later confirmed as Resolution Professional. During CIRP Resolution Plans were submitted by Arcelor Mittal India Ltd and another by Numetal Ltd which were found to be ineligible under Section 29A. Litigation regarding the same reached the Supreme Court wherein both were held to be ineligible to submit Resolution Plans but the Supreme Court invoked jurisdiction under Article 142 and gave opportunity to both Arcelor Mittal and Numetal to pay off their NPAs within two weeks failing which Corporate Debtor has to go into liquidation. Arcelor Mittal made payments but Numetal did not make payments.

Final Resolution Plan of Arcelor Mittal was approved by CoC on 23.1 0.2018 wherein upfront amount of Rs. 42,000 Crore was to be paid. Rs. 17.4 crore was to be paid to unsecured financial creditors with a claim amount of more than Rs. 10 lakhs and Rs. 30.55 Lakh to such financial creditors with claim amount of less than Rs. 10 lakhs. No change was made in respect of operational creditors. Workmen and employees were to be paid in full. Small trade creditors having claims of less than one crore were to be paid in full. Other trade and Government Creditors were to be paid in aggregate Rs. 196 Crore. Other operational creditors were to be given nothing. Allocation of Rs. 1000 Crore extra to operational creditors was approved by majority of 70.73% of Committee of Creditors.

NCLT vide its judgment dated 08.03.2019 approved the Resolution Plan. Appeals were filed before NCLAT. NCLAT in its final ordern held that (i) there cannot be any difference between financial creditor and operational creditor in matter of payment of dues (ii) Security and Security interest is irrelevant at the stage of resolution for the purpose of allocation of payment (iii) Operational Creditors by its definition have sub-classes and can be treated differently for purpose of payments (iv) Profits generated by Corporate Debtor will be distributed equally among Financial Creditors and Operational Creditors (v) A core committee or sub-committee cannot be constituted under the Code (vi) Committee of Creditors has not been empowered to decide the manner in which distribution is to be made between one or more creditors (vii) Section 53 cannot be applied during CIRP (viii) Claims which have not been decided by NCLT or NCLAT may be decided by appropriate forum (ix) Financial Creditor in whose favour guarantees were executed as their total claim stand satisfied to the extent of guarantee cannot reagitate claims as against the principal borrower.

FINDINGS OF THE SUPREME COURT

The Supreme Court discussed in detail role of Resolution Professional, Role of Prospective Resolution Applicant, Role of Committee of Creditors in the Corporate Resolution Process, Jurisdiction of the NCLAT and the NCLAT.

Equality of treatment to all creditors

The Supreme Court observed that NCLAT has held that equitable treatment demands that secured, unsecured, financial and operational creditors have to be treated equally.

The Supreme Court observed that importance of valuing security interest separately from interests of creditors who do not have security is well recognized in several jurisdictions. if "equality for all" approach in respect of all creditors is adopted, secured creditors will vote for liquidation as they would have better rights during liquidation. This will defeat the whole objective of the Code of reviving the Corporate Debtor.

The Supreme Court noted that by vesting the Committee of Creditors with the discretion of accepting Resolution Plans only with Financial Creditors , operational creditors having no vote, the Code itself creates two types of Creditors.

The Constitution of sub- committee

The Supreme Court observed that for taking decisions on questions which have vital bearing on running of business of Corporate Debtor, Section 28 (1) (h) provides that though these powers are administrative in nature, they shall not be delegated to any other body. This does not mean that sub-committees cannot be appointed for purpose of negotiating with resolution applicants or for the purpose of performance of other ministerial or other administrative acts, provided such acts are in the ultimate analysis approved and ratified by the Committee of Creditors.

Extinguishment of Personal Guarantees and Undecided Claims

The Supreme Court observed that Section 31 (1) IBC makes it clear that once Resolution Plan is approved by Committee of Creditors it shall be binding on all stakeholders including guarantors. This provision ensures that the successful Resolution Applicant starts running the business of the Corporate Debtor on a fresh slate.

The Supreme Court observed that findings of the NCLAT that claims undecided by NCLT or NCLAT can be determined by appropriate forum militates against rationale of Section 31. A successful Resolution Applicant cannot suddenly be faced with "undecided claims" after approval of Resolution Plan as this would amount to a hydra head popping up throwing uncertainty in amount payable to creditors by the Resolution Applicant.

Constitutional Validity of Sections 4 and 6 of the Amending Act, 2019

Sections 4 of Amending Act of 2019 provided that CIRP will be completed within 330 days including extension of CIRP given and legal proceedings.

The Supreme Court observed that time taken in legal proceedings cannot possibly harm a litigant if the Tribunal itself cannot take up a litigant's case within the requisite period for no fault of the litigant. A provision which mandatorily requires the CIRP to end by a certain date – without any exception thereto – may well be excessive interference with a litigant's fundamental right to non-arbitrary treatment under Article 14 and an excessive, arbitrary and therefore unreasonable restriction on a litigant's fundamental right to carry on business under Article 19 (1) (g) of the Constitution of India.

The Supreme Court while leaving the provision intact, struck down the word "mandatorily" as being manifestly arbitrary under Article 14 of the Constitution of India as being an excessive and unreasonable restriction on litigant's right to carry on business under Article 19 (1) (g) of the Constitution. But at the same time the Supreme Court observed that only in exceptional cases time can be extended, general rule being that 330 days is the outer limit within which resolution of the stressed assets of the Corporate Debtor must take place beyond which the Corporate Debtor is driven into Liquidation.

Section 6 of the Amendment Act, 2019 , which substituted Section 30 (2) (b) and made some changes in Section 30 were held to be valid. The Supreme Court noted that Section 30 (2) (b) provides better treatment to operational creditors and dissenting financial creditors as they will get minimum amount as prescribed in the amended Section.

The Supreme Court held that NCLAT judgment which substitutes its own wisdom for the commercial wisdom of the Committee of Creditors must therefore be set aside.

MAHARASHTRA SEAMLESS Vs. PADMANABHAN VENKATESH

The Supreme Court in Maharashtra Seamless Vs Padmanabhan Venkatesh (2020) 11 SCC 467 has held that the Resolution Plan amount need not match liquidation value of the Corporate Debtor. The Supreme Court also held that Resolution Plan cannot be withdrawn under Section 12A of the Insolvency and Bankruptcy Code, 2016.

> Case Title : Maharashtra Seamless Vs Padmanabhan Venkatesh
> Date of Decision : 22.01.2020
> Bench : R. F. Nariman, J; Aniruddha Bose, J; V. Ramasubramanian, J

FACTS OF THE CASE

Corporate Insolvency Resolution Process has been initiated in the matter of United Seamless Tubulaar Private Ltd (Corporate Debtor). During CIRP two registered valuers were appointed who valued the Corporate Debtor for Rs. 681 Crore and Rs. 513 Crore respectively. On account of substantial difference in their valuations the Committee appointed third valuer who valued the Corporate Debtor for Rs. 352 Crore. The Committee took the average of two closest estimates which was assessed to be Rs. 432.92 Crore.

The NCLT directed to revise valuation of the Corporate Debtor on the basis of first and second valuation. Revised valuation was enhanced from Rs. 432.92 Crore to Rs. 597.54 Crore.

The Adjudicating Authority approved the Resolution Plan vide order dated 21st January, 2019.

Appeal was filed before the NCLAT by one of the Promotors Padmanabhan Venkatesh and Indian Bank primarily on the ground that Resolution Plan amounting to Rs. 477 Crores will give Resolution Applicant windfall as liquidation value of the Corporate Debtor is Rs. 597.54 Crore. The NCLAT set aside the Resolution Plan passed by the NCLT.

FINDINGS OF THE SUPREME COURT

The Supreme Court considered two issues in this case i.e. (i) whether the Scheme of the Code contemplates that the sum forming part of Resolution Plan should match the liquidation value or not. (ii) Whether Section 12 A is the applicable route through which a successful Resolution Applicant can retreat.

The Supreme Court observed that there is no provision in the Code under which bid of any Resolution Applicant has to match the liquidation value arrived in the manner provided under Clause 35 of the IBBI (Insolvency Resolution Process for Corporate Persons) regulations, 2016. The object behind prescribing valuation process is to assist the CoC to take a decision on a Resolution Plan properly. Once Resolution Plan is approved by the CoC, the statutory mandate of on the Adjudicating Authority under Section 31 (1) of the Code is to ascertain that Resolution Plan meets requirement of Section 30 (2) and (4).

The Supreme Court observed that the Appellate Authority had proceeded on equitable considerations rather than commercial wisdom. The Court ought to cede ground to the commercial wisdom of the creditors rather than assess the resolution plan on the basis of quantitative analysis. The Code clearly lays down under Section 31 (1) of the Code that the Adjudicating Authority has to be satisfied of the requirement of Section 30 (2). The Adjudicating Authority has also to ensure that the Resolution Plan has provisions for implementation. The Supreme Court noted that in Committee of Creditor of Essar Steel Vs Satish Kumar Gupta it has been held that the scope of judicial review by the Adjudicating Authority in passing of Resolution Plan is limited.

The Supreme Court also held that the Resolution Applicant cannot withdraw the Resolution Plan under Section 12 A. The exit route prescribed in Section 12 A is not applicable to the Resolution Applicant. Section 12 A is applicable only to Section 7, 9 and 10 Applications.

The Supreme Court reversed the order of the NCLAT. The order passed by the NCLT was affirmed.

THE KARAD URBAN COOPERATIVE BANK LTD VS SWWAPNIL BHINGARDEVAY

The Supreme Court has held in Karad Urban Cooperative Bank Ltd Vs Swwapnil Bhingardevaya AIR 2020 SC 4381 that once the CoC has approved the Resolution Plan taking into account relevant factors, the Adjudicating Authority has to switch to a hands-off mode.

Case Title : Karad Urban Cooperative Bank Ltd Vs Swwapnil Bhingardevaya
Date of Decision : 04.09.2020
Bench : S. A. Bobde, J; A. S. Bopanna, J; V. Ramasubramanian

FACTS OF THE CASE

The Karad Urban Cooperative Bank Ltd, Financial Creditor, filed an application on 04.09.2017 under Section 7 of Insolvency and Bankruptcy Code, 2016 for initiating insolvency proceedings against M/s. Khandoba Prasanna Sakhar Karkhana Limited (Corporate Debtor), which was admitted by NCLT vide order dated 01.01.2018. The Committee of Creditors approved the Resolution Plan submitted by one M/s Sai Agro (India) Chemicals. Application for approval of Resolution Plan was filed before NCLT. At this stage the Director/Promoter of the Corporate Debtor also came up with an application seeking permission to file Resolution Plan. The NCLT vide order dated 01.08.2019 rejected the application filed by Director/Promoter and approved the Resolution Plan submitted by M/s Sai Agro (India) Chemicals.

An appeal was filed before the NCLAT wherein matter was remanded to the Adjudicating Authority with direction to send back the Resolution Plan to the Committee of Creditors.

FINDINGS OF THE SUPREME COURT

The Supreme Court noted that NCLAT interfered in the matter on the ground that the Resolution Plan suffered from issues of viability and feasibility. The Resolution Plan amount matched liquidation value which indicated breach of confidentiality. The ethanol plant and machinery shown as part of assets of the Corporate Debtor actually belonged to third party. The Expression of Interest (EOI) was vitiated as the same was for outright sale of the Corporate Debtor as going concern in violation of Regulation 36A.

The Supreme Court relied on K Shashidhar Vs. Padmanabhan Venkatesh (2019) 12 SCC 150 and Committee of Essar Steel India Ltd Vs Satish Kumar Gupta (2019) 2 SCC 1 and observed that if all the factors that need to be taken into account for determining whether or not the Corporate Debtor can be kept running as going concern have been placed before CoC and CoC has taken a decision to approve the Resolution Plan, the Adjudicating Authority will have to switch to the hands off mode. Corporate Debtor or its promoter/director cannot claim that some of relevant materials were not placed before the CoC. The only issue regarding feasibility and viability of resolution plan in this case was the issue of ownership and possession of ethanol plant. The CoC was well aware of this issue and it cannot be stated that the question of viability and feasibility was not examined in proper perspective.

The Supreme Court also rejected that there has been any breach of confidentiality. The Supreme Court also noted that the Liquidation value mentioned in the Resolution Plan is Rs. 13.53 Crore but the actual total payout as per the Resolution Plan is Rs. 29.74 Crore. In this case the Successful Resolution Applicant was not going to get any benefit out of breach of confidentiality.

The Supreme Court also rejected the ground that EOI has been issued in violation of Regulation 36A. The Court noted that the second meeting of the Committee of Creditors was held on 27.03.2018. It was only on 04.07.2018 when amended Regulation 36A, which required publication of Form G in newspapers, came into force. The advertising was approved in the said meeting. It was unamended Regulation 36 A which was in force at that time.

The Supreme Court found the order of NCLAT flawed and set aside the same. The order of NCLT was restored.

KALPRAJ DHARAMSHI VS KOTAK INVESTMENT ADVISORS LTD.

The Supreme Court in Kalpraj Dharamshi Vs Kotak Investment Advisors Ltd. (2021) 10 SCC 401 held that principles embodied Section 14 of Limitation Act will be applicable on IBC proceedings. The Supreme Court also reiterated that commercial wisdom of the CoC is not to be interfered with excepting the limited scope as provided under Section 30 and 31 of IBC.

> Case Title : Kalpraj Dharamshi Vs Kotak Investment Advisors Ltd.
> Date of Decision : 10.03.2021
> Bench : A. M. Khanwilkar, J; B. R. Gavai, J; Krishna Murari, J

FACTS OF THE CASE

Ricoh India Ltd. (Corporate Debtor) filed an application under Section 10 IBC for initiating CIRP. Vide order dated 14.05.2018, the application was admitted and IRP was appointed.

During CIRP, fifth and last Form G was published inviting Resolution Plans, which was to be submitted on or before 08.01.2019. Kotak Investment Advisors Ltd (KIAL) and Karvy Data Management Systems Ltd submitted their Resolution Plans on 08.01.2019. WeP Solutions Ltd submitted Resolution Plan on 13.01.2019 and Kalpraj submitted Resolution Plan on 27.01.2019.

CoC approved the Resolution Plan of Kalpraj and submitted the same to the Adjudicating Authority for approval of Resolution Plan. KIAL filed an application objecting to the Plan on the ground that permitting Kalpraj to submit Resolution Plan beyond last date mentioned in Form G was illegal. NCLT approved the Resolution Plan and rejected the application of KIAL. KIAL filed writ petition before Bombay High Court which was dismissed. KIAL filed appeal before NCLAT. NCLAT allowed the appeal and directed CoC to take a decision afresh. Against order of the NCLAT four appeals were filed before the Supreme Court.

FINDINGS OF THE SUPREME COURT

The Supreme Considered three issues in this matter – (i) Whether appeal filed by KIAL before NCLAT was within limitation ? (ii) Whether there was waiver and acquiescence by KIAL ? and (iii) Whether NCLAT was right in law in interfering with the decision of CoC approving the Resolution Plan of Kalpraj ?

Whether appeal filed by KIAL before NCLAT was within limitation ?

The Supreme Court noted that judgment of NCLAT was dated 28.11.2 019. Under Section 61 IBC Appeal was required to be filed on or prior to 28.12.2019. The appeal could have been filed within a further period of 15 days i.e. 12.01.2020 in case sufficient cause was shown. If time taken in making available certified copy is excluded then the appeal has to be filed on or before 02.02.2020. However the appeal was filed on 18.02.2020.

KIAL has filed Writ Petition before High Court on 11.12.2019 which was dismissed on 28.01.2020. Whether this period could be excluded under Section 14 of the Limitation Act ?

It has been contended that Section 14 of Limitation Act only excludes time taken in bonafide proceedings before a Court and not quasi-judicial authorities.

The Supreme Court relied on M.P. Steel Corporation Vs. Commissioner of Central Excise (2015) 7 SCC 58 and observed that principle of Section 14, which is a principle based on advancing the cause of justice would certainly apply to exclude time taken in prosecuting proceedings which are bona fide pursued with diligence but which end without a decision on the merits of the case.

One of the grounds taken by the KIAL before High Court was breach of principle of natural justice which is within the jurisdiction of High Court under Article 226 despite availability of alternative remedy. The Supreme Court held that KIAL was entitled to extension of period during which it was bona fide prosecuting a remedy before the High Court with due diligence.

Whether there was waiver and acquiescence by KIAL ?

It was contended that the KIAL had unconditionally and unequivocally agreed and accepted the terms of process memorandum and surrendered all or any claim in respect of Resolution Plan as such KIAL does not have any right to challenge the process.

The Supreme Court relied on Central Inland Water Transport Corporation Ltd Vs Brojo Nath Ganguly (1986) 3 SCC 156 and observed that Court will not enforce and will, when called upon to do so, strike down an unfair or unreasonable contract or an unfair and unreasonable clause in a contract entered into between the parties who are not equal in bargaining power. Principle will apply when a man has no choice or rather no meaningful choice, but to give his assent to the contract, or sign on the dotted line in a prescribed form or to accept a set of rules however unfair or unreasonable a clause may be.

In the instant case KIAL had no option other than to accept the terms of the Contract. The Supreme Court held that KIAL cannot be said to be bound by such unconscionable clause.

It was contended that KIAL has submitted revised plans after Kalpraj was permitted to submit Resolution Plan as such KIAL has waived its rights.

The Supreme Court observed that for constituting acquiescence or waiver it must be established that though a party knows the material facts and is conscious of his legal rights in a given matter, but fails to assert its rights at the earliest possible opportunity, it creates an effective bar or waiver against him.

KIAL has vide e-mail dated 29.01.2019 has objected to acceptance of belated Resolution Plan of the Kalpraj. It has reiterated its objection to participation of Kalpraj on many occasions. It has no other option except to submit revised plans.

The Supreme Court held that KIAL has not waived or acquiesced its right to challenge the decision of RP or CoC.

Whether NCLAT was right in law in interfering with the decision of CoC of approving the Resolution Plan of Kalpraj ?

The Supreme Court observed that scope of jurisdiction of NCLT and NCLAT has been considered in K. Sashidhar Vs. Indian Overseas Bank (2019) 12 SCC 150 , Committee of Creditors of Essar Steel India Ltd Vs. Satish Kumar Gupta (2019) SCC Online SC 1478 and Bank of Maharashtra Vs. Padmanabhan Venktesh (2020) 11 SCC 467. It is well settled that the statute has not invested jurisdiction and authority either with NCLT or NCLAT to review the commercial decision exercised by CoC of approving Resolution Plan or rejecting it. The commercial wisdom of the CoC is not to be interfered with excepting the limited scope as provided under Section 30 and 31 of IBC.

The Supreme Court observed that all decisions of the RP have been approved by the CoC. The creditor which voted in favour of KIAL is Kotak Bank which has voting rights of 0.97%.

The Supreme Court concluded that NCLAT was not justified in interfering with the decision of CoC.

JAYPEE KENSINGTON BOULEVARD APARTMENTS WELFARE ASSOCIATION Vs. NBCC (INDIA) LTD & ORS

The Supreme Court in Jaypee Kensington Boulevard Apartments Welfare Association Vs NBCC (India) Ltd & Ors (2022) 1 SCC 401 held ,inter alia, that if the Adjudicating Authority find any shortcoming in the Resolution Plan within its scope of jurisdiction, the same has to be sent back to the Committee of Creditors for reconsideration. The Supreme Court also held that dissenting Financial Creditors have to be paid in terms of money.

Case Title : Jaypee Kensington Boulevard Apartments Welfare Association Vs NBCC (India) Ltd & Ors Date of Decision : 24.03.2021 Bench : A. M. Khanwilkar, J; Dinesh Maheshwari, J; Sanjiv Khanna, J

FACTS OF THE CASE

CIRP in the matter of Jaypee Infratech Ltd (JIL) was initiated vide order dated 09.08.2017 passed by NCLT, Allahabad Bench. Some aggrieved home buyers approached the Supreme Court in the matter of Chitra Sharma Vs Union of India Writ Petition (C) No. 744/2017 wherein the Supreme Court passed direction to the holding company of the Corporate Debtor to deposit Rs. 750 Crores. After matter was disposed of, this amount was transferred to NCLT.

During CIRP two Resolution Plans were submitted for consideration of the CoC wherein the Resolution Plan submitted by NBCC (India) Ltd was approved by the CoC on 17.12.2019 by vast majority of 97% of voting share of the Financial Creditors. The Resolution Plan was submitted before NCLT which approved the same vide order dated 03.03.2020.

Several Appeals against approval of Resolution Plan reached finally to the Supreme Court.

FINDINGS OF THE SUPREME COURT

Several Issues were framed by the Supreme Court. Findings of the Supreme Court on each issue are as under.

(A) What are powers and limitation of Adjudicating Authority while dealing with Resolution Plan approved by CoC ?

The Supreme Court relied on K. Shashidhar Vs. Indian Overseas Bank (2019) 12 SCC 150 , Committee of Creditors of Essar Steel India Ltd Vs Satish Kumar Gupta (2020) 8 SCC 531 and held that the Adjudicating Authority has limited jurisdiction in the matter of approval of Resolution Plan which is defined by Section 30 (2) and 31 of IBC. There is no scope for interference with commercial aspects of CoC. If the Adjudicating Authority finds certain shortcoming in the Resolution Plan, the same has to be sent back to the Committee of Creditors for re-submission after satisfying the parameters delineated by the Adjudicating Authority.

(B) Whether Resolution Plan is vitiated on account of simultaneous voting by CoC ?

The Supreme Court observed that there is no prohibition under IBC on simultaneous voting on Resolution Plans by CoC. Legislature has made the position clear vide amendment in IBC by making provision of simultaneous voting over Resolution Plans, which is clarificatory in nature.

(C) (i) Whether the Adjudicating Authority has erred in not approving stipulations in the Resolution Plan for meeting with contingent liability of additional amount of land acquisition compensation and has also erred in modifying these stipulations ?

(ii) Whether Adjudicating Authority has erred in not approving mechanism provided in the Resolution Plan for transfer of the concessionaire's right and obligations under the concession agreement with YEIDA to the SPVs proposed to be incorporated and has also erred in modifying the relevant stipulations ?

(iii) Whether the Adjudicating Authority has erred in not approving the reliefs and concessions sought for in the Resolution Plan in relation to YEIDA ?

Rights under the land in question were provided to the original concessionaire under the concession agreement dated 07.02.2003 and later on JIL was recognized as the concessionaire. One chunk of land was provided for constructing expressway and another chunk was provided for commercial exploitation.

In the meantime Allahabad High Court passed an order for additional compensation to the land owners whose land had been acquired. YEIDA demanded the amount of additional compensation from JIL. JIL initially filed Writ Petition and later pursued arbitration proceedings which led to arbitral award which held that demand made by YEIDA was not sustainable. Award has been challenged under Section 34 of the Arbitration and Conciliation Act which is pending before District Court, Gautam Budh Nagar.

Resolution Plan provided that in case arbitral award is set aside, YIEDA will collect additional compensation amount directly from home buyers, sub-lessee etc.

The Supreme Court observed that Concessionaire Agreement is not a statutory agreement but nevertheless a contract. Any tinkering with the agreement could not be done without approval of YEIDA, an authority established by State government. Approval of YEIDA will be sine qua non for validity of Resolution Plan qua the terms related with YEIDA.

The Supreme Court held that dealing with YIEDA and terms of concession agreement has rightly not been approved by NCLT. But the correct course of action was to send the Plan back to CoC.

(D) Whether the Adjudicating Authority has erred in not approving the treatment of dissenting financial creditor like ICICI Bank Ltd. in the Resolution Plan and directing payment to dissenting Financial Creditors in monetary terms ?

The Resolution Plan provided that if the dissenting Financial Creditor would be entitled to some amount in the nature of liquidation value in terms of Section 30 and Section 53 of IBC , they would be provided such liquidation value "in form of proportionate share in the equity of the Expressway SPV and transfer of certain land parcels belonging to the Corporate Debtor" . NCLT has held that payment to dissenting Financial Creditors has to be made in cash and has itself modified the plan.

The Supreme Court noted that use of expression "payment" and "amount to be paid" when read in context or on canvas of the objects and purposes of the Code, these expressions convey only their ordinary meaning, as understood in ordinary business parlance, that is, delivery of money alone. There is no reason to construe these expressions to convey the meaning of "delivery of money or its equivalent".

The Supreme Court held that the Adjudicating Authority has not erred in disapproving the treatment of dissenting Financial Creditors but erred in modifying the related terms of Resolution Plan and not sending the matter back to CoC for consideration.

(E) Whether the Adjudicating Authority has erred in modifying provision regarding fixed deposit holders and in directing the Resolution Applicant to make provision towards dues of unclaimed fixed deposit holders ?

The Resolution Plan has provision for 100% upfront payment to the fixed deposit holders whose claims had been admitted. NCLT modified the Resolution Plan to provide that Resolution Applicant will make provision for payment to unclaimed fixed deposit holder. Right will remain in force till as long as these deposit holders are entitled to make a claim under Companies Act, 2013.

The Supreme Court observed that it has been specifically held in Essar Steel that a Resolution Applicant cannot be made to suddenly encounter undecided claims after resolution plan submitted by him has been accepted and in scheme of the Code, all claims must be submitted to and decided by Resolution Professional so that Resolution Applicant can start on a fresh slate.

The Supreme Court held that the Adjudicating Authority has erred in issuing directions to Resolution Applicant to make provisions to clear the dues of unclaimed fixed deposit holders.

(F) (i) Whether Resolution Plan unauthorizedly purports to deal with the assets of Jaypee healthcare Ltd ?

(ii) Whether the Adjudicating Authority has erred in assuming that YES Bank Ltd. has agreed for Constitution of Committee to take forward the disinvestment process of Jaypee Healthcare Limited ?

The Corporate Debtor held 100 % equity shareholding in JHL. Yes Bank, Financial Creditor of JHL, objected that assets of JHL cannot be dealt with in the Resolution Plan. It was contended that Holding Company does not own the subsidiary company.

Supreme Court left the issues to be determined by both parties.

(G) Whether stipulation in the Resolution Plan for cancellation of certain agreements/sub-leases is unfair ?

The Resolution Plan has provision for cancellation of certain instruments without valid agreement and without consideration.

The NCLT observed that when an agreement is invalid and consideration is not paid, no separate stipulation is required to be made that such agreement could be cancelled. However, at the same time NCLT observed that even though such a provision has been mentioned in the Resolution Plan, that did not mean that the agreement holders have lost their right to seek remedy before competent forum.

The Supreme Court held that stipulation in question does not seem to be unfair and observation of the Adjudicating Authority remain just and proper.

(H) Whether minority shareholders are entitled to state their claims/objections despite not having approached the Adjudicating Authority and as to whether Resolution Plan does not provide fair treatment to the minority shareholders ?

The minority shareholders had raised grievance that they are not being treated fairly. The Supreme Court observed that Resolution Plan provides an exit option to the existing public shareholders at a price which is higher than the liquidation value. They are being paid an exit price of INR one crore, which is in contrast to the treatment being accorded to promoter shareholder, whose shareholding is being extinguished and cancelled in entirety without any consideration.

The Supreme Court held that Resolution Plan has adequately dealt with interest of minority shareholders.

(I) (i) Whether after approval of Resolution Plan, any individual home buyer or any association of home buyers could maintain a challenge to the Resolution Plan and could be treated as a dissenting Financial Creditor or aggrieved person ?

(ii) Whether stipulation in the Resolution Plan stands in violation of the provisions of Real Estate (Regulation and Development) Act, 2016 ?

(iii) Whether Resolution Plan is violative of the requirements of CIRP Regulations ?

(iv) Whether housing project which is completed or nearing completion ought to be kept out of the purview of the Resolution Plan ?

The Supreme Court held that homebuyers as class having assented to the Resolution Plan of NBCC, an individual home buyer or an association of home buyers cannot maintain a challenge to Resolution Plan. When the Resolution Plan comprehensively deals with all the assets and liabilities of the Corporate Debtor, no housing project of the Corporate Debtor could be segregated merely for the reason that the same has been completed or is nearing completion.

(J) (i) Whether Rs. 750 Crore deposited by JAL on the direction of Supreme Court is property of JAL and stipulation in Resolution Plan regarding its use by NBCC or JIL is impermissible?

(ii) Whether any amount is receivable by JIL from JAL ?

The amount of Rs. 750 Crore deposited and interest accrued thereon by JAL is property of JAL . Stipulation in the Resolution Plan concerning its use by JIL or Resolution Applicant cannot be approved.

(K) (i) Whether provision in the Resolution Plan providing for extinguishment of security interest of lenders of JAL could have been approved by the Adjudicating Authority ?

(ii) Whether adequate provision is required to be made in Resolution Plan regarding utilization of Land Bank of 758 Acres ?

Whether any amount is receivable by JIL and its home buyers from JAL will be determined by NCLT after reconciliation of accounts.

(L) Whether Appellate Authority was justified in providing for an Interim Monitoring Committee for implementation of Resolution Plan in question during pendency of appeal ?

The Appellate Authority was not justified in providing for interim Monitoring Committee for implementation of Resolution Plan during pendency of appeal.

GHANASHYAM MISHRA AND SONS Vs. EDELWEISS ASSET RECONSTRUCTION LTD.

The Supreme Court held in Ghanashyam Mishra and Sons Vs. Edelweiss Asset Reconstruction Ltd. (2021) 9 SCC 6 that all claims, including the ones owed to Central Government, State Government or local authority, which do not form a part of the approved resolution plan, shall stand extinguished.

> Case Title : Ghanashyam Mishra and Sons Vs. Edelweiss Asset Reconstruction Ltd.
> Date of Decision: 13.04.2021
> Bench : R. F. Nariman, J; B. R. Gavai, J; Hrishikesh Roy, J

FACTS OF THE CASE

The case arose out of a batch of appeals involving different corporate debtors in which, after approval of the resolution plans under the Insolvency and Bankruptcy Code, 2016 (IBC), various governmental authorities, including Central and State Government departments, sought to recover statutory dues such as taxes, duties, and other government claims that were not included in the approved resolution plans. The successful resolution applicants contended that permitting such claims after approval of the resolution plan would defeat the objective of the IBC by burdening the revived corporate debtor with unforeseen liabilities.

FINDINGS OF THE SUPREME COURT

The Supreme Court was considering a bunch of matters. The issues before the Court were as under:

(i) As to whether any creditor including the Central Government, State Government or any local authority is bound by the Resolution Plan once it is approved by an Adjudicating Authority under sub-section (1) of Section 31 of the Insolvency and Bankruptcy Code, 2016 (hereinafter referred to as 'I&B Code')?

(ii) As to whether the amendment to Section 31 by Section 7 of Act 26 of 2019 is clarificatory/declaratory or substantive in nature?

(iii) As to whether after approval of the resolution plan by the Adjudicating Authority a creditor including the Central Government, State Government or any local authority is entitled to initiate any proceedings for recovery of any of the dues from the Corporate Debtor, which are not a part of the Resolution Plan approved by the Adjudicating Authority?

Limited power of NCLT/NCLAT to review CoC decision

The Supreme Court relied on K Shashidhar , Committee of Creditors of Essar Steel India Limited through Authorised Signatory vs Satish Kumar Gupta, K Shashidhar vs Indian Overseas Bank, Karad Urban Cooperative Bank Ltd vs Swappnil Bhingadevay & Ors, Kalpraj Dharamshi and Anr vs Kotak Advisors Ltd. and held that it is COC who has to take business decision and NCLT or NCLAT has limited power to review.

57. It could thus be seen, that the legislature has given paramount importance to the commercial wisdom of CoC and the scope of judicial review by the Adjudicating Authority is limited to the extent provided under Section 31 of I&B Code and of the Appellate Authority is limited to the extent provided under sub-section (3) of Section 61 of the I&B Code, is no more res integra.

Extinguishment of claims

The Supreme Court held that no surprise should be flung on the Resolution Applicant after approval of the resolution plan at para 61.

61. All these details are required to be contained in the information memorandum so that the resolution applicant is aware, as to what are the liabilities, that he may have to face and provide for a plan, which apart from satisfying a part of such liabilities would also ensure, that the Corporate Debtor is revived and made a running establishment. The legislative intent of making the resolution plan binding on all the stakeholders after it gets the seal of approval from the Adjudicating Authority upon its satisfaction, that the resolution plan approved by CoC meets the requirement as referred to in sub-section (2) of Section 30 is, that after the approval of the resolution plan, no surprise claims should be flung on the successful resolution applicant. The dominant purpose is, that he should start with fresh slate on the basis of the resolution plan approved.

The Supreme Court relied upon Committee of Creditors of Essar Steel India Limited through Authorised Signatory vs Satish Kumar Gupta and held that claim which does not form part of the resolution plan shall be extinguished. Relevant para is reproduced herein.

67. As such, with respect to the proceedings, which arise after 16.8.2019, there will be no difficulty. After the amendment, any debt in respect of the payment of dues arising under any law for the time being in force including the ones owed to the Central Government, any State Government or any local authority, which does not form a part of the approved resolution plan, shall stand extinguished.

Amendment to Section 31 (1) declaratory & clarificatory

That Supreme Court held that amendment of Section 31 (1) is declaratory and clarificatory and hence applicable with retrospective effect. Reasoning provided by the Supreme Court is given as under:

87. We have no hesitation to say, that the word "other stakeholders" would squarely cover the Central Government, any State Government or any local authorities. The legislature, noticing that on account of obvious omission, certain tax authorities were not abiding by the mandate of I&B Code and continuing with the proceedings, has brought out the 2019 amendment so as to cure the said mischief. We therefore hold, that the 2019 amendment is declaratory and clarificatory in nature and therefore retrospective in operation.

CONCLUSION

The Supreme Court observed at Para 95 as under:

95. In the result, we answer the questions framed by us as under:

(i) That once a resolution plan is duly approved by the Adjudicating Authority under sub¬ section (1) of Section 31, the claims as provided in the resolution plan shall stand frozen and will be binding on the Corporate Debtor and its employees, members, creditors, including the Central Government, any State Government or any local authority, guarantors and other stakeholders. On the date of approval of resolution plan by the Adjudicating Authority, all such claims, which are not a part of resolution plan, shall stand extinguished and no person will be entitled to initiate or continue any proceedings in respect to a claim, which is not part of the resolution plan;

(ii) 2019 amendment to Section 31 of the I&B Code is clarificatory and declaratory in nature and therefore will be effective from the date on which I&B Code has come into effect;

(iii) Consequently all the dues including the statutory dues owed to the Central Government, any State Government or any local authority, if not part of the resolution plan, shall stand extinguished and no proceedings in respect of such dues for the period prior to the date on which the Adjudicating Authority grants its approval under Section 31 could be continued.

PRATAP TECHNOCRATS (P) LTD. & ORS Vs. MONITORING COMMITTEE OF RELIANCE INFRATEL LTD. & ANR

The Supreme Court in Pratap Technocrats (P) Ltd. & Ors Vs. Monitoring Committee of Reliance Infratel Ltd & Anr (2021) SCC Online SC 569 has held that under Indian Insolvency regime, a conscious choice has been made by the legislature not to confer any independent equity based jurisdiction on the Adjudicating Authority other than statutory requirements laid down under Section 30 (2) IBC.

> Case Title : Pratap Technocrats (P) Ltd. & Ors Vs. Monitoring Committee of Reliance Infratel Ltd & Anr
> Date of Decision : 10.08.2021
> Bench: Dr. Dhananjaya Y. Chandrachud, J; M. R. Shah, J

FACTS OF THE CASE

CIRP against the Corporate Debtor was initiated by an order dated 15.05.2018 of NCLT. Subsequently, CoC was constituted on 24th May, 2019. During CIRP , the RP received resolution plans from four prospective Resolution Applicants i.e. (i) Bharti Airtel Ltd. (ii) Reliance Digital Platform & Project Services Ltd (iii) VFSI Holdings Pvt. Ltd. and (iv) UV Asset Reconstruction Company Ltd. The Resolution Plan submitted by Reliance Digital Platform and Project Services Ltd was approved by CoC in its meeting held on 2nd March, 2020 by 100 percent voting share. The NCLT approved the Resolution Plan vide order dated 3rd December, 2020.

The Appellants are Operational Creditors. Appellants were aggrieved by the fact that their claims have not received a fair and equitable treatment. Fair market value and liquidation value have not been taken into account. An amount of 800 Crore, being the value of certain preference shares did not form part of corpus. The appellants were made to suffer 90% reduction to their total claim. They challenged the approval of the Resolution

Plan before NCLAT, which was rejected by NCLAT vide order dated 4th January, 2021.

FINDINGS OF THE SUPREME COURT

The Supreme Court noted that the Resolution Professional has appointed two registered valuers as per CIRP Regulation 27 to determine fair value and liquidation value of the Corporate Debtor. The submission of the appellants , that realizable value of preference shares has been excluded, has been rebutted by specific clarification contained in the Monitoring Committee's affidavit, which was filed in these proceedings. Realizable value on account of any proceeds realized from the preference shares held by its subsidiary is included in the determination of the liquidation value of the Corporate Debtor.

On the aspect of liquidation value, the Supreme Court noted that liquidation value due to unsecured operational creditor would remain nil in all scenarios, including if the corpus of Rs. 800 Crore is separately considered.

On the aspect of application filed by Doha Bank for removing some of financial creditors has no bearing on the status of approval of the Resolution Plan as it has secured 100% voting share in CoC.

The Supreme Court relied on K. Shashidhar Vs. India Overseas Bank (2019) 12 SCC 150 , Committee of Creditor of Essar Steel India Ltd Vs Satish Kumar Gupta (2020) 8SCC 531 and reiterated that commercial or business decisions of financial creditors are not open to any judicial review by the Adjudicating Authority or Appellate Authority.

The Supreme Court observed that certain foreign jurisdictions allow resolution/reorganization plans to be challenged on grounds of fairness and equity. One of the grounds on which a company voluntary arrangement can be challenged under the United Kingdom's insolvency Act, 1986 is that it unfairly prejudices the interests of the Creditors of a company. The United States Bankruptcy Code provides that if a restructuring plan has to cram down dissenting class of creditors, one of the conditions that it should satisfy is that it does not unfairly discriminate and is fair and equitable. Under Indian Insolvency regime, it appears that a conscious choice has been made by the legislature to not confer any independent equity based jurisdiction on the Adjudicating Authority other than statutory requirements laid down under sub-section (2) of Section 30 of the Code.

The Supreme Court held that decision of the NCLT and the NCLAT are in conformity of law and dismissed the appeal.

EBIX SINGAPORE PVT LTD Vs. COMMITTEE OF CREDITORS OF EDUCOMP SOLUTIONS LIMITED & ANR

The Supreme Court in Ebix Singapore Pvt. Ltd. Vs. Committee of Creditors of Educomp Solutions Limited (2021) SCC Online 707 held that Resolution Plan cannot be modified or withdrawn after approval by the Committee of Creditors (CoC).

Case Title : Ebix Singapore Pvt. Ltd. Vs. Committee of Creditors of Educomp Solutions Limited Date of Decision : 13.09.2021 Bench : Dr. Dhananjaya Y. Chandrachud, J; M. R. Shah, J

FACTS OF THE CASE

The Supreme Court was considering three appeals wherein wherein the issue was whether a successful Resolution Applicant could withdraw or modify the Resolution Plan after its approval by the CoC.

Appeal by Ebix

Educomp filed petition for initiation of CIRP under Section 10 IBC, which was admitted by NCLT on 30th May, 2017. During CIRP, Ebix was declared successful Resolution Applicant by CoC. The RP filed Application before NCLT for approval of Resolution Plan. The Wire published an article related to irregularities in Educomp on 26th April, 2018. Some Financial Creditors filed Applications before NCLT for investigation into affairs of the Corporate Debtor. MCA also directed investigation by SFIO. NCLT dismissed these applications and directed CoC to discuss the issues raised in the applications. CoC passed resolution to appoint independent agency to conduct investigation into affairs of the Educomp. An application by RP was filed before NCLT seeking special investigation audit of Educomp. NCLT directed RP to file an affidavit in relation to transactions to be carried out by Educomp under Section 43,

45, 50 and 66. In its affidavit the RP stated that no such transaction had been found.

Ebix filed its first withdrawal application on 5th July, 2019. On 10th July, NCLT dismissed the withdrawal application. Thereafter Ebix filed second withdrawal application under Section 60 (5). NCLT dismissed the second withdrawal application. Ebix filed the third withdrawal application which was allowed by the NCLT. NCLT also dismissed the application for approval of Resolution Plan. NCLAT set aside the order of NCLT.

The Appeal by Kundan Care

Astonfield filed an application for initiation of CIRP under Section 10 IBC which was admitted by the NCLT on 27th November, 2018. Resolution Plan submitted by Kundan Care was approved with a majority of 99.28 %. RP filed an application before NCLT for approval of Resolution Plan.

Astonfield has executed PPA with GUVNL, which was valid for 25 years. This PPA formed entirety of business of Corporate Debtor. GUVNL issued notice of default, which was challenged by RP before NCLT. NCLT held the PPA cannot be terminated during CIRP but can be terminated during Liquidation. On appeal NCLAT held the PPA cannot be terminated during CIRP or Liquidation. The Supreme Court also held that PPA cannot be terminated during CIRP.

Kundan Care filed Application for withdrawal of Resolution Plan on 17th December, 2019. NCLT dismissed Kundan Care Application vide order dated 3rd July, 2020. An appeal was filed before the NCLAT, which was also dismissed.

The Appeal by Seroco

Application was filed under Section 7 IBC for initiation of CIRP by Kotak against Arya Filaments. NCLT admitted the Petition vide order dated 17th August, 2018. During CIRP , Resolution Plan of the Seroco was approved by CIRP. RP filed Resolution Plan before NCLT for approval. Seroco filed application before NCLT seeking permission to revise Resolution Plan which was rejected by the NCLT. NCLT approved the Resolution Plan submitted by RP. Seroco filed an appeal before NCLAT which was dismissed.

FINDINGS OF THE SUPREME COURT

The Supreme Court after examining scheme of the IBC in respect of Resolution Plan observed that there are three stages involved. The first stage ends with approval of Resolution Plan by CoC . The second stage is interim period after approval of Resolution Plan by CoC and before its confirmation by Adjudicating Authority. The third stage is after the approval of Resolution Plan.

Whether approval of Resolution Plan by CoC constitutes a contract ?

It was contended before the Supreme Court that Resolution Plans are in the nature of an offer, which becomes binding as a concluded contract only once Adjudicating Authority approves the Resolution Plan. Alternatively, it was contended that Resolution Plans approved by CoC are contingent contract whose enforceability is dependent on conditional approval of the Adjudicating Authority in accordance with Section 32 of the Contract Act.

The Supreme Court observed that certain stages of CIRP resembles stages of contract such as issuance of request for resolution plan, consideration of resolution plan as an offer and approval of resolution plan by CoC by acceptance of offer. However, it is the structure of IBC which confers legal force on CoC approved resolution plan. The validity of Resolution Plan is based on its compliance with the procedures established by law.

The Supreme Court surveyed several foreign jurisdictions on the issue whether instruments like Resolution Plan are statutory contracts. The Supreme Court noted that there was lack of consensus regarding the same.

The Court observed that the absence of any provisions in IBC or the regulations referring to CoC approved Resolution Plan as a contract and lack of clarity in BLRC report regarding the nature of Resolution Plan constrains it from arriving at the conclusion that CoC approved Resolution Plan will be governed by Contract Act. Statutory enabled framework for commercial negotiation is not enough to over-power the other elements of regulation that detract from view that CoC approved Resolution Plan is contract. CoC approved Resolution Plans before approval of the Adjudicating Authority under Section 31 are a function and product of IBC mechanism. Their validity, nature, legal force, and content is regulated by the procedure laid down under IBC and not Contract Act.

Whether a Resolution Plan can be withdrawn or modified ?

The Supreme Court observed that judicial restraint must not only be exercised while adjudicating upon the constitutionality of the statute relating to economic policy but also in matters of interpretation of economic statutes. If the Resolution Applicants are permitted to seek modifications after subsequent negotiations or a withdrawal after submission of Resolution Plan to the Adjudicating Authority as a matter of law, it would dictate the commercial wisdom and bargaining strategies of all prospective Resolution Applicants who are seeking to participate in the process and successful Resolution Applicants who may wish to negotiate a better deal, owing to myriad factors which are unique to their own cause.

IBC is silent whether Resolution Plan can be withdrawn or not. The absence of any exit routes being stipulated under statute for a Successful Resolution Applicant is indicative of prohibition of any attempts at withdrawal at its behest. The rule of casus omissus is an established rule of interpretation which provides that an omission in a statute cannot be supplied by judicial interpretation. In the absence of any provision under IBC allowing for withdrawal of the Resolution Plan by a successful Resolution Applicant with such a relief through a judicial interpretation would be impermissible.

The Supreme Court also examined the contention whether terms of a Resolution Plan can reserve a right to modify or withdraw its contents after submission to Adjudicating Authority.

The Supreme Court observed that if the Legislature intended to allow withdrawals or subsequent negotiations by successful Resolution Applicants, it would have prescribed specific timelines for exercise of such an option. The recognition of power of withdrawal or modification after submission of CoC approved Resolution Plan, by judicial interpretation, will have the effect of disturbing statutory timelines and delaying the CIRP, leading to depletion of values of the assets of a Corporate Debtor in the event of potential liquidation.

Whether Adjudicating Authority can permit modification or withdrawal of a Resolution Plan ?

The Supreme Court held that the Adjudicating Authority lacks the authority to allow the withdrawal or modification of Resolution Plan by a successful Resolution Applicant or to give effect to such clauses in the Resolution Plan. Power of withdrawal of resolution plan or modification of resolution plan is also not vested in NCLT under its jurisdiction under Section 60 (5) of the Code. NCLT cannot do what the IBC has consciously chosen not to confer it with the power to do.

The Supreme Court dismissed the appeal of Ebix and Seroco. In case of Kundan Care the Supreme Court granted one time relief under Article 142 and directed to convene a meeting of CoC to consider proposal submitted by Kundan Care.

NAGAITLANG DHAR Vs. PANNA PRAGATI INFRASTRUCTURE PVT. LTD. & ORS.

The Supreme Court in Nagaitlang Dhar Vs Panna Pragati Infrastructure Pvt. Ltd. (2022) 6 SCC 172 reiterated that "commercial wisdom" of CoC has been given paramount status, with minimum judicial intervention, for ensuring completion of the processes within the timelines prescribed by Insolvency and Bankruptcy Code, 2016.

Case Title : Nagaitlang Dhar Vs Panna Pragati Infrastructure Pvt. Ltd. Date of Decision : 17.12.2021 Bench : L. Nageswara Rao, J; B. R. Gavai, J

FACTS OF THE CASE

Allahabad Bank filed Application under Section 7 IBC for initiating CIRP against Meghalaya Infratech Ltd. The application was admitted vide order dated 28th August, 2019. Allahabad Bank and Corporation Bank were the only Financial Creditors. As per provisions of the Code and regulations made therein EOI was invited from prospective Resolution Applicants. Four EOI including that of Respondent No. 1 were received. The Resolution Plan submitted by the Appellant was approved by the CoC with 100% voting share. Respondent No. 1 filed IA before the NCLT for directing the CoC to consider revised plan which was rejected by NCLT. NCLT approved the Resolution Plan vide order dated 18th May, 2020. The Appeal was filed before the NCLAT, which was allowed.

FINDINGS OF THE SUPREME COURT

The Supreme Court noted that four Resolution Plans were submitted in this matter. The 5th CoC was held on 11th and 12th February, 2020. The Respondent No. 1 requested the CoC to adjourn the meeting to be held on 12th February, 2020 which was declined in light of timeline to be followed under IBC. On 12th February, 2020 Respondent No. 1 was absent in the CoC meetings. CoC decided to exclude Respondent No. 1 from the process.

Only two Resolution Applicants were present i.e. Appellant and Abhishek Agrawal. Thereafter CoC adopted open swiss challenge method. Appellant emerged as the highest bidder offering upfront amount of Rs. 64.30 Crore plus CIRP Costs. Resolution was approved by CoC with 100% voting share.

It is thus clear that Respondent No. 1 was well aware that the CoC had decided to finalise the proceedings by 12th February, 2020. When Respondent No. 1 was asked to enhance the bid amount, it has rejected and asked for adjournment.

RP and CoC had acted in transparent manner. Equal opportunity was given to all prospective Resolution Applicants. Respondent No. 1, without improving bid amount, went on insisting for more time.

It was contended by the Respondent that there was material irregularity in decision making, which was rejected by the Supreme Court. The Supreme Court observed that the procedure adopted by the RP as well as the CoC was fair, transparent and equitable. The CoC was facing timeline, which was to end on 24th February, 2020, before which it has to finalize the decision. In such circumstances refusal by CoC to grant additional time cannot be said to be irregularity.

The Supreme Court observed that it is a trite law that “commercial wisdom” of the CoC has been given paramount status without any judicial intervention for ensuring completion of the processes within the timelines prescribed by IBC.

The Supreme Court observed that in the present case there has not been any irregularity , let alone any material irregularity.

The Court observed that dominant objective of the IBC is revival of the Corporate Debtor and making it a going concern. In the present case, the said purpose is already achieved as all the dues of the Financial Creditors i.e. Allahabad Bank and the Corporation Bank have already been paid and the Corporate Debtor is a going concern.

The Supreme Court allowed the appeal and set aside the findings of theNCLAT.

SREI MULTIPLE ASSET INVESTMENT TRUST VISION INDIA FUND Vs. DECCAN MARKETEERS & ORS

Supreme Court reiterated in SREI Multiple Asset Investment Trust Vision India Fund Vs. Deccan Marketeers (2023) 7 SCC 295 that Resolution Plan after approval of NCLT cannot be modified or altered.

> Case Title : SREI Multiple Asset Investment Trust Vision India Fund Vs. Deccan Marketeers
> Date of Decision : 17.03.2023
> Bench : Ajay Rastogi, J; Bela M. Trivedi, J

FACTS OF THE CASE

Deccan Chronicle Holdings Ltd. (Corporate Debtor) was admitted to CIRP vide order of NCLT dated 5th July, 2017 on an application made by Canara Bank (Financial Creditor). SREI Multiple Asset Investment Trust Vision India Fund was successful Resolution Applicant in the matter of Deccan Chronicle Holdings Ltd. The Resolution Plan was approved by Committee of Creditors by 81.39% of voting share and subsequently approved by the NCLT vide order dated 3rd June, 2019.

At the time of approval of the Resolution Plan one application IA No. 155/2018 was pending before NCLT seeking a declaration that the Corporate Debtor is owner of the trademarks "Deccan Chronicle" and "Andhra Bhoomi". NCLT, subsequent to approval of Resolution Plan, vide order dated 14th August, 2019 declared that the trademarks "Deccan Chronicle" and "Andhra Bhoomi" belong to the Corporate Debtor.

The order of the NCLT in IA 155/2018 was challenged before NCLAT, wherein NCLAT set aside the order of NCLT and held that declaration made by NCLT holding the ownership rights of the Corporate Debtor in the trademarks "Deccan Chronicle" and "Andhra Bhoomi" amount to modification/alteration of the approved Resolution Plan which is impermissible in law.

The Successful Resolution Applicant filed an appeal before the Supreme Court.

FINDINGS OF THE SUPREME COURT

The Appellant submitted that if it gets only the right to use the trade marks and not the ownership of the trademarks, the Resolution Plan would be a non-starter. it was submitted that the declaration by the NCLT does not amount to modification of the Resolution and finding regarding the same by the NCLAT is erroneous and misconceived.

The Respondents submitted that Resolution Plan was confined to the perpetual use of trade marks. The declaration by the NCLT after approval of the Resolution Plan was tantamount to modification of the Resolution Plan which is impermissible under law. It was also submitted that determination of ownership rights was not within the jurisdiction of the NCLT.

The Supreme Court noted that the Committee of Creditors had approved the Resolution Plan to the effect that Corporate Debtor had perpetual rights to use trademarks "Deccan Chronicle" and "Andhra Bhoomi". The Resolution Plan nowhere provides that the Corporate Debtor has ownership rights over trademarks "Deccan Chronicle" or "Andhra Bhoomi". The NCLT after approval of Resolution Plan declared in IA 155/2018 that the Corporate Debtor has ownership rights in trademarks "Deccan Chronicle" and "Andhra Bhoomi". The same was modification/alteration of the Resolution Plan and hence impermissible in law.

The Supreme Court concurred with the view of the NCLAT. The Supreme Court relied on Ebix Singapore Private Ltd. Vs. Committee of Creditors of Educomp Solutions Limited & Another (2022) 2 SCC 401 which stated that enabling withdrawal or modification of the Resolution Plan, once it has been submitted to the Adjudicating Authority after complying with the provisions of the Code will create another tier of negotiations which will be totally unregulated by statute.

The Supreme Court held that right to perpetual use of the trademarks "Deccan Chronicle" and "Andhra Bhoomi" will be available to the Resolution Applicant but Resolution Applicant will not be owner of trademarks "Deccan Chronicle" and "Andhra Bhoomi".

RAMKRISHNA FORGINGS LIMITED Vs. RAVINDRA LOONKAR, RP

The Supreme Court in Ramkrishna Forgings Limited Vs. Ravindra Loonkar, RP (Civil Appeal No. 1527 /2022) held that NCLT was not justified in directing a fresh valuation after the Resolution Plan had been approved by the Committee of Creditors. The Supreme Court also emphasized the need for passing reasoned order.

Case Title : Ramkrishna Forgings Limited Vs. Ravindra Loonkar, RP Date of Decision : 21.11.2023 Bench : Vikram Nath, J; Ahsanuddin Amanullah, J

FACTS OF THE CASE

CIRP was initiated in the matter of ACIL vide order of NCLT dated 08.08.2018. Ramkrishna Forgings Ltd. submitted several revised Resolution Plans, the final one of which was submitted on 05.08.2019 having financial proposal of Rs. 129.5 crore. The Financial Creditors were to get upfront payment of Rs. 84.54 Crore. Final plan also provided for monetization of land situated at Manesar which would go to the Financial Creditors.

The Resolution Plan was approved by the Committee of Creditors on 14.08.2019 by 88.56% votes. Resolution Plan was submitted before the NCLT for approval. The haircut under the Resolution plan was about 94.25%. The Resolution Plan was kept in abeyance by the NCLT. The NCLT directed Official Liquidator to provide exact figures/value of assets. The appeal was filed against this order before the NCLAT, which upheld the order of the NCLT. Aggrieved by the same an appeal was filed before the Supreme Court.

FINDINGS OF THE SUPREME COURT

The Supreme Court observed that no objection has been raised to the Resolution Plan from any quarter regarding any irregularity/deficiency by Resolution Professional, the Resolution Applicant or Committee of Creditors. Statutory requirement of valuation by the two registered valuers had been complied with. Figures in both reports were not at great variance.

The Supreme Court relied on K Sashidhar v Indian Overseas Bank,(2019) 12 SCC 150, Committee of Creditors of Essar Steel India Ltd. v Satish Kumar Gupta (2020) 8 SCC 531, Maharastra Seamless Ltd., Kalpraj Dharamashi Vs. Kotak Investment Advisors Ltd. (2021) 10 SCC 401, Pratap Technocrats Private Limited v Monitoring Committee of Reliance Infratel Limited, (2021) 10 SCC 623 and observed that CoC decision is not to be subjected to unnecessary judicial scrutiny and intervention. Ordering a revaluation of the assets by the Official Liquidator was not justified. The Supreme Court further observed that the NCLT and the NCLAT erred in failing to recognize that under the Resolution Plan, the Corporate Debtor was set to be revived and not liquidated. Thus, the minimum mandatory component in the Resolution Plan was only a reflection of the actual money including upfront payment which would go towards FCs. The Resolution Plan also provided for the monetization proceeds of the land as also the avoidance amounts to go to the FCs of the Corporate Debtor.

The Court further observed on the limited jurisdiction of the NCLT under Section 31 (2) as under:

31. It is worthwhile to note that the Adjudicating Authority has jurisdiction only under Section 31 (2) of the Code, which gives power not to approve only when the Resolution Plan does not meet the requirement laid down under Section 31 (1) of the Code, for which a reasoned order is required to be passed. We may state that the NCLT's jurisdiction and powers as Adjudicating Authority under the Code flow from the Code and the Regulations thereunder.

The Court finally held that the order of the NCLT cannot stand judicial scrutiny either on facts or in law. The Court observed that there may have been a situation where due to glaring facts an order could be left untouched but only if detailed reasoning, disclosing the facts for being persuaded to embark on such path, was discernible in such order. The order in this case unfortunately was cryptic and bereft of detail. The Supreme Court also emphasized the importance of reasoned order and observed that recording of reasons, and not just reasons but cogent reasons, for orders is a duty on Courts and Tribunals.

KALYANI TRANSCO Vs. BHUSHAN POWER AND STEEL LTD

The Supreme Court in Kalyani Transco Vs. Bhushan Power and Steel Ltd. (Civil Appeal 1808/2020) inter alia held that CoC does not become *functus officio* after approval of Resolution Plan. The CoC continues to exist till the Resolution Plan is implemented or an order of liquidation is passed under Section 33 IBC.

Case Title : Kalyani Transco Vs. Bhushan Power and Steel Ltd. Date of Decision : 26.09.2025 Bench : B. R. Gavai, CJI; Satish Chandra Sharma, J; K. Vinod Chandran, J

FACTS OF THE CASE

Banking Regulation Act, 1949 vide 2019 amendment empowered the RBI to issue directions to Banks to initiate CIRP against major Corporate defaulters. Bhushan Power and Steel Ltd (BPSL) was one such company identified by RBI. Punjab National Bank filed Petition under Section 7 IBC, which was admitted vide order dated 26th July, 2017 by NCLT. Subsequently IRP admitted claims of Rs. 4,72,04,51,78,073 on behalf of Financial Creditors and Rs.6,21,37,61,735/- on behalf of Operational Creditors. During CIRP thirteen Resolution Applicants submitted their Resolution Plans. JSW Steel emerged as Successful Resolution Applicant (SRA). NCLT approved the Resolution Plan of JSW on 5th September, 2019. Several appeals were filed before NCLAT, which approved the Resolution Plan with some modifications.

The Supreme Court vide its judgment dated 2nd May, 2025 set aside judgments dated 5th September, 2019 and 17th February, 2020 of NCLT and NCLAT respectively. Review Petitions were filed before the Supreme Court, which were allowed on 31st July, 2025 and order dated 2nd May, 2025 was recalled.

FINDINGS OF THE SUPREME COURT

The Supreme Court rejected the argument that promoters of the Corporate Debtor donot have locus to challenge the decision of NCLAT.

The Supreme Court held that in view of explanation to Regulation 18(2) of the IBBI (Insolvency Resolution Process for Corporate Persons) Regulations, 2016 , the CoC continues to exist till the Resolution Plan is implemented or an order of liquidation is passed under Section 33 of the IBC. It will not be out of place to mention that the cloud of uncertainty exists until a finality is attained by this Court in the proceedings under Section 62 IBC.

The Supreme Court noted that the appeal has been filed against concurrent finding of NCLT and NCLAT. Supreme Court noted that no ground as provided under Section 61 IBC is made.

The Supreme Court observed that in the instant case there was not any renegotiation of any terms of Resolution Plan. Both the CoC and the SRA – JSW found it difficult to implement the Resolution Plan on account of various issues including the PMLA proceedings initiated against the Corporate Debtor - BPSL and its management, the provisional attachment of properties and the unilateral directions of NCLT to distribute EBITDA etc. It is further to be noted that both the CoC and the SRA - JSW were jointly making efforts before this Court for implementation of the Resolution Plan which was in fact implemented on 26th March, 2021. There was no deliberate delay in implementation of Resolution Plan.

The Supreme Court observed that the payments made to the OCs in the present matter are not amounts due as per the Resolution Plan and are ex – gratia payments.

The Supreme Court also rejected the contention that JSW has not paid upfront amount of Rs. 8550 Crore as equity. The JSW claimed that it has paid 100 crore and the remaining amount as Compulsory Convertible Debentures(CCD). The Supreme Court held that it is not res integra that CCD is a different type of debenture and can be considered as equity instruments.

The Supreme Court observed that for distribution of profits, provisions in the process document have to be followed. It has been reiterated on more than one occasion that since the RFRP was silent on the treatment of

EBITDA generated during CIRP and in view Essar judgment, EBITDA may be retained with the Corporate Debtor.

The Supreme Court observed, as far as admission of claim of Jaldhi as contingent claim, that in the present matter , the CoC had exercised its commercial wisdom while approving the Resolution Plan whereby the Appellant – Jaldhi was classified as a contingent creditor and such a decision is deemed to be non – justiciable by this Court in view of K. Sashidhar which has been subsequently followed in a catena of judgments.

The Supreme Court dismissed the appeal and findings of the NCLAT were affirmed.

TORRENT POWER LTD Vs ASHISH ARJUNKUMAR RATHI & ORS

The Supreme Court in Torrent Power Ltd. Vs. Ashish Arjunkumar Rathi & Ors (Civil Appeal No. 11746-11747 of 2024) reiterated that IBC leaves no scope for judicial intervention in the commercial decision of Committee of Creditors. Supreme Court further observed that predictability and finality are essential to maintaining a robust insolvency regime. Judicial intervention beyond the narrow statutory confines undermines both predictability and finality.

Case Title : Torrent Power Ltd. Vs. Ashish Arjunkumar Rathi & Ors Date of Decision : 27.02.2026 Bench : B. V. Nagarathna, J, R. Mahadevan, J

BRIEF FACTS

CIRP was initiated in respect of SKS Power Generation (Chhattisgarh) Ltd by order dated 29.04.2022 passed by NCLT. During the CIRP, seven resolution applicants including Torrent Power Ltd. submitted their Resolution Plans. CoC in its 26th meeting decided for inter se bidding. The CoC in its 31st Meeting approved the Resolution Plan of Sarda Energy and Minerals Limited (SEML).

IA 2794/2023 was filed by the Resolution Professional before the NCLT for approval of the Resolution Plan. Objections were filed by Torrent and Vantage vide IA 3336/2023 and IA 3399/2023 respectively. The NCLT remitted the Resolution Plan back to the CoC for reconsideration. The CoC in its 34th Meeting held on 19.10.2023 again approved the resolution plan of SEML. In between, Torrent and Vantage had filed appeals before NCLAT wherein their applications were revived before the NCLT.

NCLT vide order dated 13.08.2024 again allowed the application for approval of Resolution Plan and rejected IA 3336/2023 and IA 3399/2023. Unsuccessful Resolution Applicant preferred appeals before the NCLAT, which were dismissed. Finally appeals were filed before the Hon'ble Supreme Court.

FINDINGS OF THE SUPREME COURT

The Supreme Court observed that the case of the appellants was that material modifications were made in the Resolution Plan submitted by SEML after completion of the negotiation process. This was firstly, by allegedly enlarging its commitment towards Bank Guarantees of the Corporate Debtor from Rs.103.39 crores to Rs.180.05 crores, and secondly, by purportedly converting a deferred payment offer of Rs.240 crores into an upfront payment offer. According to the appellants, these changes were introduced by SEML under the guise of "clarifications" through post-bid communications between the RP/CoC and SEML, in breach of the Process Note governing the negotiation process, thus resulting in discrimination and material irregularity in the resolution process warranting interference by this Court under Section 63 of the Act.

The Supreme Court noted that an appeal before the Supreme Court is only maintainable on a question of law, which was absent in this matter. Further, there are concurrent findings of both the Tribunals below. The appeal could be dismissed on these grounds alone.

However, the Supreme Court also considered the merits. The Supreme Court noted that the Resolution Plan, from its inception, contemplated that the entire margin money of Rs.180.05 crores lying with the issuing banks would ultimately flow to the CoC for payment to secured financial creditors. Rs. 103.39 crores did not represent the "extent of SEML's offer" in relation to BGs. Rather, it represented the incremental funding requirement arising from SEML's decision to continue certain BGs. Continuing a guarantee necessarily requires substitution of collateral; discontinuing it does not. The Plan therefore required fresh infusion only for those guarantees which were to be continued. The remaining guarantees, aggregating to Rs.76.61 crores, stood on a different footing. SEML proposed extinguishment of liabilities underlying these guarantees. Once the liabilities were extinguished, the guarantees would inevitably be cancelled, and the margin money backing them would be released. The payment to the CoC was Rs.180.49 crores before clarification and remained Rs.180.49 crores even after the clarification.

On the second issue the Supreme Court noted that SEML proposed to issue NCDs at a face value of Rs.240 crores with a coupon rate of 10%. However, it also gave the CoC the option to either - (i) take the NCDs, i.e., Rs.240 crores with 10% coupon (which comes to a total of Rs.301.64 crores over three years); or (ii) take Rs.240 crores upfront. It was the CoC's choice to either take a higher value later or take its present value upfront. Hence, it is obvious that there was no change made to SEML's Resolution Plan through its clarification

The Supreme Court concluded that neither of the issues raised by the appellants establishes any modification of the Resolution Plan or any material irregularity in the conduct of the RP, the challenge stands stripped of its factual foundation.

The Supreme Court relying on K. Sashidhar vs. Indian Overseas Bank, (2019) 12 SCC 150; Kalyani Transco vs. Bhushan Power & Steel Ltd., 2025 SCC OnLine SC 2093; Committee of Creditors of Essar Steel India Limited vs. Satish Kumar Gupta, (2020) 8 SCC 531; Pratap Technocrats Private Ltd. vs. Monitoring Committee of Reliance Infratel Limited, (2021) 10 SCC 623 reiterated that IBC does not leave any scope of judicial intervention to commercial decision taken by CoC.

The Supreme Court observed that from an ex post perspective, excessive judicial review in the CIRP carries significant economic costs that run counter to the objects of IBC. From an ex ante perspective also, the expectation of expansive judicial review distorts incentives for future bidders. Future resolution applicants may price legal uncertainty into their bids, either by discounting their offers or by refraining from participation in the CIRP altogether. From an institutional design point of view, the law must secure three interdependent economic freedoms viz. entry into the market, continuation of business operations under conditions of competitive neutrality, and exit from the market. While easy entry and operation enable risk-taking and value creation, exit performs a critical function too by ensuring that failure, an inevitable byproduct of risk taking, is resolved efficiently rather than postponed indefinitely.

INDEPENDENT SUGAR CORPORATION LTD Vs. GIRISH SRIRAM JUNEJA

The Supreme Court in Independent Sugar Corporation Ltd. Vs. Girish Sriram Juneja & Ors (Civil Appeal No. 6071 /2023) held that obtaining approval by the Competition Commission of India prior to the approval of the Resolution Plan by the Committee of Creditors is mandatory in cases where there is provision for combination under the Resolution Plan. The objectives of the IBC and the Competition Act must necessarily be in harmony with one another. Expeditious resolution cannot come at the cost of disregarding statutory provisions.

Case Title : Independent Sugar Corporation Ltd. Vs, Girish Sriram Juneja & Ors.
Date of Decision: 29.01.2025
Bench : Hrishikesh Roy, J; Sudhanshu Dhulia, J; S. V. N. Bhatti, J

BRIEF FACTS

CIRP was initiated in the matter of Hindustan National Glass and Industries Ltd. (HNGIL) vide order dated 21.10.2021. HNGIL had 60% market share in glass packaging industry. During CIRP, Several Resolution Applicants including Independent Sugar Corporations Ltd. (INSCO), the appellant herein and AGI Greenpac submitted their Resolution Plans. Resolution Applicant, AGI Greenpac Ltd. was the second largest glass packaging company in India. The combination between AGI Greenpac and HNGIL would have had potential market share of 80-85% in F&B segment.

The RP in e-mail communication dated 25.08.2022 granted relaxation to Resolution Applicants to obtain CCI approval after CoC approval of the Resolution Plan but before approval by Adjudicating Authority. AGI Greenpac submitted application on 27.09.2022 before CCI seeking approval of combination which was rejected by the CCI. Subsequently, Resolution Plan was submitted for approval of CoC by AGI Greenpac.

At the time of submission of Resolution Plan, AGI Greenpac neither has approval of CCI nor any pending application before CCI.

CoC approved AGI Greenpac Resolution Plan with 98% while Resolution Plan of INSCO received 88% votes.

AGI Greenpac again filed an application before CCI for approval on 03.11.2022. On 10.03.2023 AGI Greenpac filed divestment plan in respect of one of the plants before CCI and subsequently CCI approved the combination on 15.03.2023.

Resolution Professional filed an application for approval of Resolution Plan before Adjudicating Authority. The Appellant filed an objection. On 28.04.2023, Resolution Plan of AGI Greenpac was approved by the Adjudication Authority and objection filed by INSCO was rejected.

Appellant filed an appeal before the NCLAT which was dismissed. The NCLAT observed that although approval by CCI was mandatory, prior approval by CoC was only directory. The timeline for CCI to decide upon a combination proposal is much longer and should not lead to a situation where the CIRP is frozen or halted because of a pending application before the CCI. INSCO also challenged the CCI approval before NCLAT which was also dismissed.

The decisions of NCLAT were challenged before the Supreme Court.

FINDINGS OF THE SUPREME COURT

The Supreme Court noted that the Appellant has *locus standi* to file appeal under IBC as "any person aggrieved" can file appeal. Similarly, the Appellant has locus standi to file an appeal under Competition Act as "any enterprise or any person aggrieved" can file an appeal. The Appellant as an unsuccessful Resolution Applicant satisfies the requirement of being aggrieved.

The Supreme Court noted that Section 31 (4) has been inserted by Insolvency and Bankruptcy Code (Amendment) Act, 2018 which provides that where the resolution plan contains a provision for combination, as referred to in Section 5 of the Competition Act, 2002, the Resolution Applicant shall obtain the approval of the Competition Commission of India under the Act prior to the approval of the such resolution plan by the Committee of Creditors.

The Supreme Court noted that the above provision makes it abundantly clear that the proviso creates an exception for those Resolution Plans that contain provisions for combination. The language used therein appears to be clear, precise & straightforward. As such, to understand the legislative intent, the rule of plain reading or literal interpretation should find favour rather than the rule of purposive interpretation as is suggested by the other side. The Courts should not arrogate the legislature's role by filling gaps in statutory text. Where there is no ambiguity in the words used, the question of finding a disguised intention or purpose behind the use of a particular word would not ordinarily arise.

The Supreme Court noted that a timeline was incorporated to plug a loophole and provide for a schedule to obtain necessary approvals, which was hitherto not provided. At the same time, a distinction was drawn between necessary approvals required to be received from different statutory bodies and regulatory authorities vis-à-vis the CCI's approval. In case of other statutory bodies, a timeline of one year subsequent to the CoC's approval to the Resolution Plan was deemed to be sufficient, whereas the timeline for procuring the CCI's approval was brought ahead in the sense that the same was required to be obtained prior to the approval of the Resolution Plan by the CoC.

The Supreme Court observed that to ensure that entities operate with utmost confidence in the sanctity and fairness of India's legal and regulatory system, the objectives of the IBC and the Competition Act must also necessarily be in harmony with one another. Expeditious resolution cannot come at the cost of disregarding statutory provisions. Providing relief for stressed assets must necessarily align with the statutory framework, as adherence to legal principles is fundamental to a fair and just resolution process.

The Supreme Court set aside the approval granted by the CoC to the Resolution Plan dated 28.10.2022 without the requisite CCI approval and *status quo ante* was restored.

AVOIDANCE TRANSACTIONS

ANUJ JAIN INTERIM RESOLUTION PROFESSIONAL FOR JAYPEE INFRATECH Vs. AXIS BANK LTD.

The Supreme Court in Anuj Jain Interim Resolution Professional for Jaypee Infratech Vs Axis Bank Ltd (2021) 2 SCC 799 held that mortgage transactions of the Corporate Debtor in favour of lenders of its holding company Jaiprakash Associates Ltd (JAL) are preferential transactions under Section 43 of the IBC. The Supreme Court also held that disbursement against consideration of time value of money is an essential element of Financial Debt.

Case Title : Anuj Jain Interim Resolution Professional for Jaypee Infratech Vs Axis Bank Ltd Date of Decision : 26.02.2020 Bench : A. M. Khanwilkar, J; Dinesh Maheshwari, J

FACTS OF THE CASE

JAL is a public listed company with more than 5 lakh individual shareholders. In 2003, JAL was awarded the right to construct expressway from NOIDA to Agra. A concession agreement was entered into with Yamuna Expressway Industrial Development Authority. Jaypee Infratech Limited (JIL) was set up as a special purpose vehicle. Finance was obtained from consortium of banks against partial mortgage of land acquired and a pledge of 51% of shareholding held by JAL. Housing Projects were envisaged for construction of real estate projects at two places of the land acquired – wish town, NOIDA and Mirzapur.

IDBI Bank filed an Application under Section 7 of the Code for initiating CIRP against JIL on account of committing a default of Rs. 525.11 Crore. On 09.08.2019, the NCLT admitted the Application.

The Corporate Debtor has created several security interest in favour of lenders of JAL i.e. – (i) mortgage deed dated 29.12.2016 for 167.229 acres in favour of Axis Trustee Services Limited to provide an additional security for term loans of Rs. 21081.5 crore sanctioned by consortium to JAL (ii) another mortgage deed dated 29.12.2016 for 167.9615 acres favour of Axis Trustee Services Limited (iii) mortgage deed dated 07.03.2017 for 158.1739 acres executed by JIL in favour of IDBI Trustee-ship Services Ltd for term loan of Rs. 1200 Crores granted by ICICI Bank to JAL (iv) mortgage deed dated 07.03.2017 for 151.0039 acres executed by JIL in favour of IDBI Trustee-ship Services Ltd for term loan of Rs. 1200 Crores granted by ICICI Bank to JAL (v) Mortgage deed dated 24.05.2016 for 25.0040 acres of land (Property No. 5) executed by JIL in favour of IDBI Trustee-ship Services Limited, as additional security against the facility agreement dated 29.08.2012 between Standard Chartered Bank and JAL for Rs.400 crores and other facilities, respectively for Rs.450 crores, Rs.538.16 crores and Rs.81.84 crores as also for working capital facility of Rs.297 crores (vi) Mortgage deed dated 04.03.2016 for 90 acres of land (Property No. 6), executed by JIL in favour of State Bank of India for Short Term Loan Facility to JAL to the tune of Rs.1000 crores.

The Interim Resolution Professional filed an Application under Section 66, 43 and 45 of IBC before NCLT for declaring transactions fraudulent, preferential and undervalued which was allowed by NCLT. An appeal was filed before the NCLAT, which set aside the order of the NCLT and allowed the appeal.

FINDINGS OF THE SUPREME COURT

The Supreme Court decided two major issues in this matter – (i) whether the transaction is a preferential transaction under Section 43 ? (ii) Whether Lenders of JAL could be categorized as Financial Creditors ?

Whether transaction is a preferential transaction under Section 43 ?

The Supreme Court noted that Section 43 occurs in Chapter III of Part II which deals with liquidation process, but it equally applies to Corporate Insolvency Resolution Process.

The Supreme Court while analyzing Section 43 observed that Corporate Debtor is deemed to have given preference at a relevant time if (i) the transaction is of transfer of property or the interest thereof of the Corporate Debtor, for the benefit of the Creditor or surety or guarantor for or on account of antecedent financial debt or operational debt or other liability (ii) Such transfer has the effect of putting such creditor or surety or guarantor in a beneficial position that it would have been in the event of distribution of assets in accordance with Section 53, (iii) preference is given either during the period of two years preceding the insolvency commencement date when beneficiary is a related party or during the period of one year preceding insolvency commencement date when beneficiary is an unrelated party.

The Supreme Court observed that one of the purposes of deeming provisions is to deem what may be or may not be in reality, thereby requiring the subject matter to be real. Any transactions which answer to the descriptions contained in 43 (2) and (4) is presumed to be a preferential transaction at a relevant time even though it may not be so in reality and will incur consequences under Section 44.

Deemed preference may not be offending preference it falls into any or both of the exclusions provided by sub-section 3 i.e. having entered into during ordinary course of business of the Corporate Debtor or transferee or resulting in acquisition of new value of Corporate Debtor.

The Supreme Court observed that for determining whether a transaction falls within ambit of Section 43, following questions have to be asked.

(i) Whether such transfer is for the benefit of a creditor or a surety or a guarantor?

(ii) Whether such transfer is for or on account of an antecedent financial debt or operational debt or other liabilities owed by the Corporate Debtor ?

(iii) Whether such transfer has effect of putting such creditor or surety or guarantor in a beneficial position that it would have been in the event of distribution of assets being made in accordance with Section 53?

(iv) If such transfer had been for the benefit of a related party (other than an employee) as to whether the same was made during the period of two years preceding the insolvency commencement date and if such transfer had been for the benefit of an unrelated party as to whether the same was made during the period of one year preceding the insolvency commencement date ?

(v) Whether such transfer is not an excluded transaction in terms of sub-section (3) of Section 43 ?

The mortgage deeds in question, entered by the corporate debtor JIL to secure the debts of JAL, obviously, amount to creation of security interest to the benefit of JAL.

The Supreme Court observed that JAL is holding company of the Corporate Debtor having equity shareholding of 71.64%. JAL is also operational creditor of JIL for an amount of approximately Rs. 261.77

Crore. JAL itself maintains that it had been providing financial, technical and strategic support to JIL in various ways. It is the assertion that apart from making investment in terms of equity shareholding to the tune of Rs. 995 crores, JAL had pledged its 70,83,56,087 equity shares held in JIL in favour of the lenders of JIL; had also entered into Promoter Support Agreement to the lenders of JIL to meet the DSRA obligation of JIL towards its lenders; and had further extended Bank Guarantees of Rs. 212 crores to meet the DSRA obligation of JIL. These assertions, in our view, put JAL in such capacity that it is a related party to JIL and is a creditor as also surety of JIL. In other words, the corporate debtor JIL owed antecedent financial debts as also operational debts and other liabilities towards JAL.

The Supreme Court concluded that the corporate debtor JIL has given a preference by way of the mortgage transactions in question for the benefit of its related person JAL (who has been the creditor as also surety for JIL) for and on account of antecedent financial debts, operational debts and other liabilities owed to such related person.

The Supreme Court observed that JAL is a related party as look back period will be two years preceding insolvency commencement date which is 09.08.2017 is this case. Transactions starting from 10.08.2015 up to 09.08.2017 will fall under the scanner. It has been contended that most of properties had been already under mortgage and only re-mortgage has been done. The Supreme Court observed that once mortgage is released it ceases to exist. Re-mortgage can only be treated as fresh mortgage. The Supreme Court observed that these mortgages have been created within look back period.

Whether Lenders of JAL could be categorized as Financial Creditors ?

It is the financial creditor who lends finance on term loan or for working capital that enables a Corporate Debtor to set up or operate business. Financial Creditor from the very beginning is involved in assessing the viability of the Corporate Debtor and engage in restructuring of loan as well as reorganization of Corporate Debtor's business when there is financial stress. Thus, Financial Creditor is not only about in terrorem clauses for repayment of dues but also nursing roles too.

The Supreme Court observed that the basic element of Financial Debt is that it ought to be disbursal against the consideration of time value of money. The requirement of existence of debt which is disbursed against the consideration of time value of money remains an essential part even in respect of any of the transactions/dealings stated in sub-clauses (a) to (i) of Section 5 (8) even if it is not necessarily stated therein.

A person only having security interest over assets of the Corporate Debtor, even if falling within description of "secured creditor" by virtue of collateral security extended by Corporate Debtor would stand outside category of Financial Creditor.

The Supreme Court held that debts in question are in the form of third party security given by the Corporate Debtor to secure the loan/advances/facilities obtained by JAL from the respondent lenders. Such debt cannot be a "financial debt" within the meaning of Section 5 (8) of the Code and hence mortgagees are not Financial Creditors of the Corporate Debtor.

PIRAMAL CAPITAL AND HOUSING FINANCE LTD Vs. 63 MOONS TECHNOLOGIES LTD.

The Supreme Court held in Piramal Capital and Housing Finance Ltd. Vs 63Moon Technologies Ltd. (2025INSC421) that the Avoidance Applications under Chapter III and the Applications in respect of Fraudulent trading or Wrongful trading under Chapter VI, operate in different situations.

Case Title : Piramal Capital and Housing Finance Ltd. Vs 63Moon Technologies Ltd. Date of Decision : 01.04.2025 Bench : Bela M. Trivedi, J; Satish Chandra Sharma, J

BRIEF FACTS

Dewan Housing Finance Corporation Limited (DHFC) has availed financial facilities from several lenders. DHFL was alleged of several frauds. RBI superseded the Board of Directors and filed Petition under Section 227 IBC for initiating CIRP. NCLT vide order dated 03.12.2019 admitted the petition and appointed Sh. Mr. R. Subramaniakumar as Administrator. The Administrator received the claims worth Rs.82,247 Crores. The Administrator had appointed M/s. Grant Thornton (GT) as Transaction Auditors for unearthing the transactions under Section 43 to 51 and 66 of IBC. The Administrator, based on the said report of GT, filed eight Applications before the NCLT regarding the Preferential, Undervalued, and Extortionate transactions, and the Applications with regard to the Fraudulent and Wrongful trading. The said Applications are pending for adjudication by the NCLT. The total amount involved in the Avoidance Applications pending before the NCLT is about Rs.4 5,050/- Crores. Resolution Plan of Piramal Capital was approved by an overwhelming majority of the CoC with 93.65 % votes.

The erstwhile Director Kapil Wadhawan filed I.A. No. 2431 of 2020 under Section 60(5) of the Code praying for a direction for RBI to place before CoC the 2nd Settlement proposal for consideration. 63Moon filed IA No. 623/2021 before the NCLT challenging the provision of Resolution Plan which provided that the Section 66 Recoveries will go to the benefit of the SRA. The Administrator filed an I.A. No. 449 of 2021 before the NCLT seeking approval of the Resolution Plan.

The NCLT vide its Order dated 19.05.2021 allowed the I.A. No. 2431 of 2020 filed by the erstwhile Director and directed the Administrator to place the 2nd Settlement Proposal before the CoC for consideration and voting within 10 days. the Administrator, CoC and Piramal filed Appeals under Section 61 of the Code challenging the order dated 19.05.2021. On 25.05.2021, the NCLAT while issuing notice stayed the NCLT order dated 19th May, 2021. Further, the NCLAT vide the order directed the NCLT to decide the I.A. No. 449 of 2021 (for approval of the Resolution Plan). On 06.06.2021, Mr. Kapil Wadhawan filed an I.A. No.1229 of 2021 before the NCLT for consideration of his objections to the RP.

On 07.06.2021, the NCLT passed an order granting its approval to the Plan Approval Application thereby approving the RP. The NCLT vide a separate order, dismissed the I.A. No. 623 of 2021 filed by the 63 Moons. The NCLT refused to interfere with the RP inter alia on the ground that the CoC comprising of 77 financial creditors decided in its commercial wisdom to give away the Section 66 Recoveries to the SRA after a hard bargain in exchange of a lump sum resolution amount of INR 37,250 Crores.

On 15.07.2021, erstwhile Promoter KW preferred Company Appeal No. 539 of 2021 before the NCLAT seeking a prayer to set aside the Resolution Plan.

On 23.07.2021, the NCLAT dismissed the 63 Moons' interim application for a stay on execution of the approved Resolution Plan. Following this, the 63 Moons approached this Court vide Civil Appeal Nos. 4672- 4673 of 2021. On 03.09.2021 - Roopjyot & Ors. filed a Company Appeal No. 750 of 2021 before the NCLAT challenging the Plan Approval Order raising grounds similar to those which were raised by the 63 Moons. This Appeal was also tagged with the Company Appeal No. 455 and 454 of 2021 filed by the 63 Moons. Pertinently, this was the first time that any challenge was raised by Roopjyot & Ors. against the Resolution Plan

On 06.09.2021, the Supreme Court declined to entertain the Civil Appeal Nos. 4672-4673 of 2021 and disposed of the same with a direction to the NCLAT to decide the pending Appeals expeditiously. On 30.09.2 021, the SRA implemented the Resolution Plan and discharged payment to the creditors. As per the Resolution Plan, the SRA - Piramal merged into the CD by way of a scheme of arrangement. Resultantly, the SRA - Piramal ceased to exist with effect from 30.09.2021, and the CD under the name "DHFL" continued as surviving legal entity.

On 27.01.2022, the NCLAT passed the common impugned judgment in the Appeals and held that term in the Resolution Plan that permits the SRA to appropriate recoveries, if any, from avoidance applications filed under Section 66 of the Code ought to be set aside. The Resolution Plan was sent back to the CoC for reconsideration on this aspect.

FINDINGS OF THE SUPREME COURT

The Supreme Court determined the following issues in aforesaid several appeals .

Difference between Avoidance Applications under Chapter III and applications under Section 66

The Supreme Court noted that , the Avoidance Applications under Chapter III and the Applications in respect of Fraudulent trading or Wrongful trading under Chapter VI, operate in different situations. The powers of the Adjudicating Authority in respect of the Avoidance Applications filed under Chapter III and the powers of the Adjudicating Authority in respect of the Applications pertaining to the Fraudulent and Wrongful trading filed under Chapter VI, have also been separately circumscribed.

In the cases of Preferential transactions as contemplated in Section 43, the Resolution Professional may file an Application, when he is of the opinion that the CD, at a relevant time, had given a preference in such transactions, and in such manner as laid down in sub-section (2), to any person as referred to in sub-section (4) of Section 43. The Adjudicating Authority may pass any of the orders as specified in Clauses (a) to (g) of Section 44, in such Application filed by the Resolution Professional under Section 43(1).

Similarly, in the cases of Undervalued transactions as contemplated in Section 45, the Resolution Professional may file an Avoidance Application if he determines that certain transactions were made during the relevant period prescribed under Section 46 which were undervalued. In such applications, the Resolution Professional may pray to declare such transactions as void and to reverse the effect of such transaction in accordance with Chapter III. The Adjudicating Authority may pass any of the orders specified in Clauses (a) to (d) of Section 48 in such

Application filed under Section 45(1). He may also pass orders specified in Clause (i) and (ii) of Section 49, in respect of the Undervalued transactions referred to in Section 45(2).

In case of Extortionate Credit transactions, as contemplated in Section 50, the Resolution Professional may file an Avoidance Application, where the CD had been a party to an Extortionate Credit transaction involving the receipt of financial or operational debt during the period within two years preceding the insolvency commencement date, and where the terms of such transactions required exorbitant payments to be made by the CD. In case of such Extortionate Credit transactions, the Adjudicating Authority may pass any of the orders specified in Clause (a) to (e) of Section 51. It is pertinent to note that in all these types of Avoidance Applications falling under Chapter III, the transactions in question, the properties involved and the persons with whom such transactions were made, could be ascertained by the Adjudicating Authority and therefore it is empowered to pass orders to avoid or set aside such transactions, under Sections 44, 48, 49 and 51, as the case may be.

However, in cases of "Fraudulent or Wrongful trading" in respect of the business of the CD as contemplated in Section 66, the properties and the persons involved may or may not be ascertainable and therefore the Adjudicating Authority is not empowered to pass orders to avoid or set aside such transactions, but is empowered to pass orders to the effect that any persons, who were knowingly parties to the carrying on of business in such manner, shall be liable to make such contributions to the assets of the CD, as it may deem fit. The Adjudicating Authority in such applications may also direct that the Director of the CD shall be liable to make such contribution to the assets of the CD as it may deem fit, as contemplated in Section 66(2). In case of Fraudulent trading or Wrongful trading, it would be a matter of inquiry to be made by the Adjudicating Authority as to whether the business of CD was carried on with intent to defraud creditors of the CD or was carried on for any fraudulent purpose.

In view of the above, the Applications filed in respect of "Fraudulent and Wrongful trading" carried on by the CD, could not be termed as "Avoidance Applications" used for the Applications filed under Sections 43, 45 and 50 to avoid or set aside the Preferential, Undervalued or Extortionate transactions, as the case may be. There is a clear demarcation of powers of the Adjudicating Authority to pass orders in the Avoidance Applications filed by the Resolution Professional under Section 43, 45 and 50 falling under Chapter III and the Applications filed by the Resolution Professional in respect of the Fraudulent and Wrongful trading of the Corporate Debtor, under Section 66 falling under Chapter VI of the

IBC. If the Resolution Professional has filed common applications under Sections 43, 45, 50 and also under Section 66, the Adjudicating Authority shall have to distinguish the same and decide as to which provision would be attracted to which of the Applications, and then shall exercise the powers and pass the orders in terms of the provisions of IBC.

The Supreme Court observed that having regard to the Fraudulent trading and Wrongful trading allegedly made by the DHFL, any guess work done by the RAs would have been a wild guess due to the uncertainties in recovery of the amount involved in such Fraudulent and Wrongful trading. The value of INR 1 being notional and the CoC, having considered the fact that the potential recoveries from the Section 66 Applications was very uncertain, had taken conscious decision in accepting the said clause in the Resolution Plan submitted by the SRA. The relevant Clause 2.13.2 of Resolution Plan provided that any positive monetary recovery received by the company (SRA) as a result of the orders passed in relation to avoidance transactions shall be distributed, net of costs and expenses (including taxes), to the Financial Creditors pro rata to the extent the financial debt owed provided that the CoC may in its discretion adopt a different manner of distribution. Therefore, while ascribing a notional value of INR 1 to the Applications under Section 66, the SRA had agreed for the distribution of the recoveries that may be made under the Avoidance Applications filed under Sections 43, 45, 47, 49 and 50 for the benefit of the CoC.

The Supreme Court observed that the SRA had raised its offer to the extent of Rs.37,250 crores, which had factored the potential recoveries from Section 66 Applications. Thus, the RP approved by the CoC was an outcome of the commercial bargain struck between the SRA and the CoC after several rounds of negotiations and deliberations. The said plan approved by the CoC was also further approved by the NCLT under Section 31(1) of IBC. In absence of any perversity, that was palpable on the face of the approved RP, and the CoC having taken a firm commercial decision with regard to the impugned clause of RP by voting overwhelmingly in favour of the RP, the NCLAT ought not to have interfered with the said clause of RP approved by the CoC and the NCLT.

Relying on Essar Steel and Ghanshyam Mishra, the Supreme Court observed that the NCLAT has clearly transgressed its jurisdiction under Section 61 IBC, by interfering with the clause pertaining to the treatment to the recoveries from the Fraudulent and Wrongful trading under Section 66.

Whether the Resolution Plan violated the provisions of RBI Act or NHB Act ?

Resolution Plan has provided for - i) FD Holders having an admitted claim of upto INR 2 lakhs were to be repaid their entire deposit amount; and (ii) FD Holders having an admitted claim of more than INR 2 lakhs would receive an amount equivalent to liquidation value of security created for the benefit of the Depositors for the additional aggregate claim above INR 2 lakhs.

Some of the FD Holders challenged the Resolution Plan on the ground that the treatment to the FD Holders violated their rights under the RBI Act and NHB Act to receive full payment of their deposits. The Supreme Court observed that none of the said provisions mandates full payment of deposits or confers any right upon the depositors to have full payment of such deposits. There is also nothing on record to suggest that any authorized officer under the NHB Act or the CLB under the RBI Act has passed any order to make full payment of deposits to the Appellants. Hence, it could not be said, by any stretch of the imagination, that the RP in question, providing for the Distribution mechanism, was contrary to any of the provisions of the RBI Act or of the NHB Act.

Whether erstwhile directors should have been allowed to participate in CIRP ?

The Supreme Court observed that erstwhile directors having deemed to have vacated their offices on the supersession of the Board of Directors under the RBI Act, could not have claimed any right to attend the meetings of CoC or to participate in the CIRP proceedings initiated under the IBC, which right otherwise would have been available to the Directors suspended under the IBC. In absence of any specific provision in the IBC or the Regulations 2016, they, as the members of the superseded Board of Directors, could not have made any claim to have a copy of proposed Resolution Plans submitted by the PRAs during the CIRP proceedings. Nonetheless, pertinently the RP after having been approved by the NCLT under Section 31 of IBC, would become a "Public Document" within the meaning of Section 74 of the Indian Evidence Act, and therefore, they would be entitled to get, at the most, a certified copy of the approved RP.

LIMITATION IN APPEAL

NATIONAL SPOT EXCHANGE LTD Vs. MR. ANIL KOHLI

The Supreme Court in National Spot Exchange Ltd Vs. Mr. Anil Kohli (2021) 7 SCR 2024 held that in view of the statutory scheme under Section 61(2) of the IBC, a delay beyond the additional period of 15 days is uncondonable and cannot be condoned even in exercise of the powers under Article 142 of the Constitution of India.

Case Title : National Spot Exchange Ltd Vs. Mr. Anil Kohli Date of Decision : 15.05.2025 Bench: Bela M. Trivedi, J, Satish Chandra Sharma, J

FACTS OF THE CASE

CIRP proceedings were initiated against the Dunar Foods Limited (Corporate Debtor) and IRP was appointed. The Appellant filed a claim of Rs. 673.85 Crore before the IRP, which was rejected by the IRP on the ground that there was no privity of contract between the appellant and the corporate debtor and there is no letter of guarantee issued by the Corporate Debtor in favour of the appellant. The rejection was challenged before the NCLT which was rejected by NCLT vide order dated 06.03.2019.

An appeal was filed before the NCLAT with delay of 44 days beyond maximum permissible 45 days (30 days + 15 days). The NCLAT held that it does not have jurisdiction to condone delay beyond 15 days and thereby the appeal is barred by limitation.

Aggrieved thereby, an Appeal was filed before the Supreme Court.

FINDINGS OF THE SUPREME COURT

Section 61 (2) provides limitation period of 30 days for filing appeal before NCLAT. As per proviso to Section 61 (2) of the Code, the Appellate

Tribunal may allow an appeal to be filed after expiry of the said period of 30 days if it is satisfied that there was sufficient cause for not filing the appeal, but such period shall not exceed 15 days from period of 30 days, as contemplated under Section 61 (2) of the Code.

The Court noted that Application for certified copy was filed on 8.4.2019 after delay of 34 days, which is beyond prescribed period of limitation. The certified copy was received on 11.04.2019 and appeal was preferred on 24.06.2019 after del44 days. As the Appellate Tribunal can condone the delay up to further period of 15 days only, the Appellate Tribunal refused to condone the delay which was beyond 15 days after expiry of initial 30 days.

The Supreme Court relied on Union of India Vs Popular Constructions Co. (2001) 8 SCC 470 wherein it was held that Section 34 of Arbitration and Conciliation Act, 1996 provides a limitation which is different from limitation prescribed under the Limitation Act. Section 5 of the Limitation Act will not be applicable as the Legislature has prescribed a special limitation for the purposes of Appeal as provided under Section 34 of the Arbitration and Conciliation Act.

The Supreme Court also relied on New India Assurance Company Ltd Vs. Hilli Multipurpose Cold Storage Private Ltd. (2020) 5 SCC 757 wherein it was held that the District Forum has no jurisdiction and/or power to extend the time of filing of response to the complaint beyond the period of 15 days in addition to 30 days as envisaged under Section 13 (2) (a) of the Consumer Protection Act.

The Supreme Court held unless Parliament has carved out an exception by provision of law, the period of limitation has to be given effect to.

9. It is true that in a given case there may arise a situation where the applicant/appellant may not be in a position to file the appeal even within a statutory period of Limitation prescribed under the Act and within the extended maximum period of appeal which could be condoned owing to genuineness viz. illness, accident etc. However, under the statute, the Parliament has not carved out any exception of such a situation. Therefore, in a given case, it may cause hardship, however unless Parliament has carved out any exception by a provision of law, the period of limitation has to be given effect to. Such powers are only with the Parliament and the Legislature. The Courts have no jurisdiction and/or authority to carve out any exception. If the Courts carve out an exception, it would amount to legislate which would in turn might be inserting the provision to the Statute, which is not permissible.

The Supreme Court relied on several judgments including Rohitash Kumar Vs. Om Prakash Sharma (2013) 11 SCC 451 wherein it was held that law overrides equitable considerations.

The Supreme Court also refused to condone the delay invoking its powers under Article 142 of the Constitution of India. The Supreme Court observed that what cannot be done directly considering the statutory provisions cannot be done indirectly while exercising the powers under Article 142 of the Constitution of India.

Accordingly, the appeal was dismissed by the Supreme Court.

V NAGARAJAN Vs. SKS ISPAT AND POWER LTD

The Supreme Court in V Nagarajan Vs SKS Ispat and Power Ltd (2022) 2 SCC 244 held that Limitation will start running from the date of pronouncement of order by the NCLT. The time taken in preparation of certified copy after making an application for certified copy has to be excluded.

Case Title : V Nagarajan Vs SKS Ispat and Power Ltd (2022) 2 SCC 244 Date of Decision : 22.10.2021 Bench : Dr. Dhananjaya Y. Chandrachud, J; Vikram Nath, J, B. V. Nagarathna, J

FACTS OF THE CASE

CIRP was initiated in the matter of Cethar Ltd. (Corporate Debtor) and the Appellant was appointed as IRP. CIRP was not successful as such Liquidation Order was passed and the Appellant was appointed as Liquidator. Respondent No. 10 allegedly, at behest of Respondent No. 1, sought to invoke certain bank guarantees issued by the Corporate Debtor for its failure to perform its engineering services. The Appellant filed miscellaneous application to resist the invocation of the performance guarantees until the liquidation proceedings are concluded.

The NCLT refused to grant any injunction. Order was pronounced in open court on 31st December, 2019. The order was uploaded on the NCLT website only on 12th March, 2020. There was an error in name of Judicial Member as such corrected order was uploaded on 20th march, 2020.

The Appellant was waiting for free certified copy. The Appeal before the NCLAT was filed on 8th June, 2020 along with an application for exemption from filing certified copy of the order as it had not been issued.

The NCLAT vide its order dated 13.07.2020 dismissed the Appeal on the ground that limitation period of thirty days extendable by fifteen days has already expired.

An appeal against the same was filed before the Supreme Court.

FINDINGS OF THE SUPREME COURT

The Court noted that IBC is a complete code and it has overriding effect under Section 238. Limitation Act is applicable to the Code by virtue of Section 238 A. Section 29 (2) of the Limitation Act provides that period of limitation prescribed under the special or local law shall be deemed to be the period prescribed for the purposes of Section 3 of the Limitation Act.

The Supreme Court observed that Section 61 (2) provides for a limitation period of thirty days which can be extended by a maximum of fifteen days on the demonstration of sufficient cause of delay.

The Court observed that a notable difference between Section 421 (3) of the Companies Act and Section 61 (2) of IBC is absence of the words "from the date on which a copy of the order of the Tribunal is made available to the person aggrieved". The absence of these words are not mere omissions.

Proceedings under IBC is timebound. Reading in the requirement of an "order being made available" under a general enactment (Companies Act) would do violence to the special provisions enacted under IBC where timing is critical for the workability of the mechanism, health of the economy, recovery rate of lenders and valuation of the Corporate Debtor. An appeal, if considered necessary, is expected to be filed without awaiting free copy which may be received at indefinite stage.

Rule 22 (2) of the NCLAT Rules mandates that an appeal has to be filed with a certified copy of impugned order.

Section 12 of Limitation Act provides that a person wishing to file an appeal is expected to file an application for a certified copy before expiry of the limitation period, upon which time requisite for obtaining a certified copy has to be excluded. Time taken in preparation of certified copy before making of application cannot be excluded.

The Court observed that the law required the Appellant to apply for a certified copy immediately after the order was pronounced on 31 December 2019. If the Appellant's contention that the correct order was not available until 20 March 2020 were accepted, the Appellant would not have received the certified copy and would have been entitled to the benefit of the Supreme Court's suo motu orders extending the period of limitation, which came into effect on 15 March 2020. However, since the Appellant did not apply for a certified copy, the period of limitation had expired much before the Supreme Court's suo motu directions issued in the light of the COVID-19 pandemic came into force. Consequently, the appeal was barred by limitation.

SANKET KUMAR AGARWAL Vs. APG LOGISTICS PVT. LTD.

The Supreme Court in Sanket Kumar Aggarwal & Anr Vs. APG Logistics Pvt. Ltd. (Civil Appeal No. 748/2023) has held that the time taken in preparation of certified copies and the day on which order is pronounced have to be excluded from computing period of limitation in an appeal from the National Company Law Tribunal (NCLT) to the National Company Law Appellate Tribunal (NCLAT).

Case Title : Sanket Kumar Agarwal & Anr Vs. APG Logistics Pvt. Ltd. Date of Decision : 01.05.2023 Bench : Dr. Dhananjaya Y. Chandrachud, J; Vikram Nath, J; B. V. Nagarathna, J

FACTS OF THE CASE

The Appellant has filed an application under Section 7 IBC for initiation of CIRP, which was dismissed by the National on 26th August, 2022. The Appellant filed an application for certified copy on 2nd September, 2022 which was received by the Registry of the NCLT on 5th September. On 15th September, the order was uploaded on the website of NCLT and certified copy was supplied to the Appellant. The Appellant filed an Appeal before the NCLAT on 10th October, 2022 in e-filing mode alongwith Interlocutory Application seeking condonation of 5 days. A physical copy of the appeal was filed with NCLAT on 31st October.

The NCLAT dismissed the Appeal for being barred by Limitation. The NCLAT observed that 30 days had expired on 24.09.2022. If an `Appellate Tribunal' (`NCLA T'), is satisfied on `sufficient cause', being shown to its `subjective satisfaction', in regard to the preferring of an `Appeal' (after the `Expiry of 30 days period'), then, `such period, shall not exceed 15 days', as per Section 61 (2) of the Code. The `completion of 45 days' (30 + 15 days), was on 09.10.2022. In effect, the maximum 45 days being the outer limit (30 + 15 = 45 days), beyond which, the `Appellate Tribunal' (`NCLAT), is `bereft' of any power, to `condone the delay. '

THE FINDINGS OF THE SUPREME COURT

The Supreme Court found that the appeal has been filed within limitation.

The Supreme Court held that Section 238 A of IBC makes applicable provision of Limitation Act, 1963 on proceedings before NCLT and NCLAT.

Rule 3 of the NCLAT rules, 2016 stipulates that for computation of time period the day from which the said period has to be reckoned has to be excluded. This is in line with Section 12 (1) of the Limitation Act, 1963 which states that in computing the period of limitation for any suit, appeal or application, the day from which such period is to be reckoned, shall be excluded.

Further Rule 22 requires an appeal to the NCLAT to be filed accompanied with certified copy. Rule 103 of NCLAT Rules allows filing of Appeal through electronic mode.

The Supreme Court found that of the day of order is excluded the Appeal has been filed on 45th day rather than 46th day.

Furthermore, the Supreme Court held that in terms of Section 12(2) of the Limitation Act 1963, the time requisite for obtaining a certified copy of the order appealed from has to be excluded while computing the period of limitation. As such period of 10 days from 5th September, 2022 and 15th September, 2022 taken for preparation of certified copy should have been excluded.

The Supreme Court also observed that the Union government in its rule making capacity and the administrative heads of tribunals must ensure a seamless transition to working in the electronic mode.

TATA STEEL LTD. VS RAJ KUMAR BANERJEE & ORS

The Supreme Court held in Tata Steel Ltd. Vs. Raj Kumar Banerjee (2025INSC639) that time is of the essence in statutory appeals, and the prescribed limitation period must be strictly adhered to.

Case Title : Tata Steel Ltd. Vs. Raj Kumar Banerjee Date of Decision : 07.05.2025 Bench : J. B. Pardiwala, J; R. Mahadevan, J

FACTS OF THE CASE

Respondent No. 1 filed an appeal before the NCLAT under Section 61 IBC to set aside the order dated 07.04.2022 passed by the Adjudicating Authority approving the Resolution Plan. An application for condonation of delay of 15 days was also filed. The Appellant filed e-appeal on 23.05.2022 and physical filing was done on 24.05.2022. NCLAT allowed the appeal. The Appellant approached the Supreme Court against the order of NCLAT.

The Supreme Court considered two issues :

(i) Whether the appeal filed by Respondent No. 1 was within the prescribed limitation period of 30 days, along with the additional condonable period of 15 days as provided under section 61(2) IBC ?

(ii) If not, whether the NCLAT has the power to condone the delay beyond the said prescribed and condonable period under the IBC ?

FINDINGS OF THE SUPREME COURT

(i) Whether the appeal filed by Respondent No. 1 was within the prescribed limitation period of 30 days, along with the additional condonable period of 15 days as provided under section 61(2) IBC ?

The Supreme Court noted that the total permissible period for filing an appeal under Section 61 (2) IBC is 45 days- comprising 30 days as prescribed period and an additional 15 days that may be condoned upon showing sufficient cause.

The Respondent No. 1 claimed that although the Resolution Plan was approved by the NCLT on 07.04.2022, he came to know about the order on 08.04.2022. 30 days period was to expire on 08.05.2022 however 08.05.2022 being Sunday, the prescribed period was extended to next working day on 09.05.2022. Thereafter, the additional grace period of 15 days expired on 24.05.2022. E-filing was done on 23.05.2022 and physical filing was done on 24.05.2022 as such it was claimed by the Respondent No. 1 that the Appeal was filed within 45 days.

The Supreme Court observed that benefit of exclusion of period during which the court is closed shall be available when the application is filed within "prescribed period of limitation" and shall not be available in respect of period extendable by court in exercise of its discretion.

The Supreme Court relying on Rajendra Vs. Gonugunta Madhusudan Rao noted that where judgment is pronounced in open court, the limitation starts running from that very day.

The Supreme Court observed that limitation started running on 07 .04.2022. 30 days were completed on 07.05.2022, which fell on the first working Saturday. Even otherwise, the benefit of section 4 of the Limitation Act, 1963 cannot be granted, as Respondent No. 1 filed the appeal beyond not only the prescribed period of 30 days but also the condonable period of 15 days, i.e., on 24.05.2022. In view of the same reason, Rule 3 of the NCLAT Rules, 2016 has also no application to the facts of the present case.

The Supreme Court concluded that the Appeal has been filed beyond 45 days.

(ii) If not, whether the NCLAT has the power to condone the delay beyond the said prescribed and condonable period under the IBC ?

The Supreme Court noted that Section 61 (2) clearly limits the NCLAT's jurisdiction to condone delay only up to 15 days beyond the initial 30-days period. Where a statute expressly limits the period within which delay may be condoned, an Appellate Tribunal cannot exceed that limit. The NCLAT being a creature of statute, operates strictly within the powers conferred upon it. Unlike a civil suit, it lacks inherent jurisdiction to extend time on equitable grounds.

The Supreme Court observed that time is of the essence in statutory appeals, and the prescribed limitation period must be strictly adhered to. Even a delay of a single day is fatal if the statute does not provide for its condonation. The order of NCLAT was set aside.

A. RAJENDRA VS GONUGUNTA MADHUSUDHAN RAO & ORS

The Supreme Court reiterated in A. Rajendra Vs Gonugunta Madhusudan Rao (2025 INSC 447) that a litigant must file an appeal under Section 61(2) within 30 days, which may be extended by a further period of 15 days upon showing sufficient cause, and no more

Case Title : A. Rajendra Vs Gonugunta Madhusudan Rao
Date of Decision : 04.04.2025
Bench : Abhay S. Oka, J; Ahsanuddin Amanullah, J; Augustine George Masih

BRIEF FACTS

The Appellant has filed an application before the NCLT seeking direction to place his Resolution Plan for consideration before CoC and stay on voting results on Resolution Plan, which was dismissed by the NCLT on 20.07.2023 of which free certified copy was made available on 01.08.2023. Respondent has filed application for approval of Resolution Plan, which was also approved on 20.07.2023. The Appellants filed appeals before the NCLAT against both orders on 28th August, 2023. First Appeal was filed with free certified copy and in the second appeal, application for exemption from filing certified copy was filed. Initially no applications for condonation of delay were filed but they were filed after objections were raised by Respondents. The appeals were dismissed on ground of limitation.

FINDINGS OF THE SUPREME COURT

The Supreme Court observed that statutory time limit of 30 days within which an appeal can be preferred has been provided for in sub-section (2) of Section 61 of IBC. Proviso thereto allows an additional period of 15 days to file an appeal only on the satisfaction of the NCLAT that there was sufficient cause for not filing the appeal earlier within the initial period of

30 days. The restrictions governing extension is worded in such a manner that the provisions have to be strictly followed. The first aspect is that the period is extendable by 15 days and not beyond that. The limit, therefore, has been prescribed as regards the period within which the discretion has to be exercised by the NCLAT. That apart, this period cannot be claimed as a matter of right for extension of the limitation rather it is subject to the satisfaction of the NCLAT upon having shown sufficient cause. The discretion, therefore, has further been circumscribed and not merely left at the unfettered discretion of the NCLAT. The cumulative reading of the proviso would therefore entail that the extension of period so provided for has to be strictly construed and has not to be exercised in a liberal manner which highlights the legislative intent which has to be given effect to.

The Supreme Court noted that the event which triggers limitation to commence is the date of pronouncement of the Order and in case of non-pronouncement of the Order when the hearing concludes, the date on which the Order is pronounced or uploaded on the website. However, where the judgment was pronounced in open Court, the period of limitation starts running from that very day. The appellant is however entitled to seek relief under Section 12(2) of the Limitation Act for excluding the period during which the certified copy was under preparation on an application preferred by that party.

The Supreme Court held that, in the absence of the appellant having applied for a certified copy of the impugned orders dated 20 July 2023, and in view of Rule 22 of the NCLAT Rules mandating that an appeal be accompanied by a certified copy, the appeals were rightly dismissed . The Supreme Court affirmed the decision of NCLAT and dismissed the appeal.

CIRP COST

ALOK KAUSHIK VS BHUVANESHWARI RAMANATHAN

The Supreme Court in Alok Kaushik Vs Bhuvaneshwari Ramanathan AIR (2021) SC 2216 held that the NCLT does not become *functus officio* if CIRP is set aside. NCLT has jurisdiction under Section 60 (5) to determine amount payable to the Registered Valuer even after CIRP has been set aside.

Case Title : Alok Kaushik Vs Bhuvaneshwari Ramanathan Date of decision : 15.03.2021 Bench : Dr. Dhananjaya Y. Chandrachud, J; M. R. Shah, J

FACTS OF THE CASE

The National Company Law Tribunal initiated insolvency proceedings in the matter of Kavveri Telecom Infrastructure Ltd. The NCLT vide order dated 21st March, 2019 appointed the Respondent as Resolution Professional. The Appellant was appointed as the valuer of Plant and Machinery. The appointment of the valuer was ratified by the Committee of Creditors. The Appellant conducted valuation work for eighty four sites and visited forty sites. Several outstation meetings were also conducted between the appellant and the first Respondent.

National Company Law Appellate Tribunal set aside the initiation of CIRP vide order dated 18th December, 2019.

In light of the order of the NCLAT, the appointment of the Appellant was cancelled. On request of the First Respondent , the Appellant reduced the fee by 25%. However, the First Respondent informed the Appellant that the fee agreed cannot be paid and paid a sum of Rs. 50,000/-

The Appellant filed an Application before NCLT under Section 60 (5) of the Insolvency and Bankruptcy Code, 2016 challenging the non-payment of fee. NCLT dismissed the Application by stating that it has become functus officio. The Appellant filed an appeal before the NCLAT which was also dismissed.

FINDINGS OF THE SUPREME COURT

The Supreme Court noted that "Insolvency Resolution Costs" has been defined under Section 5 (13) of the Code. Regulation 31 of IRP regulations further defines Insolvency Resolution Process Costs. Clause (c) of Regulation 31 includes expenses incurred on or by the IRP to the extent ratified under Regulation 33. Regulation 33 deals with costs of Interim Resolution Professional. Regulation 34 deals with Resolution Professional Costs.

The Supreme Court observed that the view taken by the NCLT is incorrect that it has become functus officio after setting aside of CIRP. The Supreme Court relied on Gujarat Urja Vikas Nigam Ltd Vs. Amit Gupta & Ors (2021) SCC Online SC 194 wherein it has been held that NCLT has jurisdiction to adjudicate disputes, which arise solely from or which relate to the insolvency of the Corporate Debtor.

The claim of the Appellant as registered valuer related to the period when he was discharging function as a registered valuer appointed in course of the CIRP. NCLT would have been justified in exercising its jurisdiction under Section 60 (5) of the IBC.

The Supreme Court exercised jurisdiction under Article 142 and directed that in such situations the NCLT will be empowered under Section 60 (5) to make a determination.

That Supreme Court observed that availability of grievance redressal mechanism against an insolvency professional does not divest the NCLT of its jurisdiction under Section 60(5) (c) to consider the amount payable to the appellant. The purpose of grievance redressal mechanism is to penalize errant conduct of the Insolvency Professional and not to determine claims of other professionals which form part of the CIRP Cost.

The Supreme Court allowed the appeal and remanded the matter to the NCLT for determining claim of the Appellant.

LIQUIDATION

SUNIL KUMAR JAIN Vs. SUNDARESH BHATT

The Supreme Court in Sunil Kumar Jain Vs Sundaresh Bhatt (2022) SCC OnLine SC 467 held that workmen's/employees' wages earned during Corporate Insolvency Resolution Process (CIRP) form part of CIRP Cost. The Supreme Court also held that all sums due to any workman or employee from the Provident Fund, Pension Fund and Gratuity Fund will be outside the ambit of Liquidation Estate under Section 36 (4) of the Insolvency and Bankruptcy Code, 2016.

Case Title : Sunil Kumar Jain Vs Sundaresh Bhatt Date of Decision : 19.04.2022 Bench : M. R. Shah, J; Aniruddha Bose, J

FACTS OF THE CASE

The Corporate Debtor was a ship building yard having manufacturing facility at Surat Yard and Dahej Yard in Gujarat. Prior to initiation of CIRP the Corporate Debtor had 562 workmen and 93 employees at Dahej ; and 291 workmen and 99 employees at Surat and 101 employees at Mumbai Head Office.

Corporate Insolvency Resolution Process was initiated in respect of the Corporate Debtor vide order dated 01.08.2017 passed by NCLT. 272 employees and workmen employed at Mumbai and Dahej filed application before the NCLT seeking direction to the Resolution Professional to make payment to the employees and the workmen. The NCLT directed the Resolution Professional to deposit Rs. 2,75,00,000/- subject to the outcome of the Application.

CIRP was not successful as such Liquidation Order was passed. The NCLT also disposed of the Application seeking direction to pay the workmen/employees without giving any relief. Appeal was filed before the NCLAT which refused to interfere in the order passed by the NCLT but directed the workmen/employees to file their claims.

FINDINGS OF THE SUPREME COURT

The Supreme Court observed that protection for the dues of workmen/employees have been given under Companies Act, 1956 as well as Companies Act, 2013.

Under IBC also Workmen's dues have been protected and Section 36 (4) excludes Provident Fund, Gratuity Fund and Pension Fund from Liquidation Estate.

Section 5 (13) provides that Insolvency Resolution Process Costs includes cost incurred by the Resolution Professional in running the business of the Corporate Debtor as a going concern. Section 20 imposes duty on the Resolution Professional to run the Corporate Debtor as a going concern. Wages and salaries of workmen/employee who worked during Corporate Insolvency Resolution Process will be part of the CIRP Cost and in case of Liquidation payable at first priority under Section 53 (1) (a) of the Code. Wages and salaries of only those workmen/employees who actually worked during CIRP can be included in the CIRP Costs. All other dues of Workmen/employees will be governed by Section 53 (1) (b) and Section 53 (1) (c).

The Supreme Court observed that in the instant case the Liquidator has to firstly determine whether the Corporate Debtor was a going concern and secondly whether a workman/employee has worked during Corporate Insolvency Resolution Process.

The Supreme Court observed that Section 36 (4) (iii) excludes all sums due to any workman or employee from the Provident Fund, Pension Fund and Gratuity Fund from the ambit of Liquidation Estate assets. Section 53 (1) will not be applicable to such assets. The Liquidator will have no claim over such assets. Workmen/employees will be entitled to such funds. They are not to be used for recovery.

The Supreme Court directed the appellants to file claims proving that Corporate Debtor was a going concern and they had worked during Corporate Insolvency Resolution Process. The Supreme Court also directed the Liquidator to adjudicate such claims in accordance with law. If it is found that IRP/RP managed the Corporate Debtor as going concern and the concerned workman/employee has worked during CIRP, their wages and salary will be included in CIRP cost and paid in priority under Section 53 (1) (a) of the Insolvency and Bankruptcy Code, 2016.

MOSER BAER KARAMCHARI UNION Vs. UNION OF INDIA

In another constitutional challenge to Insolvency and Bankruptcy Code, 2016, the Supreme Court in Moser Baer Karamchari Union vs Union of India and ORs (2023)5SCC720 held that waterfall distribution to stakeholders under Section 53 is valid.

Case Title : Moser Baer Karamchari Union vs Union of India and Ors Date of Decision : 02.05.2023 Bench : M. R. Shah, J; Sanjiv Khanna

FACTS OF THE CASE

The Writ Petition was filed for declaring Clause 19 (a) of Eleventh Schedule of Insolvency and Bankruptcy code, 2016 and Section 327 (7) of the Companies Act, 2013 as unconstitutional.

Clause 19(a) of the Eleventh Schedule of the IBC inserts sub-section (7) in Section 327 of the Companies Act, 2013, which puts statutory bar on the application of Sections 326 and 327 of the Companies Act, 2013, to the liquidation proceedings under the IBC.

Section 326 and Section 327 of the Companies Act deal with preferential payments to certain creditors in winding-up process. Section 271 of the Companies Act deals with situations wherein winding up process of a company can be initiated. One of the grounds of initiating winding up petition under Section 271 was inability of pay debts. In such cases distribution to creditors has to be made as per Section 326 and Section 327. After the enactment of the Insolvency and Bankruptcy Code, 2016, the ground of inability to pay debts was deleted from Section 271 of the Companies Act, 2013. On the other hand distribution under liquidation proceedings under Insolvency and Bankruptcy Code, 2016 has to be made as per Section 53 of the Code.

Distribution to workmen distribution under Section 326 & 327 of the Companies Act, 1956 is to some extent different in comparison to Section 53 of the Insolvency and Bankruptcy Code, 2016. Under the Insolvency and Bankruptcy Code, workmen dues for 24 months preceding Liquidation Commencement Date along with Secured Creditor have been given highest priority in distribution waterfall after payment of CIRP and Liquidation Cost.

Under Section 326 of the Companies Act, workmen dues has been the highest priority along with secured creditors but there is no limit of only 24 months. Further dues of workmen on account of wages, salary and accrued holidays have to be paid within a period of 30 days of sale of assets.

The Petitioners have challenged this different distribution regime before the Hon'ble Supreme Court.

FINDINGS OF THE SUPREME COURT

The Supreme Court did not find any merit in the Writ Petition and dismissed the same. The Supreme Court observed that the objectives of Companies Act and Insolvency and Bankruptcy Code are very different. The two enactments deal with two distinct situations and in our opinion, they cannot be equated when we examine whether there is discrimination or violation of Article 14 of the Constitution of India. Relevant para is as under:

As elucidated above, the Companies Act, 2013 does not deal with insolvency and bankruptcy when the companies are unable to pay their debts or the aspects relating to the revival and rehabilitation of the companies and their winding up if revival and rehabilitation is not possible. In principle, it cannot be doubted that the cases of revival or winding up of the company on the ground of insolvency and inability to pay debts are different from cases where companies are wound up under Section 271 of the Companies Act 2013. The two situations are not identical. Under Section 271 of the Companies Act, 2013, even a running and financially sound company can also be wound up for the reasons in clauses (a) to (e). The reasons and grounds for winding up under Section 271 of the Companies Act, 2013 are vastly different from the reasons and grounds for the revival and rehabilitation scheme as envisaged under the Code. The two enactments deal with two distinct situations and in our opinion, they cannot be equated when we examine whether there is discrimination or violation of Article 14 of the Constitution of India. For the revival and rehabilitation of the companies, certain sacrifices are required from all quarters, including the workmen. In case of insolvent companies, for the sake of survival and regeneration, everyone, including the secured creditors and the Central and State Government, are required to make sacrifices. The workmen also have a stake and benefit from the revival of the company, and therefore unless it is found that the sacrifices envisaged for the workmen, which certainly form a separate class, are onerous and burdensome so as to be manifestly unjust and arbitrary, we will not set aside the legislation, solely on the ground that some or marginal sacrifice is to be made by the workers. We would also reject the argument that to find out whether there was a violation of Article 14 of the Constitution of India or whether the right to life under Article 21 Constitution of India was infringed, we must word by word examine the waterfall mechanism envisaged under the Companies Act, 2013, where the company is wound up in terms of grounds (a) to (e) of Section 271 of the Companies Act, 2013; and the rights of the workmen when the insolvent company is sought to be revived, rehabilitated or wound up under the Code. The grounds and situations in the context of the objective and purpose of the two enactments are entirely different.

The Supreme Court noted that interest of workmen has been reasonably protected under the IBC. After the costs of Insolvency Resolution Process and Liquidation, secured creditors share the highest priority along with a defined period of dues of the workmen. Section 36(4)(a)(iii) of the IBC now excludes all sums due to any workman or employee from the Provident Fund, Pension Fund and Gratuity Fund from being included in the liquidation estate assets. Relevant para is as under:

17.The Code is based on the organic evolution of law and is a product of an extensive consultative process to meet the requirements of the Code governing liquidation. It introduced a comprehensive and time-bound framework to maximise the value of assets of all persons and balance the interest of the stakeholders. The guiding principle for the Code in setting the priority of payments in liquidation was to bring the practices in India in line with global practices. In the waterfall mechanism, after the costs of the insolvency resolution process and liquidation, secured creditors share the highest priority along with a defined period of dues of the workmen. The unpaid dues of the workmen are adequately and significantly protected in line with the objectives sought to be achieved by the Code and in terms of the waterfall mechanism prescribed by Section 53 of the Code. In either case of relinquishment or non-relinquishment of the security by the secured creditor, the interests of workmen are protected under the Code. In fact, the secured creditors are taking significant hair-cut and workmen are being compensated on an equitable basis in a just and proper manner as per Section 53 of the Code. The Code balances the rights of the secured creditors, who are financial institutions in which the general public has invested money, and also ensures that the economic activity and revival of a viable company is not hindered because it has suffered or fallen into a financial crisis. The Code focuses on bringing additional gains to both the economy and the exchequer through efficiency enhancement and consequent greater value capture. In economic matters, a wider latitude is given to the lawmaker and the Court allows for experimentation in such legislations based on practical experiences and other problems seen by the law-makers. In a challenge to such legislation, the Court does not adopt a doctrinaire approach. Some sacrifices have to be always made for the greater good, and unless such sacrifices are prima facie apparent and ex facie harsh and inequitable as to classify as manifestly arbitrary, these would be interfered with by the court.

PASCHIMANCHAL VIDYUT VITARAN NIGAM LTD VS RAMAN ISPAT PVT LTD

The Supreme Court in Paschimanchal Vidyut Vitaran Nigam Ltd Vs. Raman Ispat Private Ltd. (2023)10SCC60 observed that the separate and distinct treatment of amounts payable to Secured creditors on the one hand, and dues payable to the government on the other clearly signifies Parliament's intention to treat the latter differently.

Case Title : Paschimanchal Vidyut Vitaran Nigam Ltd Vs. Raman Ispat Private Ltd. Date of Decision : 17.07.2023 Bench : S. Ravindra Bhat, J; Dipankar Dutta, J

FACTS OF THE CASE

Paschimanchal Vidyut Vitaran Nigam Ltd (PVVNL) had supplied electricity to the Corporate Debtor. There were outstanding dues of Rs.4 ,32,33,883/-. The Tehsildar restrained the transfer of property by sale, donation or any other mode, and also created a charge on the properties. The Collector also initiated recovery proceedings.

The Corporate Debtor was admitted to CIRP. Resolution of the Corporate Debtor could not succeed as such liquidation of the Corporate Debtor was initiated.

The Liquidator approached the NCLT for setting aside attachment orders of property of the Corporate Debtor which was allowed. NCLAT also endorsed the view of the NCLT. Aggrieved by the same PVVNL approached the Supreme Court.

FINDINGS OF THE SUPREME COURT

There were two issues involved in the matter. Firstly,whether IBC will override Electricity Act and secondly, whether PVVNL was a secured creditor.

The Supreme Court relied on Bankruptcy Law Reforms Committee Report, 2015, Preamble of IBC etc and observed that government dues are accorded lower priority in waterfall mechanism under Section 53. The Code has provided specific category for government dues as such government dues will fall in that specific category i.e. 53 (1) (e). The Supreme Court observed asunder:

49. Rainbow Papers (supra) did not notice the 'waterfall mechanism' under Section 53 – the provision had not been adverted to or extracted in the judgment. Furthermore, Rainbow Papers (supra) was in the context of a resolution process and not during liquidation. Section 53, as held earlier, enacts the waterfall mechanism providing for the hierarchy or priority of claims of various classes of creditors. The careful design of Section 53 locates amounts payable to secured creditors and workmen at the second place, after the costs and expenses of the liquidator payable during the liquidation proceedings. However, the dues payable to the government are placed much below those of secured creditors and even unsecured and operational creditors. This design was either not brought to the notice of the court in Rainbow Papers(supra) or was missed altogether. In any event, the judgment has not taken note of the provisions of the IBC which treat the dues payable to secured creditor sat a higher footing than dues payable to Central or State Government.

50. The Gujarat Value Added Tax Act, 2003 no doubt creates a charge in respect of amounts due and payable or arrears. It would be possible to hold [in the absence of a specific enumeration of government dues as in the present case, in Section 53(1)(e)] that the State is to be treated as a'secured creditor'. However, the separate and distinct treatment of amounts payable to secured creditor on the one hand, and dues payable to the government on the other clearly signifies Parliament's intention to treat the latter differently – and in the present case, having lower priority. As noticed earlier, this intention is also evident from a reading of the preamble to the Act itself.

The Court held that IBC will override Electricity Act, 2003.Relevant Para is as under:

52. ....In a similar manner, it is held that Section 238 of the IBC overrides the provisions of the Electricity Act, 2003 despite the latter containing two specific provisions which open with non-obstante clauses(i.e., Section 173 and

174). The position of law with respect to primacy of the IBC, is identical with the position discussed in Sundaresh Bhatt and Duncan Industries (supra) [refer also: Innoventive Industries (supra), CIT v. Monnet Ispat & Energy Ltd. , Ghanashyam Mishra & Sons (P) Ltd. v. Edelweiss Asset Reconstruction Co. Ltd. , and Jagmohan Bajaj v. Shivam Fragrances Private Limited.

The Supreme Court held that in the instant case the PVVNL is not covered under the definition of State as such PVVNL will fall under category of secured creditor. The Supreme Court did not consider impact of Section 77 of the Companies Act, 2013 in light of concurrent finding of the NCLT and NCLAT that PVVNL is a secured Creditor.

This judgment has provided much needed clarity on treatment accorded to government dues under Section 53 IBC. Many government departments had started claiming that it falls under category of secured creditor under 53 (1)(b) in light of "charge" provisions in relevant Acts/Rules in case of non-payment of dues. It can be inferred from this judgment that all government dues whether they are "charge" or not will fall under 53 (1) (e).

EVA AGRO FEEDS PVT. LTD. VS. PUNJAB NATIONAL BANK

The Supreme Court in Eva Agro Feeds Pvt. Ltd. Vs. Punjab National Bank & Anr ((2023)10SCC189) has held that if the Liquidator decides not to accept the bid of the highest bidder he has to apply his mind to the relevant factors. Such application of mind must be visible or manifest in the rejection order itself. The Supreme Court has also held that disqualification under Section 29A attaches when the resolution plan is submitted by the resolution applicant thus the disqualification applies in praesenti.

Case Title : Eva Agro Feeds Pvt. Ltd. Vs. Punjab National Bank & Anr Date of Decision : 06.09.2023 Bench : B. V. Nagarathna, J; Ujjal Bhuyan, J

FACTS OF THE CASE

CIRP was initiated in the matter of M/s Amrit Feeds Ltd vide order dated 22.10.2019 of NCLT. CIRP was not successful and Liquidation Order was passed on 19.02.2021. E -auction was conducted for sale of assets of the Corporate Debtor. First auction did not materialize and hence second auction was conducted. Eva Agro Feeds Pvt. Ltd. (Appellant) participated in the e-auction and also deposited earnest money of Rs. 1 crore. The Appellant was informed that it had won the bid through an e-mail dated 20.07.2021. On 21.07.2021, the Appellant was informed that e-auction has been cancelled under clause 3 (k) of the Disclaimer Clause of the E-auction Process Information Memorandum. The Appellant was also informed that a fresh auction will take place.

The Appellant filed application before the NCLT against the decision of the Liquidator which was allowed by NCLT. NCLAT reversed the order of NCLT. Aggrieved by the same, the Appellant filed an appeal before the Supreme Court.

THE FINDINGS OF THE SUPREME COURT

The Supreme Court observed that no reasons were assigned by the Liquidator for cancellation of the E-auction held on 20.07.2021. Appellant was simply informed that the E-auction was cancelled in terms of Clause 3(k) of the E-Auction Process Information Document.

The Supreme Court relied on S. N. Mukherjee Vs. Union of India ((1990) 4 SCC 594), State of Orissa versus Dhaniram Luhar ((2004) 5 SCC 568), East Coast Railway versus Mahadev Appa Rao (2010) 7 SCC 678, Kranti Associates (P) Ltd. Versus Masood Ahmed Khan (2010) 9 SCC 496 and observed that the furnishing of reasons are integral facet of principle of natural justice. Relevant Para is as under:

29. We are afraid we cannot accept such a contention made on behalf of the intervenor. While it is true that para 1(11A) came to be inserted in Schedule 1 to the Regulations with effect from 30.09.2021, it does not imply that an auction sale or the highest bid prior to the aforesaid date could be cancelled by the Liquidator exercising unfettered discretion and without furnishing any reason. It is trite law that furnishing of reasons is an important aspect rather a check on the arbitrary exercise of power. Furnishing of reasons presupposes application of mind to the relevant factors and consideration by the concerned authority before passing an order. Absence of reasons may be a good reason to draw inference that the decision making process was arbitrary. Therefore, what para 1(11A) has done is to give statutory recognition to the requirement for furnishing reasons, if the Liquidator wishes to reject the bid of the highest bidder. Furnishing of reasons, which is an integral facet of the principles of natural justice, is embedded in a provision or action, whereby the highest bid is rejected by the Liquidator. Thus, what para 1(11A) has done is to give statutory recognition to this well-established principle. It has made explicit what was implicit.

There was another issue involved regarding ineligibility of the Appellant under Section 29A of the Code. Shri Vijay Kumar Ghidia, director and principal shareholder of the appellant, was in the past also one of the promoter director and principal shareholder of the corporate debtor. Whether he was related party and as such the Appellant was barred under under Section 29A of the Code.

The Court relied on judgments of the Supreme Court in Swiss Ribbons Private Limited and Another Versus Union of India and Others ((2019) 4 SCC 17), Phoenix ARC Private Limited versus Spade Financial Services Limited ((2021) 3 SCC 475), Arcelor Mittal (India) (P) Ltd. V. Satish Kumar Gupta ((2019) 2 SCC 1) and observed as under:

50. From the above, it is clearly manifest that the disqualification sought to be attached to the appellant is without any substance as the related party had ceased to be in the helm of affairs of the corporate debtor more than a decade ago. He was not in charge of the company or an influential member of the company i.e., the corporate debtor when the appellant had made its bid pursuant to the auction sale notice.

Finally, the order of the NCLAT was set aside and order of the NCLT was restored.

STATE BANK OF INDIA VS CONSORTIUM OF MR. MURARI LAL JALAN

The Supreme Court in State Bank of India Vs. Consortium of Mr. Murari Lal Jalan and Mr. Florian Fritsch (2024 SCC OnLine SC 3187) held that one of the key objectives of the IBC is to ensure the survival of the Corporate Debtor as a going concern, yet the same must not come at the cost of efficiency. "Timely liquidation" should be preferred over an "endless resolution process".

Case Title : State Bank of India Vs. Consortium of Mr. Murari Lal Jalan and Mr. Florian Fritsch Date of Decision : 07.11.2024 Bench : Dr. Dhananjaya Y. Chandrachud, J; J. B. Pardiwala, J; Manoj Mishra, J

FACTS OF THE CASE

NCLT vide its order dated 26.06.2019 initiated insolvency proceedings in the matter of Jet Airways. The total admitted claim against the Corporate Debtor was 7800 Crores. Request for Resolution Plan was issued during CIRP, which has inter alia provision for furnishing of performance bank guarantee or demand draft of 150 Crore or 10% of upfront amount of Resolution Plan, whichever was higher.

Resolution Plan submitted by Consortium of Murari Lal Jalan and Mr. Florian Fritsch was approved by NCLT vide order dated 22.06.2021. "Effective date" was fixed on 90th day from plan approval order dated 22.06.2021. 90 days for fulfilling of conditions precedent expired on 22.09.2021. Extension of 90 days was granted by NCLT vide order dated 29.09.2021. First extension expired on 22.12.2021. Second extension expired on 22.03.2022. Maximum extension of 180 days prescribed under the Resolution plan thus expired on 22.03.2022. On 11.04.2022, NCLT granted exclusion of 65 days which extended effective date to 25.05.2022.

The Successful Resolution Applicant had 180 days from 20.05.2022 to 16.11.2022 to infuse an amount of Rs. 350 Crore as per implementation schedule.

Appellants disputed fulfilments of conditions precedents on one ground or another. SRA filed two applications for declaration that conditions precedent had been fulfilled and exclusion of period for making payment of first tranche of Rs. 350 Crore, which were allowed vide common order dated 13.01.2023. Thus, deadline to make payment was extended to 15.05.2023.

On 30.01.2023, the Supreme Court upheld order passed by NCLAT whereunder SRA was made liable to pay gratuity and provident fund dues under 180 days of effective date.

NCLAT vide order dated 03.03.2023 declined to stay the order dated 13. 01.2023 whereby NCLT had directed that implementation of Resolution Plan has to be monitored by monitoring committee.

NCLAT vide order dated 26.05.2023 excluded period between 16.11.2 022 and 03.03.2023 for payment of first tranche under Resolution Plan. Thus, period was extended till 31.08.2023.

SRA filed Two IAs seeking adjustment of PBG against first tranche of payment of 350 Crore. NCLAT vide order dated 28.08.2023 allowed adjustment application and implementation of Resolution Plan was extended to 30.09.2023. Before expiry of 3rd implementation extension i.e. 30.09.2023 SRA deposited Rs. 200 Crore.

Three interim orders were challenged before the Supreme Court – (i) refusal of NCLAT to stay the order of NCLT wherein it was held that conditions precedent has been fulfilled (ii) Order of NCLT whereby NCLAT restrained invocation of PBG and extended implementation to 31.08.2023. (iii) order of NCLAT permitting adjustment of PBG against first tranche of 350 Crore.

The Supreme Court vide order dated 18.01.2024 held that PBG of 150 Crore could not be adjusted against first tranche of payment under Resolution Plan failing which consequences under Resolution Plan will follow. The Supreme Court directed to make payment of Rs. 150 Crore by 31.01.2024.

The NCLAT on 12.03.2024 held that conditions precedent has been fulfilled and extended period for payment of Rs. 350 Crore by 11.04. 2024. NCLAT also allowed adjustment of PBG of 150 Crore against first tranche of payment. Order of the NCLAT was challenged before the Supreme Court.

FINDINGS OF THE SUPREME COURT

The Supreme Court determined the following issues.

(i) Whether the Performance Bank Guarantee (PBG) could have been adjusted against the first tranche payment which was to be made under the Resolution Plan, within 180 days from the Effective Date in contravention of the order of this Court dated 18.01.2024, the terms of the Resolution Plan and the provisions of law ?

The Supreme Court observed that the contentions of SRA that its hands were tied since the conditions precedent were still being challenged before this Court is nothing but a reflection of its mala fide intention to not fulfil its obligations in accordance with Resolution Plan under the garb of pendency of litigation. Such an undue delay cannot be permitted especially in light of the intention of the IBC to ensure a successful and time-bound revival of the Corporate Debtor.

The Supreme Court noted that effective date has been frozen at 20.05.20 22. Several extension were granted for payment of first tranche including by the Supreme Court till 31.01.2024.

The Supreme Court observed that direction of adjustment of PBG is contrary to provision of RFRP which has been incorporated in the Resolution Plan and also Regulation 36 B (4A) of IBBI (Insolvency Resolution Process for Corporate Persons) Regulations, 2016. Once Resolution Plan is approved by Adjudicating Authority, the same is binding on every stakeholder and cannot be modified.

In view of its crystal-clear order of the Supreme Court dated 18.01.2024, the PBG of Rs. 150 Crore could not have been allowed to be adjusted with the first tranche payment of Rs. 350 Crore. Non-compliance of the SRA with the order of this Court has led to a dereliction of its obligations to implement the Resolution Plan.

(ii) Whether non-implementation of the Resolution Plan by the SRA necessarily leads to the consequence of liquidation as provided under Section 33 (3) of the IBC ?

The Supreme Court noted that the SRA has defaulted in implementation of Resolution Plan on several counts. The SRA failed to infuse first tranche of Rs. 350 Crore. The SRA also defaulted in payment of CIRP costs including Airport Dues. The Supreme Court observed that order dated 21.10.2022 of the NCLAT was unambiguous in its declaration that both Provident Fund and Gratuity dues have to be paid by the SRA in order to save the Resolution Plan from being hit by Section 30 (2)(e) of the IBC, 2016. Thus, SRA also defaulted in payment of provident fund and gratuity dues.

The Supreme Court held that although one of the key objectives of the IBC is to ensure the survival of the Corporate Debtor as a going concern, yet the same must not come at the cost of efficiency. In scenarios such as the present, "timely" liquidation is indeed preferred over an "endless resolution process". Such a view will prevent the likelihood of adversely affecting the interests of all the creditors who have been suffering due to no fault of their own and securing the maximizing of value of remaining assets.

(iii) Whether the timely implementation of the Resolution Plan is also one of the objectives of the IBC, 2016 ?

The Supreme Court observed that several decisions of this Court have highlighted the importance of a speedy resolution process under the IBC, 2016 in the context of either completing the CIRP process in a time bound manner as per Section 12 of the IBC, 2016 or ensuring that the Liquidator does not cause unnecessary delay or inefficiency in the Liquidation Process. A primary and predominant consideration behind minimizing delay is to ensure that the assets of the Corporate Debtor do not get frittered away or depreciated due to the time lag caused either during CIRP or during the liquidation process overseen by the Liquidator. Such a time bound action is also equally important and imperative while the Resolution Plan is being implemented by the successful resolution applicant. Unnecessary delay caused in implementation of the Resolution Plan would also lead to similar consequences of the assets of the Corporate Debtor diminishing in value. Therefore, there is no doubt that the timely implementation of the Resolution Plan is also one of the underlying objectives.

The Supreme Court observed that the discretion in extending the time limits fixed under the Resolution Plan must be exercised in a much more circumspect manner, especially in cases such as the present, which pertains to the aviation sector, wherein timely resolution and revival of the Corporate Debtor is all the more crucial since the sector operates in such a way that a continuous flow of cash is required to maintain the company in a position of status quo.

The Supreme Court invoked its power under Article 142 and liquidated the Corporate Debtor.

SHORTCOMING AND SUGGESTIONS

The Supreme court gave several suggestions in this case.

The Supreme Court noted that Commercial Wisdom of CoC can not be subjected to judicial review, but self-regulating guidelines have been issued by IBBI on 06.08.2024 which may go a long way in streamlining functions of CoC. The Supreme Court suggested that the Central Government or the IBBI explore the possibilities of better enforcement of the standards and practices enumerated in the guidelines through an independent mechanism under the auspices of an oversight committee instead of making them self-regulatory.

The Supreme Court observed that exercise of discretion as regards altering the binding terms of the Resolution Plan including the timelines imposed must be kept at a minimum at best. The authorities including the NCLT and NCLAT must not aid the successful resolution applicants in circumventing the strict mandates of the law by acceding to their requests to relax the terms of the plan itself.

The Supreme Court also suggested that the Adjudicating Authority while approving the Resolution Plan under Section 31 of the IBC, 2016 should record the next steps which are to be taken by the respective parties for commencement of the implementation of the approved Resolution Plan.

The Supreme Court also suggested that IBC statutorily provide for the constitution of a Monitoring Committee once the plan has been approved for a smooth handover of the Corporate Debtor to the successful Resolution Applicant.

The Supreme Court also observed that the integrity of the original timelines laid down by the code and the Resolution Plan must not be allowed to be violated since it would dilute the objective of the Code in its entirety, erode investor confidence and hinder all corporate restructuring efforts.

The Supreme Court also suggested that filing of vacancies with experts having domain knowledge in the field must be prioritized along with addressing the infrastructure needs of the Tribunals to prevent any adverse effect on the Resolution Process. There should not be any political appointment.

V. S. PALANIVEL Vs. P. SRIRAM, CS, LIQUIDATOR

The Supreme Court in V. S. Palanivel Vs. P. Sriram, CS, Liquidator (2024) 8 SCR 1263 has held that timeline prescribed under Rule 12 of Schedule I of IBBI (Liquidation Process) Regulations, 2016 is mandatory in nature.

Case Title : V. S. Palanivel Vs. P. Sriram, CS, Liquidator Date of Decision: 28.08.2024 Bench : Hima Kohli, J; Ahsanuddin Amanullah, J

FACTS OF THE CASE

Sri Lakshmi Hotels Pvt. Ltd. purchased an immovable property at Tiruchirapalli measuring 67, 533 sq feet. Lakshmi Hotels had four shareholders i.e. the appellant, his wife, son and daughter-in-law. The company started running a bar and hotel from that premise. In 2006, the company took a loan of Rs. 1,57,25,000/- from the Financial Creditor. Dispute arose between the Financial Creditor and the arbitration was invoked. The Arbitral Tribunal awarded a sum of Rs. 2,21,08,244/- in favour of Financial Creditor along with interest at the rate of 24% per annum from thea date of claim petition till date of realization. The company challenged the award before the High Court which was dismissed.

On non-payment of award amount, the Financial Creditor filed an application under Section 7 IBC which was admitted and Respondent No. 2 was appointed as Interim Resolution Professional. CIRP was not successful and Liquidation order was passed and Respondent No. 2 was appointed as Liquidator.

The Liquidation appointed two registered valuers who gave tax value and liquidation value of the Corporate Debtor. The average of Liquidation Value was Rs. 39, 41,28,500/-. Auction was scheduled on 25th November, 2019 where reserve price was kept at Rs. 39,41,28,500/-. The appellant objected to fixation of reserve price which was rejected by the Liquidator.

When the Liquidator did not receive any bid, he reduced the reserve price by 25% to Rs. 29,55,96,375/- and initiated second auction. KMC Speciality Hospitals (India) Ltd. was the sole bidder in the second auction process and on depositing an earnest amount of Rs. 2,95,59,698/- it emerged as the successful bidder. As per Liquidation Process Regulations the successful bidder was to pay the balance sale consideration within 90 days of demand. Balance sale consideration was not paid by the auction purchaser within the period of 90 days.

The Appellant filed Application before the Adjudicating Authority for setting aside the auction proceedings which was dismissed. Auction purchaser also filed an application before the Adjudicating Authority for extension of time for payment of balance amount on grounds including COVID 19 pandemic which was allowed by the Hon'ble Adjudicating Authority. The balance amount was paid on 24th August, 2020 and sale deed was executed on 28th August, 2020. One month after completion of sale transaction the Appellant filed an application for recalling the order of the Adjudicating Authority dated 5th May, 2020. By common order dated 17th November, 2021, the Adjudicating Authority dismissed both applications i.e. application for recall as well application for stalling e-auction. Appeals before the NCLAT were also dismissed.

FINDINGS OF THE SUPREME COURT

Impact of COVID 19 on Limitation

The Supreme Court observed that period for payment of balance sale consideration was to expire after 23rd March, 2020 when the lockdown was imposed. Auction purchaser was eligible to take benefit of suo motu extension of limitation by the Supreme Court as well as Regulation 47A of Liquidation Process Regulations whereby period of lockdown has been excluded from time line for every task. The Supreme Court held that suo motu extension cannot be narrowly interpreted to exclude a party such as auction purchaser.

Allegations regarding under-valuation

The Supreme Court did not find fault with fixing the reserve value at average of liquidation value determined by two registered valuers. The Supreme Court also did not find any fault in reducing the reserve price by

25% in the second auction. The Supreme Court observed that Liquidator was empowered to reduce the reserve price by 25% under Rule 4A of Schedule I under Regulation 33 of the IBBI Regulations, 2016.

Non-Constitution of Stakeholders' Consultation Committee

The Supreme Court also rejected the argument that the Liquidator has violated Regulation 31A of the Liquidation Process Regulations by not constituting Stakeholders Consultation Committee. The Supreme Court noted that Regulation 31A was introduced by amending Liquidation Process Regulations vide notification dated 25th July, 2019. By virtue of notification dated 28th April, 2022 an explanation was appended at the foot of Regulation 31A that provided that constitution of SCC was required only in those cases where liquidation proceedings were initiated after date of amending notification. In the present case Liquidation Proceedings was initiated on 19th December, 2019.

Violation of Regulation 33

The Supreme Court observed that time period prescribed under Rule 12 of Schedule I of Liquidation Process Regulations is mandatory in nature for the reason that it contemplates a consequence in the event of non-payment of the balance sale consideration by the highest bidder within the stipulated time line of 90 days, which is cancellation of the sale by Liquidator. But in the present case, the Adjudicating Authority exercised statutory powers under Section 35 of the IBC read with its inherent powers under Rule 11 of the NCLT Rules, 2016 for extending the time to deposit the balance sale consideration on sufficient cause being shown i.e. in view of the countrywide extraordinary circumstances to meet the ends of justice, cannot be faulted.

Attachment Order of Income Tax

The Supreme Court rejected the plea taken by auction purchaser that the income tax attachment order was insurmountable impediment in completion of the sale and subject property could not have been validly transferred in its favour by the Liquidator. The anxiety of the Auction Purchase was adequately addressed on the Adjudicating Authority passing an order on 10th February, 2020 lifting the attachment order despite the same Auction Purchaser delayed in payment of balance amount. COVID -19 was nowhere on horizon then. Thus, there has been glaring default in payment of balance sale consideration by the auction purchaser.

The Supreme Court observed that setting aside the auction will be harsh and directed the auction purchaser to deposit Rs. 5,00,00,000/- (50% of differential figure between the average of liquidation value and the price at which auction was done) with the Liquidator.

SHRI KARSHNI ALLOYS PRIVATE LTD Vs. RAMAKRISHNAN SADASIVAN

The Supreme Court held in Shri Karshni Alloys Private Ltd. Vs. Ramakrishnan Sadasivan (Civil Appeals No. 3625-3628 of 2025) that forfeiture condition stipulated by the NCLT in its order while granting extension of time cannot be equated with a forfeiture clause in a contract.

Case Title : Shri Karshni Alloys Private Ltd. Vs. Ramakrishnan Sadasivan Date of Decision : 10.12.2025 Bench : Sanjay Kumar, J; Alok Aradhe, J

FACTS OF THE CASE

CIRP was initiated in the matter of Surana Industries Ltd. on 02.01.2018. CIRP was not successful as such Liquidation Order was passed vide order dated 12.10.2018. The Corporate Debtor has assets in Karnataka and Tamil Nadu. Assets in Tamil Nadu could not be sold despite several auctions, as such Liquidator with the consent of Stakeholder Consultation Committee (SCC) decided to sell the said assets as scrap on 31.07.2021. On 09.09.2021, the appellant made an offer of 105.21 crore to buy the said assets as going concern. The appellant proposed to infuse 40 crore as equity infusion and balance 65.21 crore as unsecured debt. The appellant deposited 10% of the amount as advance. NCLT allowed the application filed by the Liquidator for private sale vide order dated 22.02.2022 and directed the appellant to pay within 15 days although the application had been filed on 22.09.2021. The Appellant claimed that they were facing challenges in making payments within the prescribed timeline and sought extension of time till 28.06.2022. The SCC in its meeting held on 13.04.2022 extended the timeline till 30.05.2022.

The Appellant filed an application before the NCLT seeking extension of time. The NCLT vide order dated 29.06.2022 noted that an amount of Rs. 36.30 crore has been paid. It directed for payment of 50% of balance consideration with 12% interest till 30.06.2022 and 50% of balance consideration with 12% interest till 31.07.2022. It also directed that if payment are not made as per direction, amount paid will be forfeited. Subsequently, the Appellant paid additional 1.50 crore bringing total at 37.80 crore. The Appellant could not make payment as per timeline as such the amount of Rs. 37.80 Crore was forfeited. The Appellant filed Application before NCLT against forfeiture, which was dismissed vide order dated 10.08.2022.

The Appellant filed Appeal bearing No. 443/2024 against order 2 9.06.2022. The Appellant filed another appeal bearing No. 438/2022 against order dated 10.08.2022. Appellant filed Writ Petition bearing No. 24262/2022 before the High Court of Madras against order dated 29.06. 2022. Both the appeals were dismissed by NCLAT and Writ Petition was also dismissed by the High Court. Aggrieved by the orders of NCLAT, the appellant filed appeals before the Supreme Court.

FINDINGS OF THE SUPREME COURT

The Supreme Court noted that the sale did not fall under Regulation 33 (2) (c) but under Regulation 33 (2) (d) of the Liquidation Regulations as the assets in question were sold with prior permission of NCLT. The Supreme Court noted that NCLT in its order dated 29.06.2022 had directed for forfeiture of paid amount if the balance payment is not made.

The Supreme Court noted that this was not a case of a contract between the appellant and the liquidator/stakeholders, whereby the appellant could seek to fall back on Section 74 of the Indian Contract Act,1872. The sale in question was purely under the supervision of the Adjudicating Authority, i.e., the NCLT, and the forfeiture condition stipulated by the NCLT while granting extension of time cannot be equated with a forfeiture clause in a contract. Having made an offer, coupled with a temporal commitment, which was duly accepted by the NCLT, vide its order dated 22.03.2022, the appellant went before the NCLT and sought extension of time. That extension was granted, saddled with the condition of forfeiture in the event of failure, and was duly accepted and acted upon by the appellant. The appellant actually made payments to the tune of ₹1.50 crores after the passing of the extension order dated 29.06.2022 but failed to make the full payment by 31.07.2022. The appellant cannot, therefore, seek to approbate and reprobate at this stage by assailing the forfeiture clause in the said order, having accepted and acted upon the extension granted thereunder.

The Supreme Court also observed that filing of Writ Petition suppressing the fact of appeals before NCLAT against the same orders warranted non-suiting the appellant.

The Supreme Court dismissed the appeals.

JURISDICTION OF NCLT

EMBASSY PROPERTY DEVELOPMENTS PVT. LTD. Vs. STATE OF KARNATAKA

The Supreme Court in Embassy Property Development Pvt. Ltd. Vs. State of Karnataka (2019) SCC Online SC 1542 held that wherever the Corporate Debtor has to exercise a right which falls outside the purview of the IBC ,especially in the realm of public law, they cannot take a bypass and approach NCLT. The Supreme Court also held that NCLT and NCLAT has jurisdiction to enquire in allegation of fraud.

Case Title : Embassy Property Development Pvt. Ltd. Vs. State of Karnataka
Date of Decision : 03.12.2019
Bench : R. F. Nariman, J; Aniruddha Bose, J; V. Ramasubramanian, J

FACTS OF THE CASE

Udhyaman Investments Pvt. Ltd. (Financial Creditor) filed an application under Section 7 of the Insolvency and Bankruptcy Code, 2016 against Tiffin Barytes Asbestos & Paints Ltd. (Corporate Debtor). NCLT Chennai admitted the application vide order dated 12.03.2018.

At the time the Corporate Debtor had a mining lease granted by Government of Karnataka which was to expire on 25.05.2018. Although a notice of premature termination of lease has been issued on 09.08.2017 on the allegation of violation of statutory rules and terms and conditions of the lease deed, no order of termination had been passed till initiation of Corporate Insolvency Resolution Process (CIRP).

The Interim Resolution Professional (IRP) wrote letters informing the Chairman of the Monitoring Committee as well as the Director of Mines & Geology informing them about commencement of CIRP and sought deemed extension of lease beyond 25.05.2018 to 31.03.2020 in terms of Section 8 -A (6) of the Mines and Minerals (Development and Regulation) Act, 1957.

As there was no response, IRP filed Writ Petition before the High Court of Karnataka seeking a declaration that mining lease should be deemed to be valid upto 31.03.2020 in terms of Section 8A (6) of the MMDR Act, 1957. During the pendency of the Writ Petition, Government of Karnataka passed order dated 26.09.2018 rejecting the proposal for deemed extension on ground of violation of terms and conditions of lease.

In light of rejection by Government of Karnataka, the IRP withdrew the Writ Petition with a liberty to file fresh petition. After withdrawal from High Court the RP filed Miscellaneous Application before NCLT for declaration that Lease should be deemed to be valid upto 31.03.2020 and to execute supplemental Lease Deeds for a period upto 31. 03.2020. The NCLT Chennai allowed the Application ex parte.

Government of Karnataka filed Writ Petition before High Court of Karnataka wherein the High Court directed the NCLT to consider the Application on merits after giving opportunity to the State to respond.

After hearing the State , the NCLT again allowed the Application of the Corporate Debtor.

The State of Karnataka again moved Writ Petition before the High Court of Karnataka against the order of the NCLT wherein the High Court granted stay.

Against the said order of stay of NCLT, the Resolution Applicant, the Resolution Professional and the Committee of Creditors approached the Supreme Court.

FINDINGS OF THE SUPREME COURT

The Supreme Court considered following issues

(i) Whether the High Court should have interfered with order of the NCLT when alternative remedy in form of appeal before NCLAT was available ?

The Supreme Court observed that IBC is a complete code. The code provides three-tier adjudicatory mechanism- NCLT, NCLAT and the Supreme Court.

Article 226 empowers High Court to issue writs, orders and directions to any authority or person for enforcement of any rights under Part III or for any other purpose. Traditionally, jurisdiction of High Court under Article 226 was considered to be limited to ensuring the judicial or quasi-judicial tribunals or administrative bodies do not exercise their powers in excess of statutory limits. But in view of use of words "any person" Courts recognized the jurisdiction of High Court even extended to private individuals if duties performed by such individuals are public in nature.

One of the exceptions of self-imposed restraint is review in case lack of jurisdiction on the part of statutory/quasi-judicial authority even if alternative judicial remedy is available. The Supreme Court surveyed several judgments and held that in so far as the question of exercise of the power conferred by Article 226, despite availability of statutory alternative remedy is concerned Anisminic Ltd Vs. Foreign Compensation Commission (1969) 2 WLR 163 cannot be relied upon. The distinction between the lack of jurisdiction and wrongful exercise of jurisdiction can be certainly be taken into account by High Courts when Article 226 is invoked bypassing statutory alternative remedy.

The Supreme Court observed that it has to be decided whether it is case of lack of jurisdiction of the NCLT or mere wrongful exercise of jurisdiction.

The Supreme Court went through several provisions of MMDR Act, 1957 and observed that the relationship between the Corporate Debtor and Government of Karnataka is not merely contractual but statutory. The decision of the Government of Karnataka to refuse the benefit of deemed extension of lease is in the public law domain and hence the correctness of the said decision can be called into question in superior court which is vested with power of judicial review over administrative action. The NCLT being a creature of a special statute to discharge certain specific functions, cannot be elevated to the status of a superior court having power of judicial review over administrative action. Judicial Review as observed in Sub-Committee on Judicial Accountability Vs Union of India (1991) 4 SCC 699 flows from the concept of higher law.

The Supreme Court observed that NCLT can exercise only such powers within contours of jurisdiction as prescribed by statute, the law in respect of which it is called upon to administer.

The Supreme Court observed that from a combined reading of sub-section (4) and sub-section (2) of Section 60 with Section 179, it is clear that none of them infer that NCLT would have jurisdiction over a decision taken by Government under MMDR Act, 1957. Although scope of Section 60 (5) (c) is very broad but it cannot include a decision taken by government or a statutory authority in relation to a matter which is in the realm of public law.

Duties of the Resolution Professional is entirely different from the jurisdiction of the NCLT. When the Corporate Debtor has to exercise rights in judicial, quasi- judicial proceedings, the Resolution Professional cannot short-circuit the same and bring claim before NCLT taking advantage of Section 60 (5). Wherever the Corporate Debtor has to exercise a right which falls outside the purview of the IBC, 2016 especially in the realm of public law, they cannot take a bypass and approach NCLT.

The Supreme Court concluded that NCLT did not have jurisdiction to entertain an application against Government of Karnataka in respect of lease deeds.

(ii) Whether question of fraud can be inquired by NCLT/NCLAT ?

One of the contentions of Government of Karnataka was that they have challenged the order of NCLT before High Court of Karnataka as CIRP has been initiated fraudulently and collusively. The Supreme Court observed the fraudulent trading can be inquired by Adjudicating Authority under Section 66. Corporate Debtor is liable for punishment for carrying out transactions with a view to defraud creditors. Thus, NCLT is vested with jurisdiction to inquire into (i) fraudulent initiation of proceedings as well as (ii) fraudulent transactions. As a corollary the NCLAT will also have jurisdiction to enquire into allegation of fraud.

GUJARAT URJA VIKAS NIGAM LTD VS. AMIT GUPTA

The Supreme Court in Gujarat Urja Vikas Nigam Ltd Vs Amit Gupta (2020) 5 SCC 185 held that Resolution Professional can approach the NCLT for adjudication of disputes that are related to insolvency resolution process. However, the adjudication of such disputes that arise *de hore* the insolvency of the Corporate Debtor, the Resolution Professional has to approach the relevant competent authority

Case Title : Gujarat Urja Vikas Nigam Ltd Vs Amit Gupta Date of Decision : 08.03.2021 Bench : Dr. Dhananjaya Y. Chandrachud, J; M. R. Shah, J

FACTS OF THE CASE

The Government of Gujarat notified Solar Power Policy , 2009 on 6th January, 2009 for development of solar power projects in the State. The Government of Gujarat allocated 25 megawatt capacity to the Corporate Debtor for developing and setting up a solar photovoltaic based power project in Gujarat. The Corporate Debtor set up Solar Photovoltaic Grid Interactive Power Plant and exercised its option for sale of entire electrical energy produced from the plant to the appellant for commercial purposes.

Gujarat Electricity Regulatory Commission issued Tariff Order dated 29th January, 2010 for procurement of power by the appellant from power producers.

The Appellant and the Corporate Debtor entered into PPA according to which the Appellant required to purchase all the power generated by the Corporate Debtor.

The plant of the Corporate Debtor was shut for two months due to heavy rainfall in 2015. The Plant was severaly damaged. Normalcy was restored and plant was working at capacity of 70%. Again in 2017 the plant was damaged because of flood and the plant was working at 10-15% of capacity.

On 4th May, 2018, the Second Respondent declared the Corporate Debtor to be NPA. On 20 November, 2018 the NCLT admitted the Petition under Section 10 of the Insolvency and Bankruptcy Code, 2016.

The Appellant issued two notices of default to the Corporate Debtor on 1st May, 2019 and stated that if default is not cured within the stipulated time PPA will be terminated.

1st and 2nd Respondent filed an application before the NCLT seeking injunction restraining the appellant from terminating PPA, which was allowed by the NCLT. An appeal was preferred before NCLAT which was also dismissed.

FINDINGS OF THE SUPREME COURT

The Supreme Court has to determine two issues in this matter – (i) Whether NCLT/NCLAT can exercise jurisdiction under IBC over disputes arising from contracts such as PPA ? and (ii) Whether the appellant's right to terminate the PPA is regulated by IBC ?

Section 60 (5) provides for jurisdiction of the NCLT as under :

(5) Notwithstanding anything to the contrary contained in any other law for the time being in force, the National Company Law Tribunal shall have jurisdiction to entertain or dispose of –

(a) any application or proceedings by or against the corporate debtor or corporate person

(b) any claim made by or against the Corporate Debtor or Corporate Person , including claims by or against the corporate debtor or corporate person, including claims by or against any of its subsidiaries situated in India and

(c) any question of priorities or any question of law or facts , arising out of or in relation to the insolvency resolution or liquidation proceedings of the corporate debtor or corporate person under this Code.

Section 60 (5) (c) grants wide jurisdiction to NCLT to determine any question of law or facts arising out of or in relation to insolvency resolution or liquidation proceedings. The Supreme Court held that the RP can approach the NCLT for adjudication of disputes that are related to insolvency resolution process. However, the adjudication of disputes that arise dehors the insolvency of the Corporate Debtor, the RP must approach the relevant competent authority.

The Supreme Court agreed with the view taken by NCLT. The Supreme Court observed that Section 238 is prefaced by non-obstante clause. NCLT's jurisdiction could be invoked in the present case because termination of PPA was sought solely on the ground that the Corporate Debtor has become subject to an insolvency resolution process under the IBC.

The residuary jurisdiction of the NCLT under Section 60 (5) (c) IBC provides it wide jurisdiction to determine any question of law or fact arising from or in relation to the insolvency resolution proceedings. If jurisdiction of NCLT was to be confined to actions prohibited under Section 14 IBC, there would have been no requirement for the legislature to enact Section 60 (5) (c) of the Code. However NCLT cannot exercise matters its jurisdiction over matters de hors the insolvency proceedings since such matters will fall outside the realm of IBC.

Validity of Ipso Facto Clauses

Ipso Facto clauses are contractual provisions which allow a party to terminate the contract due to occurrence of an event of default. The Supreme Court noted that Report of the Expert Committee on Company Law headed by J. J. Irani recommended need for invalidating ipso facto clauses so as to prevent the value of a Corporate Debtor's assets from becoming diluted during the insolvency process. Current IBC does not contain any clear-cut provision which invalidates ipso facto clauses.

Vide amendment in 2020 in IBC, an explanation was introduced to Section 14 (1) which prohibit some ipso facto clauses i.e. Government licenses, registrations, quotas, concessions, clearances or a similar grant or right given by central government, state government, local authority, sectoral regulator or any other authority constituted under any law for the time being in force.

Section 14 (2) and 2A prohibits termination of contracts where the counter-party supplies essential/critical goods, and services to the Corporate Debtor

The Supreme Court observed that no clear position emerges in respect of ipso facto clauses in other contracts. The Supreme Court appealed to the Legislature to give concrete guidance on this aspect.

The Supreme Court held that NCLT was empowered to restrain the appellant from terminating the PPA as it is the sole contract for sale of electricity which was entered into by the Corporate Debtor. The appellant has terminated the PPA solely on the ground of insolvency. Accordingly, the appeal was dismissed.

TATA CONSULTANCY SERVICES LTD. Vs. VISHAL GHISULAL JAIN

The Supreme Court held in Tata Consultancy Services Ltd. Vs. Vishal Ghisulal Jain (2021) SCC Online SC 1113 that NCLT does not have jurisdiction over disputes which arise *de hors* the insolvency of the Corporate Debtor.

Case Title : Tata Consultancy Services Ltd. Vs. Vishal Ghisulal Jain Date of Decision : 23.11.2021 Bench : Dr. Dhananjaya Y. Chandrachud, J; A. S. Bopanna, J

FACTS OF THE CASE

The Appellant and the Corporate Debtor entered into Build Phase Agreement followed by Facilities Agreement. Facilities Agreement obligated the Corporate Debtor to provide a facility to the Appellant for conducting examination for educational institutions. Clause 11 (b) of the Facilities Agreement provided for termination of Facilities Agreement if material breach committed by the other party is not cured within 30 days of the receipt of the notice.

The Appellant communicated to the Corporate Debtor regarding deficiency of services. The Appellant vide e-mail dated 1st August, 2018 notified the Corporate Debtor that it intended to invoke penalty clause for breaching Facilities Agreement for alleged contractual breaches. By e-mails dated 17th September, 2018, 1st October, 2018 and 11th October , 2018 the Appellant told the Corporate Debtor to take urgent steps to remedy the breaches failing which penalty and termination clauses will be invoked. Vide e-mail dated 13th October, 2018 the appellant complained about insufficiency of housekeeping staff . On 19th November, 2018, the Appellant intimated the Corporate Debtor that it will deploy its housekeeping staff and deduct the cost from invoice. On 3rd February, the Appellant wrote about issues of power supply and shortage of housekeeping staff.

In the meantime Corporate Insolvency Resolution Process was initiated against the Corporate Debtor on 29th March, 2019.

The Appellant issued notice of termination on 10th June, 2019 in terms of Clause 11 (b) of the Facilities Agreement.

The appellant claimed that the material breaches by the Corporate Debor resulted in liability of Rs. 20,78,500/-. It did not initiate recovery proceedings on account of the moratorium imposed under Section 14 of the Insolvency and Bankruptcy Code, 2016.

The Corporate Debtor filed Application under Section 60 (5) of the Code for quashing of termination notice. NCLT stayed the termination notice.

Appellant preferred appeal before the NCLAT which was also dismissed.

FINDINGS OF THE SUPREME COURT

Two issues arose before the Supreme Court for consideration – (i) whether NCLT can exercise its residuary jurisdiction under Section 60 (5) (c) IBC to adjudicate upon the contractual dispute between the parties ? , (ii) Whether in exercise of such residuary jurisdiction, it can impose an ad-interim stay on termination of Facilities Agreement ?

The Supreme Court noted that Clause 12 (d) of Facilities Agreement provided that disputes between the parties shall be subject matter of arbitration. Section 238 provides that IBC overrides other laws.

The Supreme Court observed that in Gujarat Urja Vikas Nigam Vs Amit Gupta & Ors (2021) 7 SCC 209 it has been held that the NCLT has jurisdiction over the dispute which arose in the context of insolvency proceedings. Resolution Professional can approach NCLT for adjudication of disputes which relate to the insolvency resolution process. But when dispute arise dehors the insolvency of the Corporate Debtor, the RP must approach the relevant competent authority.

In the instant case the Appellant is neither supplying any goods and services to the Corporate Debtor in terms of Section 14 (2) nor it is recovering property which is in possession of the Corporate Debtor or lessor of such property as envisioned under Section 14 (1) (d). Appellant is availing services of the Corporate Debtor and is using the property that has been leased to it by the Corporate Debtor. Hence Section 14 is not applicable in this case.

In Gujarat Urja Vikas Ltd it has been held that jurisdiction of NCLT is not limited by Section 14. It can exercise its residuary jurisdiction under Section 60 (5) (c) to adjudicate on questions of law and fact that relate to or arise during Insolvency Resolution Process.

Appellant has communicated multiple times regarding deficiencies in its services on the part of the Corporate Debtor. The Corporate Debtor was put on notice that the penalty and termination clauses of the Facilities Agreement may be invoked. In e-mail dated 13th October, 2018 the appellant specifically complained about inadequate staff. The Corporate Debtor has admitted that appellant was using its own staff. Termination notices also highlight deficiencies in the services of the Corporate Debtor.

The Supreme Court found that services the Corporate Debtor was deficient and it was falling foul of its contractual obligations. There is nothing to indicate that the termination of the Facilities Agreement was motivated by the insolvency of the Corporate Debtor. The Supreme Court concluded that in the instant case the NCLT does not have jurisdiction to entertain the present contractual dispute which has arisen dehors the insolvency of the Corporate Debtor. Without jurisdiction, NCLT could not have imposed an ad-interim stay.

The Supreme Court observed as under :

28. While in the present case, second issue formulated by this Court has no bearing, we would like to issue a note of caution to the NCLT and NCLAT regarding interference with a party's contractual right to terminate a contract. Even if the contractual dispute arises in relation to the insolvency, a party can be restrained from terminating the contract only if it is central to the success of the CIRP. Crucially, the termination of the contract should result in the corporate death of the Corporate Debtor.

The Supreme Court set aside the order of NCLAT and dismissed the proceedings against the Appellant for absence of jurisdiction.

GREATER NOIDA INDUSTRIAL DEVELOPMENT AUTHORITY Vs. PRABHJIT SINGH SONI

The Supreme Court in Greater NOIDA Industrial Development Authority Vs. Prabhjit Singh Soni & Anr (2024) SCC Online SC 122 has held that NCLT has inherent power to recall an order. The Supreme Court also held that Form prescribed under Code to submit claims is directory in nature and what is necessary is that claim should be supported by proof.

Case Title : Greater NOIDA Industrial Development Authority Vs. Prabhjit Singh Soni & Anr Date of Decision : 12.02.2024 Bench : Dr. Dhananjaya Y. Chandrachud, CJI; J. B. Pardiwala, J; Manoj Mishra, J

FACTS OF THE CASE

The Greater NOIDA Industrial Development Authority (GNIDA) being a statutory authority acquired land for setting up an urban and industrial township. On 28.10.2010 one of the plots of land acquired by it was allotted to JNC Construction Ltd. (Corporate Debtor) by way of lease for 90 years charging premium which was payable in installments. The Corporate Debtor committed default in payment of premium and was served with demand-cum-cancellation notice. CIRP was initiated against the Corporate Debtor vide order dated 30.05.2019. GNIDA filed claim of Rs. 43,40,31,951/- in the category of Financial Creditor. The RP treated GNIDA as operational creditor and requested to file claim as an Operational Creditor. The GNIDA did not file fresh claim and in the meantime Resolution Plan was approved by the NCLT on 04.08.2020. GNIDA filed an application bearing No. 344 /2021 against its treatment as operational creditor and IA 1380/2021 for recall of order approving Resolution Plan. NCLT rejected the applications of the GNIDA and Appeal filed before NCLAT was also rejected.

FINDINGS OF THE SUPREME COURT

The Supreme Court observed that a Court or a Tribunal has inherent power to recall an order to secure the ends of justice or to prevent abuse of process of the Court. IBC or regulations framed thereunder do not prohibit exercise of such inherent power. Section 60 (5) (c) of the IBC empowers NCLT to entertain or dispose of any questions of priorities or any question of law or fact arising out of or in relation to the insolvency resolution or liquidation proceedings of the Corporate Debtor or corporate person under IBC. Rule 11 of NCLT rules preserves inherent power of the Tribunal. The Supreme Court observed that even without empowering provision a Tribunal has power to recall. Power to recall has to be used sparingly on limited grounds i.e. where order is without jurisdiction, party has not been served with notice or order has been obtained on misrepresentation of facts or playing fraud on court.

The Supreme Court held that Application filed by the GNIDA for recall was maintainable as it was not informed about meeting of the CoC, the proceeding was ex parte, there was misrepresentation on the Part of the RP and the NCLT erred in approving the Resolution Plan.

The Supreme Court held that the Resolution Plan did not meet the requirements of Section 30 (2) of IBC R/w Regulations 37 and 38 of CIRP Regulations, 2016. It was undisputed fact that claim of Rs. 43,40,31,951 /- has been filed. GNIDA was advised to file claim Form B in category of Operational Creditor rather than in Form C meant for Financial Creditors. Assuming that GNIDA did not heed the advice, once the claim has been filed with proof the same could not have been overlooked. Form in which a claim is submitted is directory. What is necessary is that the claim should have support with proof. Resolution Plan has not only failed in acknowledging the claim made but also in mentioning the correct figure of the amount due and payable. Resolution Plan mentions figure at Rs. 13,47,40,819/- whereas according to GNIDA amount due was Rs. 43,40,31,951/-. These aspects have not been considered by NCLT and NCLAT.

The Resolution Plan also did not put GNIDA in the category of secured creditors although by virtue of Section 13A of 1976 Act, charge was created in favour of GNIDA. Non-placement of secured creditor in category of secured creditor has affected adversely interest of GNIDA .Regulation 38 (3) of CIRP Regulations, 2016 provides that Resolution Plan should demonstrate that it is feasible and viable and it has provisions for approvals required. When land of the Corporate Debtor belongs to a statutory body, a closer examination of Resolution Plan's feasibility has to be undertaken This aspect was also not deliberated by the NCLT or the NCLAT.

The Supreme Court sent back the Resolution Plan to the CoC for resubmission after satisfying the parameters provided under the Code.

S RAJENDRAN Vs. THE DEPUTY COMMISSIONER OF INCOME TAX (BENAMI PROHIBITION) & ORS

The Supreme Court in S Rajendran Vs. The Deputy Commissioner of Income Tax (Benami Prohibition) & Ors (2026INSC187) held that the jurisdiction of authorities under the IBC cannot be expansively construed so as to trench upon fields that are founded in the public law domain. Where the subject matter of the dispute pertains to the exercise of sovereign statutory power, particularly in relation to determination of legality of title, attachment, or confiscation and vesting thereof, the adjudicatory forums under the IBC must necessarily yield to the specialised mechanism created by such statute.

> Case Title : S Rajendran Vs. The Deputy Commissioner of Income Tax (Benami Prohibition) & Ors
> Date of Decision : 24.02.2026
> Bench : P. S. Narasimha, J; Atul S. Chandurkar, J

FACTS OF THE CASE

The promoters of the Corporate Debtor M/s Padmaadevi Sugar Ltd. transferred their 100% shareholding to the beneficial owner, V.K . Sasikala, through an intermediary, an advocate named Mr. S. Senthil, for a consideration of approximately Rs. 450 Crores, paid in demonetised high-value currency notes. As investigation disclosed commission of offence under Benami Act, as such authorities invoked Section 24 of Benami Act.

In the meantime CIRP was initiated against the M/s Padmaadevi Sugar Mills vide order dated 15.10.2018. Subsequently, an order of Liquidation was passed on 20.04.2021.

The authorities under Benami Act issued show cause notice dated 01.11. 2019 under Section 24(1) of the Benami Act to the RP as representative of Corporate Debtor characterizing the Corporate Debtor as the benamidar and the transaction as a "benami transaction". This was followed up by a provisional attachment order on 01.11.2019 under Section 24(3) of the Benami Act, attaching the immovable properties of the corporate debtor, including the factory land and plant machinery, which was confirmed by Adjudicating Authority under Benami Act.

The RP and subsequently, the Liquidator challenged the attachment order before NCLT, which said that it was not maintainable before NCLT as it lacked jurisdiction to sit in appeal over decisions of Benami Authorities. Appeals were filed before NCLAT which was also dismissed.

FINDINGS OF THE SUPREME COURT

The Supreme Court observed that the Benami Act and the IBC are special legislations operating within distinct yet potentially intersecting fields. The Benami Act is concerned with identifying and extinguishing benami holdings through a confiscatory mechanism, while the IBC is directed at resolution and liquidation of assets belonging to a Corporate Debtor within a time-bound framework. The present controversy arises at the point where property subjected to proceedings under the Benami Act is asserted to form part of the liquidation estate under the IBC. The issue, therefore, is not one of abstract supremacy, but of determining whether the two enactments can be harmoniously construed, and, if not, which statutory regime must prevail in the limited sphere of conflict. It is in this backdrop that the apparent inconsistency between the two statutory regimes requires examination.

The Supreme Court analysed judgments in State Bank India Vs Union of India 2026 INSC 153, Gujarat Urja Vikas Nigam Ltd. Vs. Amit Gupta (2021) 7 SCC 209, Embassy Property Developments (P) Ltd. Vs State of Karnataka (2020) 13SCC308 and observed that the jurisdiction of authorities under IBC cannot be expansively construed so as to trench upon fields that are founded in public law domain. Where the subject matter of the dispute pertains to the exercise of sovereign statutory power, particularly in relation to determination of legality of title, attachment, or confiscation and vesting thereof, the adjudicatory fora under the IBC must necessarily yield to the specialised mechanism created by such statute. Proceedings under Benami Act squarely fall within the public law domain. They are not in the nature of inter se disputes between private parties concerning proprietary rights, nor are they recovery proceedings capable of being subsumed within insolvency resolution. The Benami Act represents a sovereign exercise aimed at identifying and extinguishing benami transactions. The attachment and eventual confiscation of property thereunder operate in rem and culminate in vesting of the property in the Central Government free from encumbrances. Such consequences are penal and deterrent, rooted in statutory illegality, and are enforced through a distinct adjudicatory hierarchy whose jurisdiction is expressly insulated from ordinary civil fora.

The Supreme Court further observed that the liquidation estate comprises only assets beneficially owned by the corporate debtor. Property held benami is, by definition, held in a fiduciary or representative capacity for the real owner. Section 36(4)(a)(i) excludes assets held in trust for third parties from the liquidation estate. In Controller of Estate Duty, Lucknow v. Aloke Mitra (1981) 2 SCC 121 it was held that a benamidar possesses no beneficial interest and that title vests in the person who provided consideration. Where the corporate debtor is merely an ostensible holder, the property never forms part of its estate and cannot be administered in liquidation.

The Supreme Court observed that Section 32A is event-based and triggered only upon approval of a resolution plan or completion of a liquidation sale to an unconnected third party. Absent such approval, the immunity does not arise. The provision does not validate defective title nor retrospectively convert benami property into assets of the corporate debtor. Likewise, the moratorium under Section 14 is intended to preserve the debtor's estate for orderly resolution; it does not interdict sovereign proceedings in rem for attachment or confiscation under penal statutes. Such proceedings are distinct from creditor enforcement and proceed on an independent statutory footing. The contention of the appellants that the attachment order is impermissible as the moratorium under Section 14 of the Act commenced on 15.10.2018 is not acceptable because the mandate of moratorium must be understood in the context of the applicability of the Act. The moratorium is intended to protect the corporate debtor from "creditor actions" aimed at debt recovery, not to shield "tainted assets" from sovereign actions against crime. In any event, the liquidator would have power and jurisdiction to deal with the property only when the corporate debtor has a beneficial interest in the said property.

The Supreme Court dismissed appeals with exemplary costs of 5 lakh each on the appellants.

STATE BANK OF INDIA Vs. UNION OF INDIA & ORS

The Supreme Court in State Bank of India Vs Union of Bank of India & Ors. (2026 INSC153) reiterated that the jurisdiction of the NCLT and the NCLAT is confined to matters that arise purely within the insolvency framework and does not extend to adjudicating the legality of sovereign actions.

Case Title : State Bank of India Vs Union of India & Ors. Date of Decision : 12.02.2026 Bench : P. S. Narasimha, J; Atul S Chandurkar, J

FACTS OF THE CASE

Aircel Group Entities i.e. Aircel Limited, Aircel Cellular Limited and Dishnet Wireless Limited were granted telecom licenses by the DoT under Unified Access Service Licenses (UASL) pursuant to Licence Agreements dated 05.12.2006, which were valid for a term of twenty years. In spectrum auctions conducted by DoT during the years 2010, 2014, 2015 and 2016, these companies acquired rights to use spectrum in the 900 MHz, 1800 MHz and 2100 MHz bands. These companies failed to pay license fees. They initiated Corporate Insolvency Resolution Processes under Section 10 IBC and were admitted to insolvency by the NCLT, Mumbai Bench. The DoT was invited to participate in the CoC meeting held on 06.06.2018, and thereafter filed its claim in Form-F.

A resolution plan submitted by UV Asset Reconstruction Company was approved by the CoC on 13.05.2019 and thereafter approved by the NCLT by order dated 09.06.2020. DoT challenged the resolution plan before Hon'ble NCLAT.

During pendency of proceedings before NCLAT, the Supreme Court in the matter of Union of India v. Association of Unified Telecom Service Providers of India (2020) 3 SCC 525 directed the NCLAT to determine several issues arising out of treatment of spectrum licenses in

IBC proceedings. Appeals were preferred to the Supreme Court against findings of the NCLAT.

FINDINGS OF THE SUPREME COURT

The Supreme Court noted that the electromagnetic spectrum is a finite, non-renewable resource comprising of frequencies ranging from extremely low frequency (ELF) waves to gamma rays, which is owned by government in trust. The grant of a telecom license, including the right to use spectrum, does not effect a transfer of ownership or proprietary interest. What is conferred is a limited, conditional and revocable privilege to use spectrum for specified purposes and for a defined duration.

The Supreme Court noted that a cumulative reading of the License Agreement leaves no manner of doubt that effective and pervasive control over the license and spectrum vests with the Licensor notwithstanding the fixed tenure of the license and payment of consideration. The licensee's rights are circumscribed by regulatory oversight, disclosure obligations, restrictions on transfer, and the ever-present power of the Licensor to suspend or terminate the license for breach, liquidation, or winding up of the licensee. The license does not confer an unfettered or absolute right, but merely a conditional and defeasible permission to use spectrum, which remains subject to statutory control under the Telegraph Act and the regulatory framework administered by TRAI. The ability of the Licensor to withhold consent, impose conditions, and enforce compliance demonstrates that the licensee's interest is limited and subordinate to statutory and regulatory imperatives of telecommunication laws. The ownership, particularly as a trustee of the natural resource, by the Licensor, coupled with the power to suspend or terminate the license for default in payment or performance, negates any claim of proprietary ownership in the licensee. Where the licensee has defaulted in payment of license fees or failed to perform its obligations, the very substratum of its right to use spectrum stands impaired.

The Supreme Court noted that recognition of licensing rights as an intangible asset in the balance sheet is not determinative of recognition/transfer of ownership of the spectrum to TSPs. It only indicates control over the future economic benefits flowing from the grant of the right to use the spectrum. Hence, even if the right to use spectrum exhibits property-like features such as longer licensing terms, exclusivity, transferability, tradability, etc., they merely represent different sticks in the bundle of rights and falls short of conferring complete ownership of the spectrum on TSPs.

The Supreme Court observed that IBC explicitly excludes from the scope of insolvency and liquidation framework, assets over which corporate debtor does not have ownership rights. The Supreme Court noted that explanation to Section 18 specifically provides that for the purpose of this section, assets shall not include those assets owned by a third party but are in possession of the corporate debtor held under trust or under other contractual agreements. Similarly, Section 36 (4) provides that the liquidation estate shall exclude assets owned by a third party in possession of the corporate debtor, including under other contractual arrangements which do not stipulate transfer of title but only the use of the assets.

The Supreme Court concluded that the framework of IBC is clear in excluding assets over which the corporate debtor has no ownership rights. Mere recognition of spectrum licensing rights as an intangible asset by TSPs in the Financial Statements is not conclusive of their ownership, as it only represents control over future economic benefits. Even assuming that licensing of spectrum rights is one among the bundle of rights, in the absence of transfer of title over the spectrum, no ownership rights are created in TSPs either in the spectrum or in its right to use as governed by licensing conditions. Hence, under the IBC framework, spectrum licensing rights is not a part of the pool of assets for insolvency or liquidation.

The Supreme Court observed that its decision in Embassy Property Developments (P) Ltd. v. State of Karnataka (2020) 13 SCC 308 is a case in point to put substance into the view that the jurisdiction of authorities under the Code, 2016 must take a backseat when the same is in conflict with public law. The jurisdiction of the NCLT and NCLAT is confined to matters that arise purely within the insolvency framework and does not extend to adjudicating the legality of sovereign actions.

The Supreme Court observed that the statutory regime under IBC cannot be permitted to make inroads into telecom sector and re-write and restructure the rights and liabilities arising out of administration, usage, and transfers of spectrum which operate under exclusive legal regime concerning telecommunications. The disharmony caused by applying IBC to the telecom sector which operates under a different legal regime was never intended by the Parliament.

The Supreme Court held that spectrum allocated to TSPs and shown in their books of account as an "asset" cannot be subjected to proceedings under Insolvency and Bankruptcy Code, 2016.

GLOSTER LTD Vs. GLOSTER CABLES LIMITED & ORS

The Supreme Court held in Gloster Ltd. Vs. Gloster Cables Limited & Ors (2026INSC81) that the NCLT does not have jurisdiction to adjudicate on the title of trademark under Section 60 (5) IBC as it is not "in relation to the insolvency proceedings".

Case Title : Gloster Ltd. Vs. Gloster Cables Limited & Ors Date of Decision : 22.01.2026 Bench : J. B. Pardiwala, J; K. V. Viswanathan, J

FACTS OF THE CASE

CIRP was admitted against Fort Gloster Industries Limited (Corporate Debtor) vide order dated 09.08.2018. During the pendency of the application seeking approval of Resolution Plan, Gloster Cable Ltd. (GCL) filed an application for excluding the trademark "Gloster".

The trademark "Gloster" was registered in the name of the Corporate Debtor. Corporate Debtor had granted an exclusive, non-transferrable, long term license to GCL to use the Trademark for an Initial period of 33 years with effect from the date of execution of the said agreement for a fee of Rs. 3,00,00,000 (Three crore only) apart from annual royalty of Rs. 2,00,000 (Two lakhs only) during the existence of the said agreement. The Corporate Debtor also created first and exclusive charge over the Trademark in favour of GCL as security against a loan of Rs. 10 crore granted by GCL to FGIL pursuant to the loan agreement dated 10th November 2006. The Corporate Debtor had entered into Supplemental Trade Mark Agreement on 15th July 2008 with GCL wherein the Corporate Debtor inter alia agreed to assign the Trademark in favour of GCL for an aggregate consideration of Rs, 10,00,000 (ten lakhs only) and the said assignment was to become effective without any further act or deed if the order dated 10th September, 2001 passed by BIFR declaring FGIL as sick undertaking stood vacated and / or discharged or FGIL is wound up under the provisions of the Companies Act,1956. Finally, GCL & FGIL entered into deed of assignment dated 20th September 2017 wherein the abovementioned Trade Mark "GLOSTER" has been assigned and/or transferred to and vested to GCL with effect from the end of the statutory period from 1st December, 2016 under the Sick Industrial Companies (Special Provisions) Repeal Act, 2003.

Resolution Plan was approved by Hon'ble NCLT and application filed by Gloster Cable Ltd. was rejected. Appeal was preferred by GCL before NCLAT, which was allowed.

FINDINGS OF THE SUPREME COURT

The Supreme Court noted that the RP has not moved any application challenging the assignment agreement. The Supreme Court relying on Embassy Property Developments Pvt. Ltd. Vs. State of Karnatka & Ors (2020) 13 SCC 308, Gujarat Urja Vikas Nigam Vs Amit Gupta (2021) 7 SCC 209, Tata Consultancy Services Ltd. Vs. SK Wheels (p) Ltd. (2022) 2SCC583 held that the NCLT did not have jurisdiction under Section 60 (5) to entrain application filed by Gloster Cable Ltd. The issue of the title of the Trademark was not "in relation to the insolvency proceedings", on the facts of the present case.

The Supreme Court observed that under the insolvency regime, a plan approved by the CoC and ultimately by the Adjudicating Authority is the charter by which stakeholders are governed. As rightly held in SREI Multiple Asset, the ultimate order of the NCLT recognizing the title in the trademark "Gloster" with the SRA does not reconcile with the resolution plan as approved by the CoC and later by the Adjudicating Authority. Further, any grant of further rights over and above what is recognized in the plan would amount to modification or alteration of the approved plan. It should be remembered that the plan as it exists is the one duly approved by the CoC and while adjudicating an application of GCL, no directions could be made by the NCLT conferring better rights. In a case like the present where the SRA has perceived clouds hovering over its title, it is for the SRA to resort to remedies and protect its rights. On the facts of the present case, while adjudicating an application under Section 60(5) of GCL, NCLT could not have passed the direction it ultimately passed.

The Supreme Court also disapproved the approach of the NCLT in falling back on Sections 43(2)(a) and 45(2)(b) of the IBC to hold that the Assignment Deed dated 20.09.2017 would fall foul of those provisions. The Supreme Court observed that while adjudicating the application of

GCL and in the process of approving the plan, they could have resorted to an enquiry under Sections 43 and 45 of the IBC.

EXCLUSION OF CIRP PERIOD

NEW DELHI MUNICIPAL COUNCIL Vs. MINOSHA INDIA LTD

The Supreme Court held in New Delhi Municipal Council Vs Minosha India Ltd (Civil Appeal No. 3470/2022) that by virtue of Section 60(6) of the Insolvency and Bankruptcy Code, 2016, the period during which the moratorium remained in force is liable to be excluded while computing limitation for any suit or application by or against the Corporate Debtor.

Case Title : New Delhi Municipal Council Vs Minosha India Ltd Date of Decision : 27.04.2022 Bench : K. M. Joseph, J; Hrishikesh Roy, J

FACTS OF THE CASE

Appellant placed purchase order of Rs. 16, 20, 00,000 with the Respondent. The appellant issued a termination notice on alleged account of inaction and unresponsiveness of the Respondent. The Respondent invoked the arbitration clause and sent communication to the Appellant to appoint arbitrator. The Appellant did not consent to names suggested by the Respondent and proposed to proceed for arbitration through the Delhi Arbitration Centre. On 14.05.2018 insolvency proceedings were admitted in the matter of the Respondent under Section 10 of the Insolvency and Bankruptcy Code, 2016 and Resolution Plan was approved on 28.11.2019. High Court allowed the Petition under Section 11 (6) vide order dated 14.12.2020 and appointed Arbitrator in the matter. The same was challenged before the Supreme Court.

FINDINGS OF THE SUPREME COURT

It was argued by the appellant before the Supreme Court that no reliance should be permitted on Section 60 (5) of the Code. Section 14 does not put any embargo on the Corporate Debtor to initiate any proceedings against third party. It was contended that if the Resolution Professional can launch proceeding before judicial, quasi-judicial or arbitral forums during moratorium, exclusion cannot be granted to the Corporate Debtor. Court should interpret in a manner which should advance object and purposes of the law. Acceptance of the Respondent's case will give free rein to those who sleep on their rights and bring a delayed claim much beyond period of limitation.

The Court observed that Section 14 of the Insolvency and Bankruptcy Code, 2016 does not bar Corporate Debtor to initiate any proceedings including Application under Section 11 (6) of Arbitration and Conciliation Act, 1996 during moratorium. There is no express exclusion of the jurisdiction of the court or authorities to entertain any such proceedings at the hands of the Corporate Debtor.

The Supreme Court observed that there cannot be the slightest doubt that period of moratorium is excluded in case of suit or application by the Corporate Debtor under Section 60 (6). The Supreme Court noted that ambiguity emerges in respect of exclusion of period of limitation for a suit or application at the instance of the Corporate Debtor when moratorium does not bar any suit or application at the instance of the Corporate Debtor. The Supreme Court noted that Section 60 (6) is integral part of scheme which will benefit Resolution Applicant who is enabled to take suitable measures to ventilate its legitimate grievances by excluding the period during which moratorium was enforced.

The Court observed that the Court would not indulge in interpretation of a report when there is better material available in the form of the Act itself. If words of statute are not ambiguous, the scope of interpretation dwindles. It is not for a Court to rewrite the statute. The Court cannot sit in judgment over the wisdom of law giver.

The Court concluded that Appellant should be debarred from raising the plea of limitation and dismissed the appeal.

LIABILITY OF PERSONAL GUARANTORS

LALIT KUMAR JAIN VS UNION OF INDIA

The Supreme Court in Lalit Kumar Jain Vs. Union of India (2021 SCC OnLine 396) upheld the validity of the notification dated 15.1.2019 issued by Central Government, whereby certain provisions were made applicable to the personal guarantors to Corporate Debtor.

Case Title : Lalit Kumar Jain Vs. Union of India
Date of Decision : 21.05.2021
Bench : L. Nageswara Rao, J ; S. Ravindra Bhat, J

FACTS OF THE CASE

The Central Government issued notification dated 15.11.2019 which brought into force Section 2(e) , Section 78 (except with regard to fresh start process), Sections 79, Section 94-187 and some other provisions of the Code in force in relation to personal guarantor to corporate debtors.

It is pertinent to mention that Section 2 (e) introduced separate category of "personal guarantors to Corporate Debtors" under the Code vide 2018 amendment.

Part III of the Code deals with insolvency and bankruptcy of individuals and partnership firms. These provisions have as yet not been notified by the Government. Notification dated 15.11.2019 brought into force certain provisions i.e. Section 2(e) , Section 78 (except with regard to fresh start process), Sections 79, Section 94-187 relating to insolvency and bankruptcy of individual and partnership firms in respect of only "personal guarantors to Corporate Debtors". These provisions have not been made applicable to other individual and partnership firms.

FINDINGS OF THE SUPREME COURT

The Writ Petitioners challenged the notification on following major grounds.

It was argued that impugned notification as having been issued in excess of the authority conferred upon the Union of India. The petitioners contended that the power conferred upon the Union under Section 1 (3) of the Code could not have been resorted to in the manner as to extend the provisions of the Code only as far as they relate to personal guarantors to the Corporate Debtor. It was argued that the provision of the code brought into effect by the impugned notification are not severable as they do not specifically or separately deal with or govern insolvency proceedings against personal guarantors of the Corporate Debtor.

It was also argued that the notification suffers from non-application of mind because the Central Government failed to bring into effect Section 243 of the Code which could have repealed the Presidency Town Insolvency Act, 1909 and Provincial Insolvency Act, 1920. Since 243 has not been brought into force, the impugned notification has the illogical effect of creating two self-contradictory legal regimes for insolvency proceedings against personal guarantors of the Corporate Debtor.

It was also argued that liability of a guarantor is coextensive with that of the principal debtor. Upon conclusion of the insolvency proceedings all the claims get extinguished as such personal guarantors are no more liable to pay any money.

The Supreme Court held that the method adopted by the Central Government was to bring into force different provisions of the Code having regard to priorities. Parliament vide 2018 Amendment Act altered Section 2 (e) and subcategorized three categories of individuals resulting in Sections 2 (e), (f) and (g). This amendment introduced Section 2 (e) i.e. personal guarantors to the Corporate Debtor as a distinct category to whom the code applied. The Supreme Court held that there was sufficient legislative guidance to distinguish and classify personal guarantors separately from other individuals. Relevant Para is as under:

97. In the opinion of this Court, there was sufficient legislative guidance for the Central Government, before the amendment of 2018 was made effective, to distinguish and classify personal guarantors separately form other individuals. This is evident from Section 5 (22), 60, 234, 235 and unamended Section 60. In V. Rama Krishnana (Supra) this court noted the effect of various provisions of the Code and how they applied to the personal guarantors.

The Supreme Court held that impugned notification is not an instance of legislative exercise or amounting to impermissible and selective application of provisions of the Code. Relevant Para is as under:

101. In view of the above discussion, it is held that the impugned notification is not an instance of legislative exercise, or amounting to impermissible and selective application of provisions of the Code. There is no compulsion in the Code that it should, at the same time, be made applicable to all individuals (including personal guarantors) or not at all. There is sufficient indication in the Code by Section 2 (e) Section 5 (22), Section 60 and Section 179 indicating that persona guarantors, though forming part of the larger grouping of individuals, were to be , in view of their intrinsic connection with corporate debtors, dealt with differently, through the same adjudicatory process and by the same forum (though not insolvency provisions) sa such corporate debtors. The notifications under Section 1 (3) (issued before the impugned notification was issued) disclose that the Code was brought into force in stages, regard being has to the categories of persons to whom its provisions were to be applied. The impugned notifications, similarly inter alia makes the provisions of the Code applicable in respect of personal guarantors to corporate debtors, as another such category of persons to whom the code has been extended. It is held that the impugned notification was issued within the power granted by Parliamentand in valid exercise of it. The exercise of power in issuing the impugned notification under Section 1 (3) is therefore, not ultra virus; the notification is valid.

The Supreme Court also justified that rationale for not notifying Section 243 as far as personal guarantors to corporate persons are concerned. Section 243 (2) saves pending proceedings under the Acts repealed (PIA and PTI Act) to be undertaken in accordance with those enactments. As of now, Section 243 has not been notified. In the event Section 243 is notified and those two Acts repealed, then the present notification would not have had the effect of covering pending proceedings against individuals, such as personal guarantors in other forums, and would bring them under the Provisions of the Code pertaining to Insolvency and bankruptcy of personal guarantors. The impugned notification, as a consequence of the non-obstante clause in Section 238, has the result that if any proceeding were to be initiated against personal guarantors it would be under the Code.

The Supreme Court also rejected the contention that liability of the personal guarantors of the Corporate Debtor gets extinguished with the approval of the Resolution Plan by the Adjudicating Authority. Relevant Para is as under:

111. In view of the above discussion, it is held that approval of a resolution plan does not ipso facto discharge a personal guarantor (of a corporate debtor) or her of his liabilities under the contract of guarantee. As held by this Court, release or discharge of a principal borrower for the debt owed by it to its creditor, by an involuntary process, i.e. by operation of law or due to liquidation or insolvency proceedings, does not absolve the surety/guarantor of his or her liability, which arises out of an independent contract.

DILIP B. JIWRAJKA VS. UNION OF INDIA

The Supreme Court in Dilip B Jiwrajka vs. Union of India & Others (2023 SCC OnLine SC 1530) upheld the validity of Sections 95 to 100 of the Insolvency and Bankruptcy Code, 2016.

Case Title : Dilip B Jiwrajka vs. Union of India & Ors. Date of Decision : 09.11.2023 Bench : Dr. Dhananjaya Y. Chandrachud, CJI; J. B. Pardiwala, J; Manoj Misra

FACTS OF THE CASE

This case involved a batch of 384 writ petitions challenging the constitutional validity of Sections 95 to 100 of Part III of the Insolvency and Bankruptcy Code, 2016, which govern the insolvency resolution process for individuals and partnership firms. Most of the petitioners were personal guarantors to corporate debtors against whom creditors had initiated or proposed to initiate insolvency proceedings.

Section 95 -100 falls under Chapter III of Part III of the Code providing for Insolvency Resolution Process for individual and partnership firms. These provisions came into prominence when the Central Government notified various provisions for initiating insolvency and bankruptcy proceeding against personal guarantors to Corporate Debtor in 2019 which was challenged in Lalit Kumar Jain Vs. Union of India (Transferred Case (Civil) No. 245/2020) and which was upheld by the Supreme Court.

Section 95 empowers a Creditor to file application for initiating Insolvency Resolution Process either by himself or through a Resolution Professional. Section 96 provides for Interim Moratorium from the date of application under Section 94 or 95. Under Section 98, the Adjudicating Authority can appoint the Resolution Professional through whom the Application has been filed or Resolution Professional recommended by the Board in case the Application has been filed by Creditor or debtor himself. The Adjudicating Authority has been empowered under Section 98 to replace the Resolution Professional. Section 99 empowers the Resolution Professional to examine the application within 10 days of his appointment and seek relevant information from the Debtor, Creditor or any other person in connection with the application. After examination of the Application, the Resolution Professional has to prepare a report recommending the Adjudicating Authority for acceptance or rejection of the Application.

FINDINGS OF THE SUPREME COURT

Aforesaid provisions were challenged before the Supreme Court interalia on following grounds:

- Judicial determination is involved even before the Resolution Professional begins the task outlined in Section 99, for determining the jurisdictional requirements for the existence and continuity of a debt.
- Following the appointment of the Resolution Professional under Section 97(5), wide-ranging powers are granted by Section 99(4) to demand information not only from the debtor but also from third parties
- Without incorporating a requirement for a hearing before the Adjudicating Authority prior to the appointment of a Resolution Professional, the provisions of Sections 95 to 100 would be arbitrary and violative of Article 14.

The Supreme Court noticed that Part II of the IBC, on one hand, and Part III, on the other, deal with distinct processes for the resolution of insolvencies. The former deals with resolution of insolvencies of corporate entities, whereas the latter deals with the resolution of insolvencies of individuals and partnership firms.

The Supreme Court observed that the Resolution Professional does not perform any adjudicatory function. The powers of Resolution Professional under Part III is not as comprehensive as in the case of his counterpart under Part II. The role under Section 99 which is ascribed to the esolution professional is that of a facilitator and is to gather relevant information on the basis of the application which has been submitted under Section 94 or Section 95 and after carrying out the process which is referred to in sub-section (2), sub-section (4) and sub-section (6) of Section 99, to submit a report recommending the acceptance or rejection of the application. Significantly, the statute has used the expression "examine the application", "ascertain" and "satisfies the requirements" and "recommend" the acceptance or rejection of the application. The use of these expressions leaves no manner of doubt that the Resolution Professional is not intended to perform an adjudicatory function or to arrive at binding conclusions on facts. The role of the Resolution Professional is purely recommendatory in nature and cannot bind the creditor, the debtor or, the Adjudicating Authority.

The Supreme Court noted that default amount for initiating insolvency proceedings in case of Individual and Partnerships is not less than one thousand rupees or any amount which the Central Government may specify, not exceeding one lakh rupees. The Adjudicating Authority will be inundated if all such defaults are judicially determined. Relevant para is as under:

55. This distinction between the role of the Resolution Professional in a CIRP under Part II, and an IRP under Part III is of crucial importance. The reason why the legislature has chosen it fit to interpose the function of the Resolution Professional even before the Adjudicating Authority under Section 100 comes, is that the application under Section 94 or Section 95, is sought to be moved principally against an individual or a partnership. In terms of Section 78, Part III applies to individuals or partnership firms where the amount of default is not less than one thousand rupees or any amount which the Central Government may specify, not exceeding one lakh rupees. The Adjudicating Authority would be inundated if all amounts of alleged defaults as low as one thousand rupees were to be judicially determined. Bearing in mind the nature and context of the insolvency resolution, the legislature has stepped in by providing an intermediate stage where the Resolution Professional will collate and compile the relevant materials and submit it in the form of a report to the Adjudicating Authority recommending either the acceptance or the rejection of the application for initiating insolvency.

The Supreme Court further observed that the purpose of interim moratorium under Section 96 is protective. The impact of the interim-moratorium under Section 96 is that a legal action or proceeding pending in respect of any debt is deemed to have been stayed and the creditors or the debtors shall not initiate any legal action or proceedings in respect of any debt. The crucial words which are used both in clause (b)(i) and clause (b)(ii) of sub-section (1) of Section 96 are "in respect of any debt". These words indicate that the interim-moratorium which is intended to operate by the legislature is primarily in respect of a debt as opposed to a debtor. Clause (b) of sub-section (1) indicates that the purpose of the interim-moratorium is to restrain the initiation or the continuation of legal action or proceedings against the debt.

The Supreme Court also held that the difference in the role of Resolution Professional, the imposition of moratorium and role of Adjudicating Authority under Part III is based on an intelligible differentia between the nature of the insolvency resolution process in the case of a corporate debtor, on one hand, and individuals or partnerships, on the other.

The Court noted that there is no violation of principles of natural justice as Debtor is engaged at various levels. Relevant para is as under:

The legislature has evidently made provisions in Section 99, as we have construed earlier, to allow for the engagement of the debtor with the Resolution Professional before a report is submitted to the Adjudicating Authority. The process under Section 100 before the Adjudicating Authority must be compliant with the principles of natural justice. The Adjudicating Authority is duty bound to hear the person against whom an application has been filed under Section 94 or Section 95 before it comes to the conclusion as to whether the application should be admitted or rejected. The duty of the Adjudicating Authority to furnish a hearing attaches to its role and function as an authority which is entrusted to decide questions of law and fact and to arrive at a conclusion on either to admit or reject the application filed by the debtor or the creditor under Chapter III of Part III.

The Court finally concluded that the impugned provisions of the IBC do not suffer from any manifest arbitrariness so as to offend Article 14 of the Constitution.

About the author

Mukesh Kumar Suman is an advocate and legal author based in Delhi. He has completed an LL.B. from the Faculty of Law, University of Delhi, and also holds a master's degree in Personnel Management and Industrial Relations from Patna University.

He has authored several legal books, including *Fundamentals of Indian Constitution, Insolvency and Bankruptcy Code, 2016: A Paradigm Shift, Protection of Women from Domestic Violence Act, 2005: A Concise Commentary, Supreme Court Judgments on Indian Constitution*, and *The Industrial Relations Code, 2020: The New Framework for Industrial Peace.*

His legal articles are available at www.mukeshsuman.com.

www.ingramcontent.com/pod-product-compliance
Ingram Content Group UK Ltd.
Pitfield, Milton Keynes, MK11 3LW, UK
UKHW020838290926
15470UKWH00004B/1427

9 798895 193365